Technology, Innovation and Competitiveness

Technology, Innovation and Competitiveness

Edited by

Jeremy Howells

Associate Director, PREST/Centre for Research in Innovation and Competition, University of Manchester and UMIST, UK

and

Jonathan Michie

Professor of Management and Business, Birkbeck College, University of London, UK

Edward Elgar
Cheltenham, UK • Lyme, US

Published by
Edward Elgar Publishing Limited
8 Lansdown Place
Cheltenham
Glos GL50 2HU
UK

Edward Elgar Publishing, Inc
1 Pinnacle Hill Road
Lyme
NH 03768
US

HC
79
.T4
T445
1997

A catalogue record for this book
is available from the British Library

Library of Congress Cataloguing in Publication Data
Technology, innovation, and competitiveness / edited by Jeremy
   Howells, Jonathan Michie
      All draft versions of papers in this book were discussed at a
   working conference in June 1995 at Robinson College, Cambridge.
      Includes index.
      1. Technological innovations—Economic aspects—Congresses.
   2. Competition, International—Congresses.   I. Howells. Jeremy,
   1956–   .   II. Michie, Jonathan.
   HC79.T4T445   1997
   338'.064—dc21   97–5357
                                                             CIP

ISBN 1 85898 428 9

Typeset by Manton Typesetters, 5–7 Eastfield Road, Louth, Lincolnshire LN11 7AJ, UK.
Printed and bound in Great Britain by Bookcraft (Bath) Limited.

Contents

v

List of Figures

List of Tables

List of Contributors

Mr Jørn B. Andersen	European Commission Directorate-General III – Industry
Dr Susan Bartholomew	Judge Institute of Management Studies, University of Cambridge
Professor John Cantwell	University of Reading
Dr Hariolf Grupp	FhG-ISI, Karlsruhe, Germany
Dr Jeremy Howells	University of Manchester/UMIST
Dr Michael F. Kluth	University of Roskilde
Miss Usha Kotecha	University of Reading
Professor Stan Metcalfe	University of Manchester
Professor Jonathan Michie	Birkbeck College, University of London
Dr Renée Prendergast	Queen's University of Belfast
Dr Vivien Walsh	Manchester School of Management, UMIST

Preface and Acknowledgements

All the chapters in this book were commissioned specifically for this volume and draft versions were discussed at a working conference in June 1995 at Robinson College, Cambridge. This conference marked the first in a series of Euroconferences entitled, 'The Globalization of Technology: Lessons for the Public and Business Sectors' co-funded by DGXII of the European Commission as part of the Human Capital Mobility (HCM) Programme (Grant No. ERBCHECCT940230), organized by Daniel Archibugi, Jeremy Howells and Jonathan Michie. The overall Euroconference initiative has a number of objectives, but a key aim is to help to inform, involve and support young scientists and researchers in the field of industrial innovation and technology policy. The Cambridge conference therefore sought to bring together a small and informal group of some young and not so young researchers working in this field, to have a lively and interesting debate surrounding the issue of the globalization of technology which is of such crucial strategic importance to both private and public sectors alike.

Obviously a vital role was played by all the conference presenters, many of whom have subsequently become contributors to this book. We would therefore like to thank Jørn Andersen, Susan Bartholomew, John Cantwell, Francoise Chesnais, David Connell, Hariolf Grupp, Michael Kluth, Usha Kotecha, Renée Prendergast and Vivien Walsh for presenting papers and participating in the discussions.

In addition to the financial support from the European Commission for the conferences, additional support came from Robinson College and The Judge Institute of Management Studies, University of Cambridge. John Grieve Smith provided a vital link not only between the Advisory Committee of this Euroconference project and ourselves, but also in dealing with the inner workings of Robinson College. Special thanks go to Carol Jones and Shay Ramalingam for helping to organize the event and for ensuring it ran smoothly.

Our thanks go to the authors for revising their chapters; to Dymphna Evans and Julie Leppard from Edward Elgar for their speedy turnaround of the final manuscript; Carol Jones for help on various stages of the manuscript; Ann Rooke for drawing work; and to Stan Metcalfe for contributing the Foreword.

xv

Our personal thanks go to our patient families for all the spare time that has been given up in the preparation of this book.

Jeremy Howells
Jonathan Michie

Foreword

J.S. Metcalfe

The essential point to grasp is that in dealing with capitalism we are dealing with an evolutionary process

So wrote Schumpeter in 1942 when expounding his justly famous theory about the evolutionary nature of capitalism and the principle of creative destruction. However, even he could not have foreseen how, due in part to the international trading and financial institutions established at Bretton Woods, the operation of the capitalist system was about to become global on a hitherto unimagined scale. The rapid and sustained growth of trade and investment was to link together the underlying dynamics of production and consumption growth in a mosaic of divergent and convergent phenomena; an ever-present medley of structural change involving nations, regions, cities, communities and individuals. Change built upon change became the spirit of the age, with all the concomitant opportunity and anxiety that this entails. Thus globalization and competition go hand in hand with specific, local effects which are often extreme in their intensity.

To a considerable degree scholars agree that a unique set of particular technological opportunities has provided the basis for many of these changes. This being so, the question arises naturally about the extent to which the differential exploitation of these opportunities is nationally embedded or whether it reflects wider dissipative forces. Hence the central concern of these lively and timely essays which seek to establish the nature and meaning of globalization in the modern world of technological change.

One realization of globalization trends is found in statistics of world trade. Taking the trading system as a whole, the proportion of world production which is traded in the form of goods or services has risen from 17 per cent to 24 per cent in the last decade. In all the major trading blocs the ratio of trade to GDP continues to increase, although there remain large differences in the contribution which different regions make to aggregate trade. In round terms, Western Europe accounted in 1994 for 44 per cent of world merchandise trade exports, Asia for 35 per cent and the USA for 15 per cent. The former communist bloc in Europe and the USSR combined account for some 3 per

cent. But trade is only part of the picture. By far the most significant development of the past 25 years has not been the growth of trade alone, but the
growth of direct foreign investment and long-term capital flows more generally. Between 1986 and 1993, the flows of direct foreign investment grew at
roughly twice the rate of world exports of goods and services, with the great
bulk of the investment, whether inflows or outflows, being located in developed countries. The sectoral composition of world foreign direct investment
stocks has also changed dramatically, with a declining proportion invested in
natural resource industries and an increasing proportion in services. Of course,
this has implications for the pattern of trade since overseas investment in
local facilities can be trade-destroying or trade-creating. Broadly speaking,
an expansion of a locality's share in world production, given its share in
world consumption, has a pro-trade bias if that locality is a net exporter but
not otherwise. The significance of foreign investment has been to influence,
in some cases considerably, the inter-country distribution of shares of world
productive activity. A particularly important and modern aspect of globalization is picked up by many contributors to this volume, namely the location of
the accumulation of knowledge capital, those invisible assets which are widely
agreed to be of deep significance in shaping the future development of the
world economy. This emphasis is surely correct in that the growth and transfer of productive knowledge is a principal determinant of comparative and
absolute advantage. But contrary to the traditional perspective, comparative
advantages are not readily comprehensible in a world in which technological
opportunities are shared equally or in which those opportunities remain constant over time. It is not that the concept of comparative advantage is wrong,
far from it, rather it is that the comparative advantages of localities and their
industries are transient and shaped by intentional investments in capacity and
technology. All this reflects the inherent nature of capitalism in which market
institutions coordinate a decentralized, distributed system for promoting technological, organizational and social innovation. Globalization implies that
more and more distinct localities are embedded in this system that coordination processes become more competitive and that investment decisions have
consequences which diffuse far beyond the bounds of a specific locality. This
has many of the features of an evolutionary process in which the rate of
change of the system, measured in terms of the changing proportions of
different activities, is driven by the market coordination of competing rival
behaviours. As Adam Smith and many others have emphasized, competition
is a process driven by variety in behaviour. Competitive advantage means
acting better than one's rivals and, of course, innovation is intended precisely
to generate these advantages. All of these themes interact as the contributors
to this volume tease out the meanings which can be attached to globalization.
They are right to emphasize the implications for our understanding of the

behaviour of firms and governments in coping with the dynamics of competition. Policy-makers want firms with strong competitive behaviours to be located within their domain, and they have a range of instruments at their disposal to compete in terms of locational advantage. Leaving purely monetary inducements aside, one of these is the education system; another is the national research system since the outputs of skills and knowledge bear directly on the capabilities of firms to produce efficiently and innovate successfully. If capabilities are customer-driven one location policy will be required; if they are technology-driven then the policy will need to be different. Hence what this book directs us to is the interaction between policy and management strategy perspectives in shaping the warp and the weft of modern capitalism. Just as managers must think beyond the national domain, so must policy-makers. It is not only macroeconomic and monetary policy which is a casualty of the interpenetration of markets, it is also the micro policy of industrial and technological development. This collection of essays makes this clear: they pose the right questions and, most significantly of all, they show how the answers must integrate the contribution of different disciplinary perspectives. Globalization is simultaneously the economics, the geography, the sociology, the politics and the management of change in capitalism.

PART I

Globalization in Context

1. The globalization of technology: precepts and prospects

Jeremy Howells and Jonathan Michie

INTRODUCTION

Although there remains considerable debate about the nature, extent and implications of the globalization of technology, there is no doubting that the generation, diffusion and utilization of technology is being played out on an increasingly global arena and that this in turn is having a profound impact on both the shape and character of national innovation systems and upon local growth prospects. Thus whether technology generation is still largely 'local' or now more 'global' in character, the patterns of trade and investment embodying such technology, its utilization and consumption are certainly more international in character. Debates around the globalization of technology are still wide-ranging and the literature offers quite contrasting views on the landscape of technological innovation within the 'global economy'.

One aim of this book, which emanates as it does from a series of conferences run by the two editors together with Daniele Archibugi (see also Archibugi and Michie, 1997a,b,c), is to promote this dialogue and to explore the policy implications of these developments. We also seek to highlight those areas where, although we do have some knowledge about the issue, much remains to be done. Indeed, in some areas the data and indicators remain of poor quality or are even non-existent (on which, see Chapter 2).

The issue of the globalization of technology, however, is not just the repository of narrow academic debate, but holds truly critical implications for both policy-makers and industrialists in terms of fostering competitiveness and maintaining industrial growth. What then are the key factors in analysing the internationalization of technology? And if there is in some sense a globalization of technology, how should supranational (especially here the European Union but also the OECD and other key international agencies), national and regional policy-makers react to such changes? More particularly, what key ingredients do national governments have to focus on to create a successful environment for growth in a global economy (Chapter 8)? What should industrialists do? How should they reconfigure their companies so that they can face these new challenges? What new strategies should they pursue or what old ones should they rediscover? The following chapters of this book do not claim to answer all these questions, but they do at least suggest some possible avenues and routes which policy-makers, strategists and academics might fruitfully be taking (or at least exploring).

THE GLOBALIZATION OF TECHNOLOGY AND COMPETITION

What is striking about debates around the issue of globalization and the globalization of technology is not that there should be different evaluations regarding its extent, but rather the dramatically different policy options that are 'read off' by those that have similar views about its existing nature and scope. This is particularly true in terms of what the best approach would be in this situation for pursuing technological competitiveness. In this context, Lazonick (1993) highlights the fact that although Porter (1990) and Reich (1991; see also 1990) may hold roughly similar views about the extent of globalization and the nature of technical change, their opinions about what the best policy agenda would be for a nation to retain and build upon its competitive advantage within this new world situation are dramatically different. Thus Michael Porter argues that for indigenous industry, the building of a domestic base within a nation, or within a region of a nation, represents the organizational foundation for global competitive advantage. Here the establishment of strong indigenously owned 'industry clusters' is all-important. Even if the globalization of technology is continuing apace and the national system of innovation is under threat, the national system of innovation should be defended all the more and built up again, although on newer, more competitive structures.

By contrast, Robert Reich argues that the globalization of industrial competition has led to a global fragmentation of industry, thus making national industries and the national enterprises within them, less and less important entities in attaining and sustaining global competitive advantage. For Reich the emphasis lies here in having a trained, knowledge-based workforce that can tap into, but also attract, 'global webs' of stateless innovative corporations. Reich would accept this sort of general prognosis but would argue that the treatment is not to defend the ailing national system of innovation, but rather to enable its constituent parts, above all its workforce, to remain both competitive and attractive to outsiders.

This debate hinges on the issue of where technological competitiveness does (or perhaps should) reside: firms, people or places? Clearly the nature and status of geographical place in relation to the globalization of technology has become recognized to be an important element. Will localities and regions become less important as economies become more open in terms of trade and investment, as distances 'shrink' (Vernon, 1977, p. 3) and as enterprises become 'wired up', 'virtual organizations' seeking to compete in the global economy (Ohmae, 1990)? Or, as Porter infers, do they become more important as they evolve into unique, local institutional systems, based on close, informal knowledge flows that are difficult to re-create elsewhere? More fundamentally, is this locational 'stickiness' (Von Hippel, 1990, pp. 1–2) associated with the cost of communicating and transferring knowledge (Hu, 1995), the reason why the globalization of technology has not really taken off and remains fundamentally national (Patel, 1995) or, indeed, local in its orientation? The role of tacit knowledge in its localized patterns of learning and knowledge-sharing still provides a strong element in this spatial stickiness of innovation and technology transfer (Howells, 1996). The global–local dimension is important here (Dicken, 1994, p. 102), but what shape it takes, and the social and economic relations that are associated with it, remains unclear. Is a mix of late 19th century Marshallian districts and mid 20th century growth poles and innovation agglomerations going to prove to be the pattern of industrial organization of the future? Can there be readily identifiable technology districts (Storper, 1992 – see Chapter 2 refs) that emerge as the centres of competitive advantage in a future global context? And perhaps more fundamentally, at what geographical scale should technological competitiveness be seen to be residing: at a national, regional (Ohmae, 1993) or even, as some would suggest, urban level (Brezis *et al.*, 1993, p. 1213)? As Metcalfe (1995, p. 41) suggests, the national unit may be too broad a category to allow a clear understanding of the complete dynamics of a technological system and instead the focus should be on, 'a number of distinct technology-based systems each of which is geographically and institutionally localised within the nation but with links into the supporting national and international system'.[1]

These technology-based systems not only apply to a specifically geographical setting but also to a sectoral context. National systems of innovation can be viewed as a set of dynamic sectoral systems of innovation. More fundamentally, if national systems of innovation are breaking down, will sectoral (industry- and/or technology-based) systems of innovation (Kitschelt, 1991) become more important over time? Industry associations are moving into pan-continental groupings, such as in the chemical industry with the Conseil Europeen des Federations de l'Industrie Chimique and the pharmaceutical industry with the European Federation of Pharmaceutical Industries' Associations, and this is increasingly the key 'policy community' arena where important decisions are being made (Grant *et al.*, 1988, p. 317) in terms of shaping the industry and the technologies within them. Equally, as public procurement, pricing and intellectual property right regimes start to converge internationally, will innovation frameworks become more a set of interlocking international sectoral regimes rather than national systems of innovation with some degree of international harmonization?

There are two final elements to this discussion of competitiveness and the globalization of technology. The first is that under such increasingly competitive regimes only some places will prosper and be winners (Dicken, 1992). Moreover, in this dynamic context of competition, winners – whether they be firms or places – may, and often do, become losers (Rosegrant and Laupe, 1992). Equally it is often assumed that firms and places will do best by trying to be *similar* to other previously successful firms and places, imitating them in an attempt to tread the same path. However, an evolutionary theory of diversity would suggest that being *different* should perhaps be seen as the key to competitive advantage. Only a few firms and places will be able to follow successfully similar routines and patterns.

The second issue is that of technological competitiveness and appropriability. Who benefits from the competitive process is not always straightforward; the assumption of the co-location of innovation generation and its commercialization is a precarious one (Jevons and Saupin, 1991; see also Howells, 1990). This has recently been exemplified by Sigurdson and Reddy's (1995 – see Chapter 2 refs) study of ink jet technologies in Sweden. Swedish universities led the field in developing these technologies, but they were not successfully incorporated into the Swedish industrial structure and were instead commercialized elsewhere by foreign companies. A country may therefore be outwardly technologically successful competitively, but problems of absorption and the nation's inability to provide complementary assets for the appropriation of such innovations may prevent such successes from being translated into direct commercial benefits.

These are some of the key theoretical and policy issues which flow from an investigation of the globalization of technology, representing not simply the consequences of the globalization of technology but also representing important factors in the driving of the very process of technological globalization. While this book of course does not claim to answer all these questions, it can perhaps indicate where we might look for the answers and points to areas where the debate needs to be pushed further.

PERSPECTIVES ON THE GLOBALIZATION OF TECHNOLOGY

At the start of this chapter we highlighted the wide range of perspectives that could be taken when analysing the issue of the globalization of technology, and we indicated that, taken together, researchers were indeed taking just such a heterodox approach. This book seeks to present this diversity of approaches and opinions about the globalization of technology. However, while the following chapters do therefore portray such differences, they are at the same time linked together through a number of broad themes.

The contributions by Howells (Chapter 2) and Bartholomew (Chapter 3) consider the wider scenarios within which the phenomenon of the globalization of technology needs to be viewed. Jeremy Howells' chapter emphasizes the large gaps that still exist in our knowledge about the globalization of technology, ranging from an inadequate conceptualization of what precisely the globalization of technology amounts to, through to the lack of adequate indicators to measure satisfactorily any such globalization. Again, the issue of perspective is raised by Howells' chapter; for some industries, technologies and countries the globalization of technology remains of relatively minor importance, while for other sectors, countries and regions the internationalization of research and technology is, of course, profound. Chapter 3, by Susan Bartholomew, seeks to view the globalization of technology through the lens of a socio-cultural perspective, an aspect of globalization within the context of technological innovation which has to date been largely neglected by researchers. Bartholomew's thesis here, taking the example of biotechnology, is that differences in the socio-cultural characteristics of countries help to shape their national technological capability and their institutional system. This influences not only how countries approach research and technology and the way they do it, but also their degree of internationalization in terms of technology. Only by understanding what are often subtle differences in cultural and social patterns of interaction within countries can we understand the propensity and character of their international links and networks in technology.

The next three chapters, constituting Part II, take contrasting approaches to the nature and impact of the globalization of technology. They range from the perspective of a particular organizational form (Chapter 4), to a sectoral perspective (Chapter 5), through to a country view (Chapter 6). Chapter 4, by Michael Kluth and Jørn Andersen, is valuable in presenting the issue of the globalization of technology not from a traditional firm-based viewpoint but from an institutional perspective focusing on research and technology organizations (RTOs) across Europe which have different organizational goals and structures, and which in turn form an important element of a country's innovation system. The authors conclude that RTOs are indeed affected differently and are responding differently to the pattern of the internalization of technology and in a sense are following their own development trajectory. Research by Vivien Walsh (Chapter 5) on the globalization of the chemical industry indicates that the industry has traditionally had a long history of international collaboration in science and investment. However, in this piece, Walsh highlights the recent wave of mergers and acquisitions, joint ventures and research links, in particular with the rise of biotechnology. The notion that there is one homogeneous pattern to the globalization of technology within the sector is readily dispelled. Rather, the highly differentiated national, corporate and sub-sector nature of this internationalization is demonstrated.

The study by John Cantwell and Usha Kotecha (Chapter 6) provides an in-depth appraisal of how one country, France, has reacted to the process of the internationalization of research and technology. Presenting evidence on the internationalization of technological activity by the major French industrial firms – as well as by the largest foreign multinationals in France – and comparing this with the equivalent evidence for other countries over the period 1969–90, the chapter extends similar studies previously carried out on the UK (Cantwell and Hodson, 1991; Cantwell, 1992). Using data on the US patenting of the world's largest firms, variations between industries in the extent of the internationalization of their technological activity are analysed and the French case is compared with that of the USA, Japan, Germany and the UK, with changes between the early 1970s and the late 1980s also investigated. Their findings are broadly what might be expected on the basis of the experience of the formation of international networks for technological development by other multinational corporations, originating from the UK and elsewhere, with the leading French firms tending to concentrate outside France on selected existing fields of strength in which their technological competence has already been established. If so then we might expect over time to see the technological profile of the French-owned foreign affiliates becoming more dispersed in accordance with their local conditions to take advantage of local sources of expertise and innovation.

After the detailed sectoral and corporate analysis and descriptions contained in Part II, the last part of the book investigates some of the key dynamic elements underlying and shaping the globalization of technology. The chapter by Hariolf Grupp (Chapter 7) on external effects as a microeconomic determinant of innovative efficiency, contributes to the understanding of the often invisible mechanisms of the global creation and appropriation of technological knowledge by innovative firms. Using new indicators for technology measurement that reflect among other things sources of tacit knowledge, Grupp demonstrates that innovative search processes for problem-solving are important; it is not the case that the most advanced technology is always the most appropriate.

Jonathan Michie and Renée Prendergast (Chapter 8) then consider what fundamental economic and institutional attributes make for successful, dynamic and competitive national economies in an increasingly open world economy. The institutional setting is particularly important here, as is the short-term versus long-term nature of institutional and financial practice. The ability to be allowed to take the long-term view and to have time and space to learn and to practise trial and error becomes more, not less, important in an ever faster, short-term economic planet. Being able to create these 'oases' of long-term knowledge centres may be the competitive weapon for economies in the 21st century.

In the final chapter we reflect on the uneven development of this thing called 'technological globalization' – an uneven development well illustrated by the authors of the various chapters within this volume. Drawing together some of the lessons from the research reported in those chapters, we see that there is certainly still a significant local dimension to the processes of technological development and innovative activity, and that institutions and policy action, whether these be national or regional in orientation, remain key.

NOTE

1. On which see also Archibugi *et al.* (1995).

BIBLIOGRAPHY

Archibugi, D. and Michie, J. (1997a), 'Technological Globalisation or National Systems of Innovation?', *Futures*, **29**, 121–37.

Archibugi, D. and Michie, J. (eds) (1997b), *Technology, Globalisation and Economic Performance*, Cambridge: Cambridge University Press.

Archibugi, D. and Michie, J. (eds) (1997c), *Trade, Growth and Technical Change*, Cambridge: Cambridge University Press.

Archibugi, D., Carlsson, B., Jacobsson, S., Metcalfe, J.S. and Michie, J. (1995), *The Internationalization of the Innovation Process and National Innovation Policies: A Survey of the Literature*, Cambridge: ESRC Centre for Business Research.

Brezis, E.S., Krugman, P.R. and Tsiddon, D. (1993), 'Leapfrogging in International Competition: A Theory of Cycles in National Technological Leadership', *American Economic Review*, **83**, 1211–19.

Cantwell, J.A. (1992), 'The Internationalisation of Technological Activity and its Implications for Competitiveness', in O. Grantrand, L. Hakanson and S. Sjolander (eds), *Technology Management and International Business: Internationalisation of R&D and Technology*, Chichester: John Wiley.

Cantwell, J.A. and Hodson, C. (1991), 'Global R&D and UK Competitiveness', in M.C. Casson (ed.), *Global Research Strategy and International Competitiveness*, Oxford: Basil Blackwell.

Dicken, P. (1992), *The Global Shift: The Internationalisation of Economic Activity*, second edition, London: Paul Chapman.

Dicken, P. (1994), 'Global–Local Tensions: Firms and States in the Global Space Economy', *Economic Geography*, **70**, 101–28.

Grant, W., Paterson, W. and Whitson, C. (1988), *Government and the Chemical Industry: A Comparative Study of Britain and West Germany*, Oxford: Clarendon Press.

Howells, J. (1990), 'The Internationalisation of R&D and the Development of Global Research Networks', *Regional Studies*, **24**, 495–512.

Howells, J. (1996), 'Tacit Knowledge, Innovation and Technology Transfer', *Technology Analysis & Strategic Management*, **8**(2), 91–106.

Hu, Y.-S. (1995), 'The International Transferability of the Firm's Advantage', *California Management Review*, **37**(4), 73–88.

Jevons, F. and Saupin, M. (1991), 'Capturing Regional Benefits from Science and Technology: The Question of Regional Appropriability', *Prometheus*, **9**, 265–73.

Kitschelt, H. (1991), 'Industrial Governance Structures, Innovation Strategies, and the Case of Japan: Sectoral or Cross-National Comparative Analysis?', *International Organization*, **45**, 453–93.

Lazonick, W. (1993), 'Industry Clusters Versus Global Webs: Organizational Capabilities in the American Economy,' *Industrial and Corporate Change*, **2**, 1–24.

Metcalfe, J.S. (1995), 'Technology Systems and Technology Policy in an Evolutionary Framework', *Cambridge Journal of Economics*, **19**(1), 25–46 (and reprinted in Archibugi and Michie (eds), 1997b).

Ohmae, K. (1990), *The Borderless World*, London: Collins.

Ohmae, K. (1993), 'The Rise of the Region State', *Foreign Affairs*, **71**, 78–87.

Patel, P. (1995), 'Localised Production of Technology for Global Markets', *Cambridge Journal of Economics*, **19**, 141–54 (and reprinted in Archibugi and Michie (eds), 1997b).

Porter, M.E. (1990), *The Competitive Advantage of Nations*, New York: Free Press.

Reich, R.B. (1990), 'Who Is Us?', *Harvard Business Review*, **68**(1), 53–64.

Reich, R.B. (1991), *The Work of Nations: Preparing Ourselves for 21st-Century Capitalism*, New York: Knopf.

Rosegrant, S. and Laupe, D.R. (1992), *Route 128: Lessons from Boston's High-Tech Community*, Boston, Mass: MIT Press.

Vernon, R. (1977), *Storm Over Multinationals: The Real Issues*, Harvard: Harvard University Press.

Von Hippel, E. (1990), *The Sources of Innovation*, New York: Oxford University Press.

2. The globalization of research and technological innovation: a new agenda?

Jeremy Howells

INTRODUCTION

The origins of research into the globalization of technology have been mirrored and influenced by the wider study of globalization, which in turn was rooted in the study of international trade and foreign direct establishment by multinational corporations (MNCs). The first major strand of studies examining the globalization of technology arose from work centred on the internationalization of R&D and more specifically the spread of research activity overseas by US multinationals (Creamer, 1976; Ronstadt, 1977; Behrman and Fischer, 1980). Here the analysis was focused on the spread, locational decision-making and type of managerial structures involved in a firm's international R&D operations (see, for example, Håkanson, 1981). Subsequently this sphere of work expanded not only to cover R&D through the establishment of overseas laboratories but also to include internationalization of research via joint ventures and collaboration (Hagedoorn and Schakenraad, 1991). The focus of study therefore extended from examining research activity *per se* (that is, innovation *generation*) to studying technology more generally (that is, encompassing innovation *outputs,* such as technology licences). Patent data, already well established in analysis of other science and technology policy issues, was also subsequently brought to bear in the analysis of the internationalization of technological innovation (Patel and Pavitt, 1991). This therefore forms the first raft of studies relating to the globalization of technology, marked by its gradual evolution away from a specific focus on R&D towards much wider aspects of technology and from its focus on direct establishment to other aspects of globalization, including joint ventures and licensing. This strand of research can be described as an *agent*-based approach, with the focus on the firm itself, as well as its organization and control of technology over national boundaries.

The second strand, or tradition, embedded in current analysis of the globalization of technology is the product life-cycle model, which seeks to present the evolutionary shift of new, high technology products from home to overseas markets. Although currently not popular, it still retains a strong hold on academics. In brief, the product life-cycle model, stemming from the law of industrial growth, is associated with three stages of production where manufacturing capacity will shift from innovation markets to foreign markets as products move from an 'early' or 'development' phase through to a 'growth' stage and into a 'mature' phase of their life-cycles (Vernon, 1966). A number of studies have suggested that R&D in turn lags behind the internationalization phases of the production process, although once the early, home-based phase of production involving the major technological work is over, the amount of research and technology inputs required with overseas production is seen as minimal (indeed the model provides an explanation of why multinationals *do not* shift their R&D and technical capacity abroad; Vernon, 1977, pp. 41–5). The focus of the model is very much a *process-led* view of describing the globalization of technology.

However, there is a third, neglected strand of studies examining the globalization of technology, still from the basis of the firm, but with another focus, an *area-* or *place*-based perspective. Work in this field also stemmed from early trade and foreign investment studies, but here the focus was on the *impact* of increased international trade and investment on national and regional economic development. One factor in economic development was technological innovation, and studies began to examine the impact of multinational and multilocational firms on the development of nations and regions. In particular the concern was focused on the role of multinationals and technological development in peripheral or disadvantaged areas, covering: less favoured regions in advanced economies (see, for example, Firn, 1975; Thwaites, 1978; Oakey *et al.*, 1980; Hood and Young, 1982; Haug *et al.*, 1983); less developed countries (see, for example, Fuenzalida, 1979; Marton, 1986); or small, open economies, such as Canada, New Zealand and Australia (see, for example, Duerr, 1970; Cordell, 1971; Globerman, 1973; Britton *et al.*, 1978; Le Heron, 1978; Lewis and Mangan, 1987).

At the outset interest was not just focused on the lack of R&D investment in terms of direct *establishment* by multinational companies in these localities (although this was important), but also on intra-firm technology *flows* and barriers to technology transfer within these economies. These studies were therefore very much more directly focused on the policy issues and how the globalization of technology would affect the competitive performance of their economies. Thus the 'branch plant' economies of Scotland and northern England in the late 1960s and early 1970s were already having to face the fact of non-local, and indeed non-national, control of their technological destiny (Firn, 1975; Thwaites, 1978; Hood and Young, 1982).

Over time all three strands have merged together with, for example, interest being focused on an agent-based approach on international intra-firm technology flows, as well as taking on a more specific policy focus on the implications of the globalization of technology on national or regional innovation systems. In our understanding of the phenomenon of the globalization of technology, all three elements – the *agent*, *process* and the *place*-based focus of global innovation – are important foundations and provide key conceptual and policy-oriented insights into its dynamics and effects. The following section of this chapter will provide a more general overview of the globalization of technology and identify those areas where there is common agreement and those which can be said to be still 'in play'. The chapter then outlines studies that have analysed some of the factors and processes behind the dynamics of the internationalization of technological innovation. Those areas in the study of the globalization of technology where there are knowledge gaps which need further exploration are then highlighted.

THE BASIC PARAMETERS OF GLOBALIZATION OF TECHNOLOGY STUDIES: CONSENSUS AND DISSENSION

There are three main areas where there is some kind of common agreement emerging between researchers relating to the general description and basic parameters regarding the globalization of technology, although, as will be seen, there are still some areas of dissension. These three areas cover the definition, the measurement and focus, and the extent of globalization.

Definition

In relation to the issue of accepted definition, the problem of a commonly understood definition or term 'globalization of technology' centres on the word 'globalization' rather than 'technology'. Leaving aside more specific issues to do with interpretation, measurement and coverage (see below), 'technology' is defined to cover the whole spectrum of technological knowledge as seen in the old linear model of technological innovation (Kline and Rosenberg, 1986, p. 290), although it has never really encompassed the process of technology diffusion or indeed the supply and consumption of technology. In this sense the word 'innovation', encompassing the whole breadth of scientific and technical change is more applicable, although to conform to other contributors in the debate, the term 'globalization of technology' will continue to be used here (rather than the 'globalization of innovation'). However, rather surprisingly the word 'technology', at least specifically within the wider globalization of technology field, has not attracted much discussion or debate. The issue here, however, is not about the breadth of the word 'technology' but rather the focus and measurement of the phenomenon.

However, the word 'globalization' has engendered much more debate. This stems from two issues. First, there are those who treat the use of the word 'globalization' as only describing an end-state where technology generation, flows and absorption are almost completely internationalized (see also Dicken, 1994, p. 102). At the other extreme, there is the more general use of the word 'globalization' as a verb denoting an ongoing process; with indeed some describing it as a journey not as a destination (Neff, 1995, p. 19). The second area of conflict stems from those who seek to define the words 'globalization' and 'global' within a wider framework of terms denoting internationalization. Here 'globalization' and 'global' are seen as the end point of a continuum, starting with 'transnational' and moving to 'multinational', 'international' and finally 'global'. The problem with this *a posteriori* attempt at providing a wider definitional framework for the word is that it has never gained widespread currency. As such, ambiguity over the use of the word 'globalization' has reigned in the absence of a common language among scholars working in the field (Worthington, 1993, p. 177).

Measurement and Focus

By way of illustration, taking the traditional linear model of technological innovation for a moment, most researchers have concentrated on R&D (technical 'inputs') and patent (regarded as representing technical 'intermediates'; Comanor and Scherer 1969, p. 397) data, as well as including at the other end a more general discussion and analysis of patterns of high technology trade and investment. However, the more one moves down the linear model towards specific new product and process innovations (technology 'outputs'); adoption, consumption and diffusion of existing technologies; and nontangible and tacit technologies, the evidence and analysis is much more fragmentary.

If we divide aspects of technology measurement according to the traditional linear view, we move from indicators associated with innovation inputs (R&D), through to intermediate technology measures, such as patents, and specific new product and process innovations. Below that there are the more technical, design, test and engineering activities associated with general production patterns (Figure 2.1).

Starting from a geographical perspective in terms of the spatial phenomenon of globalization there are three main components. They involve those indicators which measure the 'sources' of technology; the 'flows' (both intra- and inter-firm) of technology; and the 'sinks' of technology. If one takes a diagonal line from the top left-hand corner of Figure 2.1 to the bottom right,

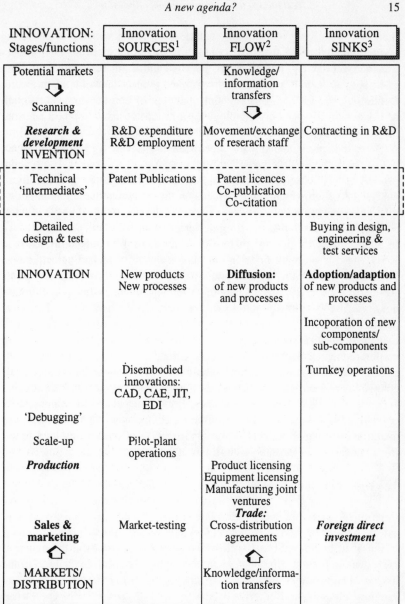

INNOVATION: Stages/functions	Innovation SOURCES[1]	Innovation FLOW[2]	Innovation SINKS[3]
Potential markets ⇩ Scanning		Knowledge/ information transfers ⇩	
Research & development INVENTION	R&D expenditure R&D employment	Movement/exchange of reserach staff	Contracting in R&D
Technical 'intermediates'	Patent Publications	Patent licences Co-publication Co-citation	
Detailed design & test			Buying in design, engineering & test services
INNOVATION	New products New processes	**Diffusion:** of new products and processes	**Adoption/adaption** of new products and processes
			Incoporation of new components/ sub-components
	Disembodied innovations: CAD, CAE, JIT, EDI		Turnkey operations
'Debugging'			
Scale-up	Pi!ot-plant operations		
Production		Product licensing Equipment licensing Manufacturing joint ventures **Trade:**	
Sales & marketing ⇧	Market-testing	Cross-distribution agreements ⇧	**Foreign direct investment**
MARKETS/ DISTRIBUTION		Knowledge/informa- tion transfers	

Notes:
1. Indicators of location of generation/source of innovative activity.
2. Indicators of location of innovation transfers and linkages.
3. Indicators of location of innovation consumption and use.
4. CAD (Computer-Aided Design); CAE (Computer-Aided Engineering); JIT (Just In Time); EDI (Electronic Data Interchange).

Figure 2.1   Model of globalization of technology

there is generally a good amount of data, information and interest, covering 'source' inputs and intermediates, inter-firm flows and more general production and capital equipment diffusion. By contrast there is much less on international 'source' patterns of product and process innovations, intra-firm technology 'flows' and general 'sink' patterns of consumption, absorption and diffusion of specific technologies (or artefacts) and disembodied, non-tangible elements of technological innovation.

These hidden elements of the globalization of technology arise, however, not so much through the view that they are not proper elements of the wider process of technological innovation, but because of neglect and difficulty of analysis. As such we continue to focus on those aspects that are readily and relatively easy to measure. By concentrating on these 'higher' levels of basic and applied research and more sophisticated technical elements, we also are in danger of distorting our picture of technological globalization. Thus in R&D, the role of small firms in our picture of global technological change (Kleinecht, 1993) still remains underplayed. Equally, in relation to patents we neglect the ever-growing part of technological innovation which either does not use patents for intellectual property protection or is of no real defence in a fast-moving technological area such as computer software and biotechnology (Patel, 1995, p. 144). Similarly there is a growing belief in corporate management circles of the importance of cross-border tacit knowledge flows, both on an intra-firm basis between sites of major multinational companies and on an inter-firm basis (Oujian and Carne, 1987; Gupta and Govindarajan, 1995; Menzler-Hokkanen, 1995), and this again remains largely ignored in studies of the globalization of technology. All these harder to quantify, but crucial, aspects of the globalization of technology tend to get lost or neglected in the analysis of the situation.

The Extent of Globalization

In terms of extent, there are three elements here. First, there is geographical extent in terms of the spatial spread and intensity (or 'depth') of the globalization of technology. Secondly, there are sectoral variations in the extent of globalization in terms of industry and technology variations in the level of the internationalization of innovation. Lastly, there is the issue of the temporal extent of globalization in terms of how far back it goes in time. Thus when did the globalization of technology effectively first appear and what is the nature and extent of its development?

Geographical Extent
In relation to studies analysing R&D and patent data, there is now (and generally always was) common agreement on their scale and reach. Thus

Pearce's comments in the late 1980s that the internationalization of R&D, 'has been by no means a persistent or generalised phenomenon' (Pearce, 1989, p. 12) has been echoed by a whole series of subsequent studies investigating the internationalization of R&D using large-scale surveys and more specific case study work (see, for example, Pearce and Singh, 1992, p. 188; De Meyer, 1993, p. 109; Granstrand *et al.*, 1993, p. 427; Howells and Wood, 1993, pp. 21 and 23).

Similarly, in relation to patent analyses, Patel and Pavitt's (1991, p. 17) conclusion that, 'the production of technology remains far from globalised' has also been confirmed by other patent studies using similar US patent data (Cantwell 1995; Patel 1995). Thus Patel (1995, pp. 148–9) found that, regarding the US patenting activity of 569 large firms (selected from *Who Owns Whom* in 1988), on average 89.1 per cent of US patenting activity during 1985–90 took place in their home country. This ranged from Japanese firms which had 99.0 per cent of their US patenting originating from Japan down to Belgium with 37.2 per cent. However, Patel did find that over time, from the period 1979–84 to 1985–90, all firms (except those from Canada) increased the proportion of US patenting originating from abroad. Indeed, Niosi and Bellon (1994, 186–7) in their analysis of patenting trends between 1975 and 1990 went further, noting, 'foreign patents have rapidly increased as a proportion of national patent applications in the G-7 countries except for Canada, in which the internationalization process was already very advanced, and Japan'.

As noted above, a number of other indicators have been used, such as analysis of scientific publications, but on a more limited basis. Thus Hicks *et al.* (1994), investigating publication and citation patterns in an admittedly domestically oriented Japanese corporate sector, found that the publication of papers by Japanese companies was from laboratories located in Japan and staffed by Japanese, with Japanese companies also overwhelmingly citing Japanese sources. However, Hicks *et al.* (1994, p. 384) acknowledge that trends in papers published abroad and in collaboration are towards increased globalization, and this is borne out by similar studies (Luukkonen *et al.*, 1992; although national collaboration is still important; see Debackere and Rappa, 1993). Again these suggest a limited and gradual extension of technological globalization.

Sectoral Extent
A host of in-depth and larger-scale studies have indicated that not only are there geographical variations in the extent of globalization of technology, but also sectoral differences. Thus in terms of sectoral concentrations, petroleum products, chemicals (and in particular pharmaceuticals) and food show the highest level of overseas research activity, while primary metal manufacture

and aerospace show least expansion abroad (although there are notable variations between studies; see, for example, Creamer, 1976; Pearce, 1989, 12–20;
Pearce and Singh, 1992, 189; Cantwell, 1995, 162–3). Patel (1996), using US
patent data from 1969–90 rather than R&D activity, has discovered that firms
having a higher R&D intensity in fact produced relatively less of their technology (as measured by patents) outside their home country.

Temporal Extent

There is also substantial agreement on the temporal extent of the appearance
and development of the globalization of technology. Up until the early 1980s
the stated view was that 'globalization', at least in terms of overseas R&D,
first appeared after the Second World War and began to take off in the 1960s.
In part this view was influenced by R&D studies investigating mainly US
multinational R&D. However, as economic historians began exploring early
multinationals via detailed case study work, both the origins of their first
overseas expansions and, in turn, their research activity got pushed further
back to the turn of the 20th century (Liebanau, 1984; Davenport-Hines, 1986;
Hounshell and Smith, 1988; Freeman, 1995). This was confirmed on a more
comprehensive basis by Cantwell (1993, 1995) using US patent data. Thus
Cantwell (1993, p. 275) notes:

> For the largest US, Swedish and British firms the degree of internationalization of
> technological activity was relatively high as early as the interwar period. Indeed,
> if one was to look further back in time it may be that European firms were
> technologically active in their operations in the US at the end of the last century.

There is now therefore a consensus from both in-depth case study work and
aggregate statistical analysis that the origins of the globalization of technology began much earlier than previously thought, at the start of the 20th
century.

Conclusions

Although there are some who feel they can identify the full-blooded rhetoric
of the pro-globalization protagonists in terms of the overall globalization
debate (Hirst and Thompson, 1994), it is difficult to identify full-blown
protagonists within the more specific research arena of the globalization of
technology. It is equally hard to find what may be termed as a total 'anti-
globalist' sceptic. Thus Patel and Pavitt in their paper outlining the case of
'non-globalization', which some have seen as coming perhaps closest to a
global-sceptic stance, ended up acknowledging that Belgian, Dutch, British,
Canadian, Swedish and Swiss large firms all executed over 30 per cent of
their technological activities outside their home country (Patel and Pavitt,

1991, pp. 10–11). Nonetheless there is still a tendency among some studies to use the academic device of a 'straw man' to push forward the rhetoric of full-blown globalization of technology which can then be satisfyingly knocked down. This is despite the surprisingly high level of agreement regarding the basic parameters of the globalization debate relating to the descriptive assessment of the nature and extent of the globalization of technology, as indicated above. Based primarily on R&D and patent data, the process of the globalization of technology for most countries and firms remains limited, and its progress has been gradual and uneven.

THE DYNAMICS AND PROCESSES BEHIND THE GLOBALIZATION OF TECHNOLOGY

For many studies, trying to ascertain the basic extent and nature of the globalization of technology has been hard enough in itself and has remained the essential focus of study. For some studies there has been an attempt to go further and to try and discover the underlying factors driving such globalization, the processes and decisions behind such moves and, more speculatively, what the future scenario of the globalization of technology might be.

Taking this latter point first, few studies have suggested in relation to globalization what the end state of a truly globalized technological world might look like. Here those pushing forward the 'straw man' rhetoric of the globalization of technology would perhaps suggest giant, stateless corporations generating technology wherever they require across the globe, where information and communication technologies (ICTs) make geography an irrelevance and where technology flows unimpeded across boundaries. However, it is difficult to find any such proponents for this 'end state'. Even at the level of the wider globalization debate it is difficult to find protagonists enveloping the concept of the uncoupling of companies and markets from distinct national bases and the move towards a genuine global economy centred upon truly global companies, heralding a new stage of TNC (Trans National Corporations) evolution. Hirst and Thompson (1994, pp. 287–8) find Ohmae (1990, 1993) leaning nearest to this, with his vision of the inter-linked economy. Here the prime movers are indeed stateless corporations based in North America, Europe and Japan, with developments in ICTs and the 'electronic superhighways' enabling everyone to plug into a global marketplace and with the shackles of nationally oriented bureaucracies being lifted, enabling a new world of open global marketing and production. However, the picture of technology in this remains blurred; technology is seen primarily as a facilitator (via the use of ICTs), with corporations being able to generate, tap and distribute technology more freely across the globe; but there is not much beyond this. A detailed vision of what a truly globalized technology system might present still awaits.

In relation to the underlying factors driving the globalization of technology are a number of general and more specific factors. Two key general factors have played an important driving and shaping role in cross-border technology activity. The first is the strong association between the globalization of production and technology, and the second is the strong, but mainly indirect, role played by cross-border merger and acquisition activity on the increase in foreign research and technical capacity controlled by firms.

There have been a series of studies that have identified the expansion of overseas production with an accompanying rise in the level of research and technology being undertaken abroad. Hirschey and Caves (1981, p. 128), for example, found that the proportion that US multinationals devoted to overseas R&D outlays was positively associated with the extent of the multinationals' foreign markets served by their subsidiaries' local production. This is associated with a strong evolutionary process observed in the research and technical capabilities of overseas plants (Cordell, 1971; Steele, 1975; Behrman and Fischer, 1980; Håkanson, 1990). Thus Steele (1975, p. 212) notes: 'There is an almost irresistible creepage from production engineering upstream into design and development', and this is echoed by Håkanson (1990, p. 260) who comments that, 'engineering capabilities acquired to perform routine technical activities – service, maintenance and customisation of products to individual buyer needs – often evolve into proper R&D'. There is often therefore a strong evolutionary time sequence involved with the build-up of research, technical and engineering knowhow which the establishment of an overseas manufacturing plant creates (Haug, Hood and Young, 1983, p. 391).

A second general, and more indirect, factor driving the globalization of technology, at least in terms of international R&D activity, has been cross-border acquisition activity by firms. Thus Ronstadt (1977, p. 94) found that in his sample of US companies nearly a quarter of the overseas R&D establishments originated as an indirect consequence of takeover activity, while Pearce and Singh (1992, pp. 124–5) discovered that 20 per cent of the overseas R&D units they surveyed had been acquired by merger or takeover activity. Indeed Patel (1995, p. 149) notes that 60 per cent of the growth in the total number of patents granted to large British firms from outside the UK between the periods 1979–84 and 1985–90 was due to acquisitions.

Other studies have suggested that the factors driving the internationalization of technology have changed over time. Cantwell (1995, pp. 171–2) sums this up best in his reinterpretation and adaption of the product life-cycle model noting that:

In the past, foreign technological activity exploited domestic strengths abroad, it was located in response to local demand conditions, it assisted in the growth of other high income areas, and its role ranged from the adaptation of products to suit local tastes through to the establishment of new local industries ... By contrast, today, for companies of the leading centres, foreign technological activity now increasingly aims to tap into local fields of expertise, and to provide a further source of new technology that can be utilised internationally in the other operations of the MNC.

The argument here, therefore, is that the *raison d'être* for locating R&D overseas changes over time from one of satisfying individual national *demand* requirements, to local technical adaption, to one of satisfying *supply criteria* to tap into national centres of expertise and specialist scientific and technical personnel. Indeed, this neatly combines the two different theoretical perspectives that have attempted to explain the internationalization of R&D (Howells, 1990, pp. 496–7). The former perspective sees technology as a tool which firms use to defend and develop their market power across national boundaries. On this basis, R&D is seen as a corporate weapon in terms of a demand or market control mechanism. The organization and location of technological assets is therefore seen largely as a 'market pull' response, where R&D and technology are deployed in the most optimal way to defend and secure market power. The second perspective has focused on the needs and requirements of R&D and technology in order to fulfil their role as elements in the competitive advantage of the firm. The focus here is on the supply-side requirements of research and technical activities and the problems associated with organizing these inputs to optimize innovative output and efficiency. The ability to tap into pools of scientific and technical expertise is seen as an important element in this process.

Certainly there is some indication to suggest that supply-side factors are becoming more important over time, not least the predicted world-wide shortage of skilled scientific and technical personnel (Swinbanks, 1992). A shift away from simple developmental, adaptive R&D to more basic and applied research also has major implications in terms of changing the weighting of different locational factors in R&D (Malecki, 1979, 1980; Howells, 1984; Kenney and Florida, 1994). Equally demand-type defensive adaptation work may be declining with the rise, not so much of what may be termed truly 'global products' (where absolutely no modification is needed for particular countries), but rather the emergence of products with increasing numbers of shared components requiring less local market adaptation work. This can be seen in the case of new car models, with increasing standardization of 'underbodies' but some customization of 'upper-bodies' still being undertaken (Miller, 1994, pp. 37–9). This shift, however, may still have a long way to go, with Patel (1995, p. 151), for example, noting the most internationalized firms are not in the 'high tech' product groups, but in product groups where adaptation for serving local markets is the most important.

More definable trends and processes in terms of more globalized patterns and networks of technology still, however, remain to be articulated and conceptualized, although again this is hampered by the problems of undertaking more detailed longitudinal studies of technology across borders. Such problems and gaps will now be explored in more detail.

KNOWLEDGE GAPS

Despite the undoubted progress made in the study of the globalization of technology, today it is still difficult not to reject the conclusion made by Mansfield *et al.* (1979, p. 194), in their study of overseas R&D activity, when they noted that, 'despite the magnitude and importance of these overseas R&D activities, little is known about their purpose, nature or effects' and apply it to the study of the whole of overseas technological activity. The following discussion seeks to outline those areas where the author believes further work needs to be done before the purposes, nature or effects of the internationalization of technology can be more adequately described and conceptual progress can be made.

Indicators, Non-Tangibles, the Small-Scale and the 'Other End'

The problem of developing new and refining existing indicators to provide a more complete and realistic picture of technological innovation does not remain confined to studies examining the process of the globalization of technology. Progress continues in this area with, for example, work on the revision of the OECD 'Oslo Manual'. The implementation of the Community Innovation Survey by the European Commission is just one strand of this. However, although the problem is not unique, the picture of the globalization of technology still remains restricted because of a lack of suitable indicators and of interest in non-R&D/patent activity. R&D and activities associated with patenting only remain a part of the whole technology process. Thus as far back as the 1970s Crum and Gudgin (1977, p. 7) noted that within UK manufacturing, scientific personnel associated with R&D only made up just over 11 per cent of the total number of people employed in activities classified as scientific and technical.

Similarly, taking a 'sink' rather than a 'source' perspective can also alter our perspective on the globalization of technology. Thus Le Heron (1978), in a survey of New Zealand manufacturing companies, found that domestically generated technology only formed a small part of the technology base that the firms used and developed. Nearly 35 per cent of firms were adopting or adapting overseas technology already in use in New Zealand. Another 47 per cent were directly introducing overseas technology into the country, but only 18 per cent were developing totally new technology by themselves or in collaboration with other New Zealand firms. The Australian Economic Planning Advisory Council (1986) has emphasized an even more limited role for domestic technology in Australia, noting that only 2 per cent of new technology used by Australian industry will originate from domestic R&D, the balance coming from overseas. Indeed, there is a whole range of technical and knowledge-based support activities which, although crucial to the competitive and technological success of the firm, have been excluded from studies of the internationalization of innovation and diffusion because of measurement problems and lack of data. A key area here is non-tangible, tacit and disembodied technical change, which has been increasingly recognized as the key competitive technological weapon for firms (Howells, 1996). However, studies of the globalization of technology have little, if anything, to say about these crucial innovative activities and there remains little progress in this area. As Chesnais (1992, p. 291) has noted, studies of national and international innovation systems need to be involved in the analysis of much wider linkage patterns, sourcing policies (see Levy, 1993) and strategic alliances of firms.

Predictive Ability: Future Scenarios of Globalization

A number of researchers suggest that the national specialization in technology, as suggested by the national systems of innovation (NSI) model, would under conditions of the globalization of technology become 'irrelevant' (Patel, 1995, p. 152), if it really did take place. However, it is difficult to identify any specific references which actually suggest under real, or perceived, conditions of globalization of technology that technological generation and production across the world are characterized by increasing homogeneity. Technological specialization has been shown to have increased over time (Archibugi and Michie, 1995), but indeed it would be strange if it had not, given the obvious and direct parallel with the laws of comparative advantage which has underpinned models of trade theory. With increasing growth and freedom in international trade the law of comparative advantage would suggest *increased* specialization in terms of production and trade, rather than increased homogeneity. This was highlighted by Porter (1990, p. 1) who noted that, 'the international integration of economic systems leads to the emergence of specific fields of national specialisation in industrial production', with global competition leading countries to focus on their areas of international excellence (Porter, 1990, p. 149). Why should this be any different for technology? Even the strongest exponent of economic and technological globalization has inferred that national technological specialization will decline, being in turn replaced by some kind of homogeneous, delocalized world of technology generation and diffusion (see below). Rather, NSIs will become more open but still 'trade' on their particular strengths and specialisms (Niosi and Bellon, 1994, p. 194).

However, the problem with the concept of national technological specialization, like the law of comparative advantage, is that it has little, if any, predictive ability. Japan in 1950 had a trade advantage only in textiles (over a quarter of all exports) and, later in the decade, textile machinery (Eatwell, 1982, p. 136). On the basis of the law of comparative advantage, predictions about Japan's trade growth and specialization would suggest that Japan would continue to strengthen and consolidate in the field of textiles and related products. In fact the notion of comparative advantage has had nothing to say about where Japan has gone since the late 1950s in terms of trade or industry specialization and its virtual world domination in such areas as consumer electronics, electrical engineering and the automotive sector. This applies equally to the predictive abilities of national technological specialization. Will Japan continue to be pre-eminent in electronics and electrical engineering? Will it become even more specialized in research and technological terms in this field? Will the UK remain strong and further build on its research specialization in pharmaceuticals? Who will win and sustain new technologies arising from an increasingly specialized, differentiated global technology system? At one level the notion of technological specialization is a useful descriptor; on another level it offers little in the way of explanation or prediction.

Global–Local Interface and Closed Spatial Innovation Systems

Linked to the debate about NSIs and national technological specialization are the implications for local economies under increased globalization of technology. The general assumption is that certain regions and localities which are already 'centres of excellence' for certain technologies will further develop these specialisms under processes of cumulative causation linked back to the old debates about the advantages of innovation agglomeration and more general Marshallian districts (Marshall, 1932, pp. 151–78). These are familiar themes to economic geographers and planners who tried to develop and implement 'growth pole' theory from the 1950s onwards (Perroux, 1955; Thomas, 1975) and who then subsequently sought to measure local technological linkages and benefits at the local level (see, for example, Taylor, 1973; McDermott, 1976). More recently it has resurfaced under the discussion of industrial districts and the opportunities of small and medium-sized enterprises to develop a dense fabric and technological and industrial links generating favourable long-term regional growth trajectories. Again these were heavily criticized and have been abandoned for lack of empirical evidence and conceptual consistency (Amin and Robins, 1990; Harrison, 1992).

Undoubtedly, at the level of knowledge generation and sharing there are strong and highly localized knowledge and information flows (see, for example, Thorngren, 1970; Allen 1977; Pred 1977) reflected in turn in spatially concentrated citation patterns (Jaffe *et al.*, 1993) and research links (Gibson *et al.*, 1994). Equally, at the other level, there are strong spatial elements within innovation diffusion (Hagerstrand, 1952; Malecki, 1977; Brown, 1981). However, these should not be equated with highly localized and closed systems of technology throughout the whole innovation process. When it comes to investigating locational development paths of particular innovations, basic and applied research activity may remain highly localized (although drawing in knowledge and information sources from a wide area), but the development, testing, scale-up and production (all involving key research, technical, engineering and design skills) may be undertaken over a wide, sometimes global, geographical basis. The case of salmeterol, a new anti-asthma drug discovered and produced by Glaxo Wellcome is just one example of this (Howells, 1993, p. 225). In terms of academic and scientific standing, basic research represents the 'top flight' research activity and is likely to be spatially concentrated, but the more widely dispersed 'lower level' design, engineering and technical activities required in an innovation's eventual production should not be neglected. Skills at this lower level in terms of timeliness, quality, precision, reproducibility and efficiency can be just as important to the eventual success of the product as the basic research which led to the initial invention.

More recent studies in advanced economies have found very little evidence for the technological agglomeration with dense technical or material linkages and spillover effects in terms of productivity or performance (see, for example, Anderson, 1995; Angel and Engstrom, 1995; Appold, 1995). Thus in the Canadian aerospace industry, Anderson (1995, p. 71) found that close technical relationships, 'are not those developed within regions but rather those created between regions and nations that link local economies with one another'. Similarly Angel and Engstrom (1995, p. 79) have noted in the context of the US personal computer industry that linkages between manufacturers and component suppliers are predominantly interregional and international in scope and that there is little evidence of locational clustering of assemblers and suppliers in the USA. Certainly there appears little material or technical sourcing between branch plants and the local or regional economy (Phelps, 1993; Turock, 1993; Munday *et al.*, 1995), although there may be some evidence of such integration in high performing Asian economies (Wong,

1992). Indeed Phelps (1993) found a decline in the local procurement of branch plants over time, while other studies have highlighted the depressing effects of foreign multinationals on the R&D activity of indigenous local firms (Veughelers and Vanden Houte, 1990, p. 12). The notion of 'technological dependency' effects is one which many less favoured countries and regions still strongly adhere to.

Important issues still remain here in terms of what may be termed the global–local interface. Although spatial and locational factors are important in research and technical activity, they are certainly more subtle and complex than has been traditionally conceived. If further national technological specialization is occurring within a period of continued (albeit slow) globalization of technology, such processes may be expected at the regional level as well (Cooke *et al.*, 1992). Moreover, 'the image of the global economy as a sort of delocalised "space of flows" of human, physical and financial capital' (Storper, 1992, p. 91) is belied by examples of multinationals still seeking to locate key research and technical facilities in centres of excellence, and by such companies allowing local subsidiaries to take on 'strategic leader' (Bartlett and Ghoshal, 1989) or 'global innovator' (Gupta and Govindarajan, 1991) roles.

However, although 'vicious cycles' of restructuring associated with the presence of foreign multinationals in the technological and competitive profile of indigenous companies may be evident, there is also evidence of 'virtuous cycles' of localized learning and technological accumulation. This is associated with the dynamic interaction between inward investment by foreign multinationals and the indigenous sector that has strengthened the competitive and technological position of firms (see, for example, Dunning 1988; Cantwell, 1989). Thus, for example, Dunning (1988, pp. 137–8) outlines the beneficial effect of inward investment on the UK pharmaceutical industry in terms of its industrial and technological capability. More detailed work is required here at both the national and regional scale. A central issue is what makes the difference between 'vicious' and 'virtuous' cycles.

Global Technology Regimes?

One feature of the globalization of technology which is frequently overlooked is in the area of regulatory and bureaucratic regimes relating to technology. Regulatory regimes relating to technology include not only such direct areas as the regulatory system covering intellectual property rights, but also public procurement (traditionally important in such high technology sectors as defence, aerospace and telecommunications), accountancy legislation and pricing controls (which are still common in sectors such as pharmaceuticals, for example, the Pharmaceutical Price Regulatory Scheme in the

UK). An important element of NSIs is their regulatory and bureaucratic regimes relating to science and technology. However, although these national technology regulatory regimes are still important, they are becoming less so with the agreement under GATT and the emergence of the WTO (World Trade Organization) moving towards gradual international harmonization of patenting and copyrights. Thus by the early 1990s the UK's national system of patenting and its institutional framework was already giving way to a pan-European regime. In turn the three main patent regulatory systems of the USA, Japan and Europe are moving towards global harmonization of systems under the impetus of the recent TRIPS (Trade Related Aspects of International Property Rights) agreement of the GATT Uruguay Round. This establishes a comprehensive and binding agreement on intellectual property rights, with a 20 year minimum patent life from filing date. While the international harmonization of patenting systems is still some way off (Carey 1994, p. 31), with the effective pan-national implementation of international standards even further away (see, for example, General Accounting Office, 1993), there is increasingly less scope for the use of idiosyncratic patent and standards systems to give covert protection to local industries and distinctive national systems in these two important areas of technological regulation (Howells and Neary, 1995, p. 165).

Equally, in the area of public procurement, legislation under the Completion of the Internal Market programme of the European Union has led to stringent new rules on public procurement within Europe, which are being paralleled under the North American Free Trade Agreement. This has now been followed by calls for the harmonization of competition policy between the major world trading blocs to make it more of a 'level playing field' (Hoekman and Mauroidis, 1994). Movement towards regulatory harmonization may be a gradual and uneven process, with many less developed countries still resisting the new GATT system (and more particularly open to wide variations of interpretation and policing); it will, however, undoubtedly diminish one aspect of NSIs over time. Here the research issue is therefore what are the implications for NSIs of the gradual harmonization of regulatory frameworks and what role will international technical regulation play in the overall development of technological globalization?

New Organizational Modes

Although the numbers of firms having to deal with the coordination and management of technological innovation across national boundaries may still be comparatively small, this represents a vitally important issue for multinationals seeking to manage innovation on a global basis. A series of studies in the late 1980s outlined the move of multinational companies from centralized, top-down, hierarchical structures of command from the parent to the subsidiaries towards flatter, decentralized and autonomous networks with two-way flows of information and control in what Hedlund has termed 'heterarchies' (Hedlund 1986; see also, Bartlett, 1986; Hakansson, 1987; Prahalad and Doz, 1987; Kogut, 1990). These more general 'global' management trends (Rhinesmith, 1993) have been replicated in terms of how firms have sought to manage their technological activities across borders. The emphasis here is on how firms have sought to improve their global intra-organizational research and technical links, allowing more local autonomy and flexibility (such as acquiring world-wide research charters; De Meyer, 1993) while maintaining the advantages of scale and scope that multinationals possess (Neff, 1995). Nevertheless, even in relation to R&D there remains a wide diversity of international organizational structures between multinational companies (Industrial Research Institute, 1995).

A few major multinational corporations have succeeded in developing strategies and techniques that allow the effective generation and transfer of technology between different functions of the firm and key suppliers on an international basis. However, even within these companies such successful global technology management 'repertoires' may not be widely dispersed or codified and shared between different Strategic Business Units or divisions. Much of this action-oriented learning (De Meyer, 1993, p. 111) and memory remains embedded in only small fragments of the wider corporation. Still less are these 'best practice' methods more widely diffused between firms. Indeed for many firms this is the very essence of their competitive advantage over other companies.

While some of these general trends may therefore have been charted by researchers within certain firms, very little is known about the international patterns of innovation generation and intra- and inter-firm linkages associated with a new product and the way that this process is managed by the firm. However, these practices and strategies are the very processes that actually influence and drive the process of globalization of technology within the world economy. Research here should not only help us to understand such processes, but also help to improve their efficiency and effectiveness for the firm, as well as to expand the economic development prospects for disadvantaged economies and societies.

CONCLUSIONS

This chapter has indicated that in those areas where there has been analysis of the globalization of technology, namely in terms of technology inputs and intermediates, there has been surprising agreement between academics over its nature and extent. In short, the internationalization of technology has been gradual but 'lumpy', while innovation generation still remains a largely 'domestic' (national) affair. This view in turn has been influenced by two important factors: that much of the dominant analysis of this phenomenon has been within the tradition of the agency-based perspective outlined above; and secondly (and perhaps more critically) that such studies have been influenced by the availability of data. However, there remains much which is hidden in the debate over the globalization of technology, and changing the perspective of analysis can generate substantially different views. The place-based perspective suggests that, for many, the domestic (national) nature of technology may be less well placed. Major industrial corporations located in the major advanced industrial economies of the world, such as the USA, Japan and Germany, that generate technology, may still operate in largely national contexts. Nonetheless for many countries in the less developed world; for smaller industrialized economies; for less favoured regions in major advanced economies; and, indeed, for many smaller firms and plants themselves, such a 'national-centric' view of technology may be not so applicable. Much of the technology for these countries, regions and firms comes from overseas before being used and adapted locally. Indeed closer examination of specific innovations suggests that they do not necessarily operate within strictly closed national innovation spatial systems. Moreover, the wider international technological framework also becomes more applicable when the focus of attention moves from technology generation (a 'source' view) to technology use (a 'sink' perspective). In such places the term 'technology dependence' (see Erb and Kallab, 1975; Thomas, 1979) remains a major concern and continues to hold a central place in policy debates, irrespective of the more academic debates on the globalization of technology. The 'branch plant syndrome' of dependence on foreign, imported technology; the 'shadow effect' that large foreign multinationals have on indigenously generated technology; and the acquisition and takeover of successful, innovative domestic companies by foreign firms are still very much an issue. Lack of indigenous capability and control over technology is seen as a major constraint on long-term economic development.

The spectre that the globalization of technology leads to international homogenization of technology generation and use is also held up, but unlikely actually to happen. Both national and regional differentiation in technological capability will undoubtedly remain and, indeed, show propensity to increase over time. Indeed in many respects the competitive advantage of major multinationals that are leading the trend towards the globalization of technology is their ability to harness this differentiation to their firm-specific benefit. National systems of innovation and regional systems of innovation (RSIs) will continue to provide crucial institutional, economic and cultural frameworks for the technological competitiveness of firms. There will be certain facets between different NSIs that will become more similar over time through harmonization, in particular through the trend towards a more global pattern of regulation affecting technological innovation. However, there will be other elements of NSIs and RSIs that will remain distinctive and difficult for other national and regional economies to copy successfully.

The importance of NSIs has, however, led governments further into what the OECD (1990, p. 13) has termed 'techno-nationalism'. This has led the USA in particular to impose restrictions on foreign firms in participating in US technology programmes, associated with such recent legislation as the Defense Authorization Legislation, the National Critical Technologies Act (1991), the Advanced Manufacturing Technology Act (1991) and the American Technology Preeminence Act. This is despite the fact that foreign investment in research and technology has played an important role in revitalizing key areas of US business (Florida, 1995, pp. 52–5). Although the rationale is to protect domestic technological assets, it also limits the potential of indigenous firms to collaborate and use much-needed foreign sources of technology.

Trying to achieve a balance between stimulating (rather than necessarily protecting) the indigenous technology base of an economy while allowing ready access and flow of foreign technology is a problem that smaller and peripheral economies have had to battle with for several decades. However, it is still relatively new for other larger economies, most notably the USA. There are still many policy issues in this global–local technology balance that need to be explored. Much attention has rightly been focused on systems of innovation successes; however, much can also be learnt from failures. The lack of effective national or regional appropriation of indigenous innovations is one such area (Sigurdson and Reddy, 1995), with still too little being known about the absorptive capacity of indigenous firms at a national (Teece, 1987) or regional (Jevons and Saupin, 1991) scale. Indeed for many countries, particularly in developing countries, there is a danger that a 'dual technology' environment is emerging, with a small, elite, high-tech base with strong complementarities with Western firms and a dominant portion of the economy with little or no technical capabilities and non-existent contact with the Westernized elite of the nation concerned (Reddy and Sigurdson, 1994). Globalization of technology does not imply the need for the abolition of national or regional policies, or an attempt to create a protectionist barrier around an economy's technology base; rather it requires sensitive policies that seek to engage the wider economic base of the nation or region with both indigenous and foreign technological capabilities.

BIBLIOGRAPHY

Allen, T.J. (1977), *Managing the Flow of Technology*, Cambridge, Mass: MIT Press.

Amin, A. and Robins, K. (1990), 'The Reemergence of Regional Economics? The Mythical Geography of Flexible Accumulation', *Environment and Planning*, **D8**, 7–34.

Anderson, M. (1995), 'The Role of Collaborative Integration in Industrial Organization: Observations from the Canadian Aerospace Industry', *Economic Geography*, **71**, 55–78.

Angel, D.P. and Engstrom, J. (1995), 'Manufacturing Systems and Technological Change: The US Personal Computer Industry', *Economic Geography*, **71**, 79–101.

Appold, S.J. (1995), 'Agglomeration, Interorganizational Networks and Competitive Performance in the US Metalworking Sector', *Economic Geography*, **71**, 49–54.

Archibugi, D. and Michie, J. (1995), 'The Globalization of Technology: A New Taxonomy', *Cambridge Journal of Economics*, **19**, 121–40.

Bartlett, C.A. (1986), 'Building and Managing the Transnational: The New Organizational Challenge', in M.E. Porter (ed.), *Competition in Global Industries*, Boston, Mass: Harvard Business School Press, pp. 367–401.

Bartlett, C.A. and Ghoshal, S. (1989), *Managing Across Borders: The Transnational Solution*, Boston, Mass: Harvard Business School Press.

Behrman, J.N. and Fischer, W.A. (1980), *Overseas R&D Activities of Transnational Companies*, Cambridge, Mass: Oelgeschlager, Gunn & Hain.

Britton, J.N., Gilmour, J.M. and Murphy, M.G. (1978), *The Weakest Link: A Technological Perspective on Canadian Industrial Underdevelopment*, Ottawa: Science Council of Canada.

Brown, L.A. (1981), *Innovation Diffusion: A New Perspective*, New York: Methuen.

Cantwell, J.A. (1989), *Technological Innovation and Multinational Corporations*, Oxford: Basil Blackwell.

Cantwell, J. (1993), 'The Internationalization of Technological Activity in Historical Perspective', in J. Simoes (ed.), *International Business and Europe after 1992: Volume 1*. Proceedings of the 19th Annual Conference of the European International Business Association, 12–14 December, Lisboa, pp. 263–83.

Cantwell, J. (1995), 'The Globalization of Technology: What Remains of the Product Cycle Model?', *Cambridge Journal of Economics*, **19**, 155–74.

Cantwell, J. and Hodson, C. (1991), 'Global R&D and UK Competitiveness', in M.C. Casson (ed.), *Global Research Strategy and Global Competitiveness*, Oxford: Basil Blackwell.

Carey, J. (1994), 'Inching Towards a Borderless Patent', *Business Week*, **3373**, 703.

Chesnais, F. (1992), 'National Systems of Innovation, Foreign Direct Investment and the Operations of Foreign Multinational Enterprises', in B.-Å. Lundvall (ed.), *National Systems of Innovation: Towards a Theory of Innovation and Interactive Learning*, London: Pinter, pp. 265–95.

Comanor, W.S. and Scherer, F.M. (1969), 'Patent Statistics as a Measure of Technical Change', *Journal of Political Economy*, **77**, 392–8.

Cooke, P., Mouleart, F., Swyngedouw, E., Weinstein, O. and Wells, P. (1992), *Towards Global Localisation*, London: UCL Press.

Cordell, A.J. (1971), *The Multinational Firm, Foreign Direct Investment and Canadian Science Policy*, Ottawa: Science Council of Canada.

Creamer, D. (1976), *Overseas Research and Development by United States*

Multinationals, 1966–1995: Estimates of Expenditures and a Statistical Profile, New York: The Conference Board.

Crum, R.E. and Gudgin, G. (1977), *Non-Production Activities in UK Manufacturing Industry Collection Studies*, Regional Policy Series 3, Brussels: Commission of the European Communities.

Davenport-Hines, R.P.T. (1986), 'Glaxo as a Multinational before 1965', in G. Jones (ed.), *British Multinationals: Origins, Management and Performance*, Aldershot: Gower, pp. 137–63.

De Meyer, A. (1993), 'Management of an International Network of Industrial R&D Laboratories', *R&D Management*, **23**, 109–20.

Debackere, K. and Rappa, M.A. (1993), 'An International Comparison of Scientists in an Emerging Field', *International Journal of Technology Management*, **8**, 740–63.

Dicken, P. (1994), 'Global–Local Tensions: Firms and States in the Global Space-Economy', *Economic Geography*, **70**, 101–28.

Duerr, M.G. (1970), *R&D in the Multinational Company: A Survey*, Montreal: National Conference Board.

Dunning, J.H. (1988), *Multinationals, Technology and Competitiveness*, London: Unwin Hyman.

Eatwell, J. (1982), *Whatever Happened to Britain?*, London: Duckworth.

Economic Planning Advisory Council (1986), *Technology and Innovation*, Council Paper 19, Canberra: Commonwealth of Australia.

Erb, G.F. and Kallab, V. (eds) (1975), *Beyond Dependency: The Developing World Speaks Out*, Washington, DC: Overseas Development Council.

Firn, J.R. (1975), 'External Control and Regional Development: the Case of Scotland', *Environment and Planning*, **A7**, 393–414.

Fischer, M.M., Frohilch, J. and Gassler, H. (1994), 'An Explanation into the Determinants of Patent Activities', *Regional Studies*, **28**, 1–12.

Florida, R. (1995), 'Technology Policy for a Global Economy', *Issues in Science and Technology*, **11**(3), 49–56.

Freeman, C. (1995), 'The "National System of Innovation" in historical perspective', *Cambridge Journal of Economics*, **19**(1), February, 5–24.

Fuenzalida, E.E. (1979), 'The Problem of Technological Innovation in Latin America', in J. Villamil (ed.), *Transnational Capitalism and National Development*, Atlantic Highlands, NJ: Humanities Press, pp. 115–27.

General Accounting Office (1993), *US Companies Patent Experience in Japan*, Washington, DC: US General Accounting Office, US Congress, Government Printing Office.

Gibson, D.V., Kehoe, C.A. and Lee, S.-Y.K. (1994), 'Collaborative Research as a Function of Proximity, Industry, and Company: A Case Study of an R&D Consortium', *IEEE Transactions on Engineering Management*, **41**, 255–63.

Globerman, S. (1973), 'Market Structure and R&D in Canadian Manufacturing Industries', *Quarterly Review of Economics and Business*, **13**(2), 59–67.

Granstrand, O., Håkanson, L. and Sjölander, S. (1993), 'Internationalization of R&D – a Survey of some Recent Research', *Research Policy*, **22**, 413–30.

Gupta, A.K. and Govindarajan, V. (1991), 'Knowledge Flows and the Structure of Control within Multinational Corporations', *Academy of Management Review*, **16**, 768–92.

Gupta, A.K. and Govindarajan, V. (1995), 'Organizing Knowledge Flows within MNCs', *International Business Review*, **3**, 443–57.

Hagedoorn, J. and Schakenraad, J. (1991), *The Role of Interfirm Cooperation Agreements in the Globalization of Economic and Technology*, FAST Occasional Paper 280, Brussels: Directorate General for Science, Research and Development (DGXII), Commission of the European Communities.

Hagerstrand, T. (1952), 'The Propagation of Innovation Waves', *Lund Studies in Geography, Series B*, **4**, 3–19.

Håkanson, L. (1981), 'Organization and Evolution of Foreign Multinationals', *Geografiska Annaler*, **63B**, 47–56.

Håkanson, L. (1990), 'International Decentralization of R&D – The Organizational Challenges', in C.A. Bartlett, Y. Doz and G. Hedlund (eds), *Managing the Global Firm*, London: Routledge, pp. 256–78.

Hakansson, H. (1987), *Industrial Technological Development: A Network Approach*, London: Croom Helm.

Harrison, B. (1992), 'Industrial Districts: Old Wine in New Bottles', *Regional Studies*, **26**, 469–83.

Haug, P., Hood, N. and Young, S. (1983), 'R&D Intensity in the Affiliates of US Owned Electronics Companies Manufacturing in Scotland', *Regional Studies*, **17**, 383–92.

Hedlund, G. (1986), 'The Hypermodern MNC – a Heterarchy', *Human Resource Management*, **25**, 9–35.

Hicks, D., Ishizuka, T., Keen, P. and Sweet, S. (1994), 'Japanese Corporations, Scientific Research and Globalization', *Research Policy*, **23**, 375–84.

Hirschey, R.C. and Caves, R.E. (1981), 'Research and Transfer of Technology by Multinational Enterprises', *Oxford Bulletin of Economics and Statistics*, **43**, 115–30.

Hirst, P. and Thompson, G. (1994), 'Globalization, Foreign Direct Investment and International Governance', *Organization*, **1**, 277–303.

Hoekman, B.M. and Mauroidis, P.C. (1994), 'Competition, Competition Policy and GATT', *The World Economy*, **17**, 121–50.

Hood, N. and Young, S. (1982), 'US Multinational R&D: Corporate Strategies and Policy Implications for the UK', *Multinational Business*, **2**, 10–23.

Hounshell, D.A. and Smith, J.K. (1988), *Science and Corporate Strategy: Du Pont R&D, 1902–1980*, Cambridge: Cambridge University Press.

Howells, J. (1984), 'The Location of Research and Development', *Regional Studies*, **18**, 13–29.

Howells, J. (1990), 'The Internationalization of R&D and the Development of Global Research Networks', *Regional Studies*, **24**, 495–512.

Howells, J. (1993), 'Emerging Global Strategies in Innovation Management', in Humbert, M. (ed.), *The Impact of Globalisation on Europe's Firms and Industries*, London: Pinter, 219–28.

Howells, J. (1996), 'Tacit Knowledge, Innovation and Technology Transfer', *Technology Analysis & Strategic Management*, **8**, 91–106.

Howells, J. and Neary, I. (1995), *Intervention and Technological Innovation: Government and the Pharmaceutical Industry in the UK*, Basingstoke: Macmillan.

Howells, J. and Wood, M. (1993), *The Globalization of Production and Technology*, London: Wiley.

Industrial Research Institute (1995), *Industrial R&D Organization and Funding Charts*, Washington, DC: IRI.

Jaffe, A.B., Trajtenberg, M. and Henderson, R. (1993), 'Geographic Localization of Knowledge Spillovers as Evidenced by Patent Citations', *Quarterly Journal of Economics*, **108**, 577–98.

Jevons, F. and Saupin, M. (1991), 'Capturing Regional Benefits from Science and Technology: the Question of Regional Appropriability', *Prometheus*, **9**, 265–73.

Kenney, M. and Florida, R. (1994), 'The Organization and Geography of Japanese R&D: Results from a Survey of Japanese Electronics and Biotechnology Firms', *Research Policy*, **23**, 305–23.

Kitschelt, H. (1991), 'Industrial Governance Structures, Innovation Strategies, and the Case of Japan: Sectoral or Cross-National Comparative Analysis?', *International Organization*, **45**, 453–93.

Kleinecht, A. (1987), 'Measuring R&D in Small Firms: How Much are we Missing?', *Journal of Industrial Economics*, **36**, 253–6.

Kline, S.J. and Rosenberg, N. (1986), 'An Overview of Innovation', in R. Landau and N. Rosenberg (eds), *The Positive Sum Strategy*, Washington, DC: National Academy Press, pp. 275–305.

Kogut, B. (1990), 'International Sequencing Advantages and Network Flexibility', in C.A.Bartlett, Y. Doz and G. Hedlund (eds), *Managing the Global Firm*, London: Routledge, pp. 47–68.

Lall, S. (1979), 'The International Allocation of Research Activity by US Multinationals', *Oxford Bulletin of Economics and Statistics*, **41**, 313–31.

Le Heron, R.B. (1978), 'R and D in New Zealand Manufacturing Firms', *Pacific Viewpoint*, **19**, 149–171.

Levy, D. (1993), 'International Production and Sourcing: Trends and Issues', *STI Review*, **13**, 13–59.

Lewis, D.F. and Mangan, J. (1987), 'Research and Development in Australia: the Role of Multinational Corporations', *Prometheus*, **5**, 368–85.

Liebenau, J. (1984), 'International R&D in Pharmaceutical Firms in the Early Twentieth Century', *Business History*, **26**, 329–46.

Link, A.N. and Tassey, G. (1993), 'The Technology Infrastructure of Firms: Investments in Infratechnology', *IEEE Transactions on Engineering Management*, **40**, 312–15.

Luukkonen, T. Persson, D. and Siertsen, G. (1992), 'Understanding Patterns of International Scientific Collaboration', *Science, Technology & Human Values*, **17**(1), 101–26.

Malecki, E.J. (1977), 'Firms and Innovation Diffusion', *Environment and Planning*, **A9**, 1291–1305.

Malecki, E.J. (1979), 'Locational Trends in R&D by Large US Corporations, 1965–1977', *Economic Geography*, **55**, 309–23.

Malecki, E.J. (1980), 'Corporate Organization of R and D and the Location of Technological Activities', *Regional Studies*, **14**, 219–34.

Mansfield, E. and Romeo, A. (1984), '"Reverse" Transfers of Technology from Overseas Subsidiaries to American Firms', *IEEE Transactions on Engineering Management*, **EM31**, 122–7.

Mansfield, E., Teece, D. and Romeo, A. (1979), 'Overseas Research and Development by US-Based Firms' *Economica*, **46**, 187–96.

Marshall, A. (1932), *Elements of Economics, Volume 1: Elements of Economics of Industry*, 3rd edition, London: Macmillan (first published 1892).

Marton, K. (1986), *Multinationals, Technology and Industrialization: Implications and Impact in Third World Countries*, Lexington, MA: Lexington Books.

McDermott, P.J. (1976), 'Ownership, Organization and Regional Dependence in the Scottish Electronics Industry', *Regional Studies*, **10**, 319–35.

Menzler-Hokkanen, I. (1995), 'Multinational Enterprises and Technology Transfer', *International Journal of Technology Management*, **10**, 293–310.

Miller, R. (1994), 'Global R&D Networks and Large-Scale Innovations: The Case of the Automobile Industry', *Research Policy*, **23**, 27–46.

Munday, M., Morris, J. and Wilkinson, B. (1995), 'Factories or Warehouses? A Welsh Perspective on Japanese Transplant Manufacturing', *Regional Studies*, **29**, 1–18.

Neff, P.J. (1995) 'Cross-Cultural Research Teams in a Global Enterprise', *Research Technology Management*, **38**(3), 15–19.

Niosi, J. and Bellon, B. (1994), 'The Global Interdependence of National Innovation Systems: Evidence, Limits and Implications', *Technology in Society*, **16**, 173–97.

Oakey, R.P., Thwaites, A.T. and Nash, P.A. (1980), 'The Regional Distribution of Innovative Manufacturing Establishments in Britain', *Regional Studies*, **14**, 235–53.

OECD (1990), *Towards Techno-Globalization*, Summary Paper on the OECD Colloquium, 6–9 March, Tokyo, Paris: OECD.

Ohmae, K. (1990), *The Borderless World*, London: Collins.

Ohmae, K. (1993), 'The rise of the region state', *Foreign Affairs*, **71**, 78–87.

Oujian, M.I. and Carne, B. (1987), 'A Study of the Factors which Affect Technology Transfer in a Multilocational Multibusiness Unit Corporation', *IEEE Transactions on Engineering Management*, **34**, 194–201.

Parker, J.E.S. (1974), *The Economics of Innovation: The National and Multinational Enterprises in Technological Change*, London: Longman.

Patel, P. (1995), 'Localised Production of Technology for Global Markets', *Cambridge Journal of Economics*, **19**, 141–54 (reprinted in D. Archibugi and J. Michie (eds), *Technology, Globalization and Economic Performance*, Cambridge: Cambridge University Press, 1997).

Patel, P. (1996), 'Are Large Firms Internationalising the Generation of Technology? Some New Evidence', *IEEE Transactions in Engineering Management*, **43**(1), 41–7.

Patel, P. and Pavitt, K. (1991), 'Large Firms in the Production of the World's Technology: An Important Case of "Non-globalization"', *Journal of International Business Studies*, **22**, 1–21.

Pearce, R.D. (1989), *The Internationalization of Research and Development by Multinational Enterprises*, Basingstoke: Macmillan.

Pearce, R.D. and Singh, S. (1992), *Globalising Research and Development*, Basingstoke: Macmillan.

Perroux, F. (1955), 'Note sur la Notion de "Pôle de Croissance"', *Economie Appliquée*, Jan–June, 307–20.

Phelps, N.A. (1993), 'Branch Plants and the Evolving Spatial Division of Labour: A Study of Material Linkage in the Northern Region of England', *Regional Studies*, **27**, 87–102.

Porter, M.E. (1990), *The Competitive Advantage of Nations*, London and Basingstoke: Macmillan.

Prahalad, C.K. and Doz, Y.L. (1987), *The Multinational Mission: Balancing Global Demands and Global Vision*, New York: Free Press.

Pred, A.R. (1975), 'Diffusion, Organizational, Spatial Structure and City System Development', *Economic Geography*, **51**, 252–68.

Reddy, A.S.P. and Sigurdson, J. (1994), 'Emerging Patterns of Globalization of Corporate R&D and Scope for Innovative Capability Building in Developing Countries', *Science and Public Policy*, **21**, 283–94.

Rhinesmith, S. (1993), *A Manager's Guide to Globalization*, Burr Ridge, IL: Erwin Professional Press.

Ronstadt, R. (1977), *Research and Development Abroad by US Multinationals*, New York: Praeger.

Schott, T. (1993), 'World Science: Globalization of Institutions and Participation', *Science, Technology, & Human Values*, **18**, 196–208.

Sigurdson, J. and Reddy, P. (1995), 'National Appropriation of University Innovations: The Failure of Ink Jet Technologies in Sweden', *Technology Analysis & Strategic Management*, **7**, 41–62.

Steele, L.W. (1975), *Innovation in Big Business*, New York: Eisner.

Storper, M. (1992), 'The Limits of Globalization: Technology Districts and International Trade', *Economic Geography*, **68**, 60–92.

Swinbanks, D. (1992), 'More Yen for Japan's University Research System', *Research Technology Management*, **35**, 3–4.

Taylor, M.J. (1973), 'Local Linkage, External Economies and the Ironfoundry Industry of the West Midlands and East Lancashire Conurbations', *Regional Studies*, **7**, 387–400.

Teece, D.J. (1987), 'Capturing Value from Technological Innovation: Integration, Strategic Partnering and Licensing Decisions', in B.R. Guile and H. Brooks (eds), *Technology and Global Industry: Companies and Nations in the World Economy*, Washington, DC: National Academy Press.

Terpstra, V. (1977), 'International Product Policy: The Role of Foreign R&D', *Columbia Journal of World Business*, **12**, 24–32.

Thomas, M.D. (1975), 'Growth Pole Theory, Technological Change and Regional Economic Growth', *Papers of the Regional Science Association*, **34**, 3–25.

Thomas, M.D. (1979), 'Economic Development, Technological Change and the New International Economic Order', *Geoforum*, **10**, 129–40.

Thorngren, B. (1970), 'How Do Contact Systems Affect Regional Development?', *Environment and Planning*, **A2**, 409–27.

Thwaites, A.T. (1978), 'The Future Development of R&D Activity in the Northern Region: A Comment', *Discussion Paper 12*, Newcastle-upon-Tyne: Centre for Urban and Regional Development Studies, University of Newcastle-upon-Tyne.

Turock, I. (1993), 'Inward Investment and Local Linkages: How Deeply Embedded Is "Silicon Glen"?', *Regional Studies*, **27**, 401–17.

Vernon, R. (1966), 'International Investment and International Trade in the Product Cycle', *Quarterly Journal of Economics*, **80**, 190–207.

Vernon, R. (1977), *Storm over the Multinationals: The Real Issues*, London: Macmillan.

Vernon, R. (1979), 'The Product Cycle Hypothesis in a New Institutional Environment', *Oxford Bulletin of Economics and Statistics*, **4**, 255–67.

Vernon, R. and Davidson, W.H. (1979), 'Foreign Production of Technology-Intensive Products by US-Based Multinational Enterprises', *Working Paper No. 79-5*, Harvard: Division of Research, Graduate School of Business Administration, Harvard University.

Veughelers, R. and Vanden Houte, P. (1990), 'Domestic R&D in the Presence of Multinational Enterprises', *International Journal of Industrial Organization*, **8**, 1–15.

Wong, P.K. (1992), 'Technological Development Through Sub-Contracting Linkages', *Scandinavian International Business Review*, **1**, 28–40.

Worthington, R. (1993), 'Introduction: Science and Technology as a Global System', *Science, Technology & Human Values*, **18**, 176–85.

Young, S., Hood, N. and Peters, E. (1994), 'Multinational Enterprises and Regional Economic Development', *Regional Studies*, **28**, 657–77.

3. The globalization of technology: a socio-cultural perspective

Susan Bartholomew

INTRODUCTION

As global competition intensifies and becomes increasingly driven by technology and innovation, there has emerged a heightened interest in the technological and competitive advantage of nations (for example, Cohen *et al.*, 1984; Scott and Lodge, 1984; Kennedy, 1987; Porter, 1990; Beck, 1992). A recent body of scholarship has underscored the importance of nation-specific factors in shaping technological development and change (for example, Dosi *et al.*, 1990; Lundvall, 1992; Kogut, 1993; Nelson, 1993). From this perspective, technological development is considered a country-specific phenomenon, rooted in the skills, capabilities and knowledge which accumulate over time (Archibugi and Michie, 1995a). However, at the same time, 'the whole concept of *national* differences in innovative capabilities determining national performance has been recently challenged on the grounds that transnational corporations (TNCs) are changing the face of the world economy in the direction of globalization' (Freeman, 1995, p. 15; emphasis in original). Ohmae (1990) and Kobrin (1995) argue that national borders are losing their meaning as economic frontiers, and technology is increasingly a product of what Ohmae calls the 'ILE' (interlinked economy). The inevitable debate thus emerges: does increasing techno-globalism signal the eventual convergence of approaches to technological development? Or will national innovation systems maintain their diversity in the face of the inter-linked economy?

The analysis of the competing forces of global integration and local differentiation has been at the core of academic discourse in a number of fields, including political science (for example, Keohayne and Nye, 1973; Kindleberger, 1975), strategic management (for example, Prahalad and Doz, 1987; Bartlett and Ghoshal, 1989), and organizational behaviour (for example, Child, 1981; Hofstede, 1983; Laurent, 1983). Increasingly the conceptualization of 'globalization' and 'local differentiation' as opposite poles of a single continuum is being viewed as outmoded. Strategic management in the contemporary environment calls for firms to manage the requirements for global-scale efficiency and local responsiveness simultaneously (Bartlett and Ghoshal, 1989). While firms' human resource management systems are becoming more global in scope, recognizing and valuing diversity in management approaches is increasingly central to firms' competitive success (Adler and Bartholomew, 1992).

The global/local dichotomy would also appear to be a limited concept for understanding the dynamics of technological development and change (Archibugi and Michie, 1995a). Indeed it is suggested that persistent national differences in technological capabilities are in fact a driving force of the globalization of technology. International technological cooperation derives from the *complementarity* of knowledge and capabilities embedded in firms from different national contexts (Shan and Hamilton, 1991). Dosi *et al.* (1990, p. 269) argue that, 'the significant growth of such international technology agreements is precisely the illustration of the crucial firm- and country-specific technological advantages rooted in skills and knowledge'. Thus as Archibugi and Michie (1995b: p. 136) conclude: 'The effects of techno-globalism on national technological specialisation does not seem ... to be leading to any greater uniformity in patterns of strength and weaknesses. Nations are becoming *increasingly* different and the international operations of large firms are exploiting and developing this diversity' (emphasis in original).

The strength of this argument hinges on the extent to which technological trajectories may be considered societally embedded. Yet the empirical analysis of national technological accumulation and international technology agreements remains curiously detached from an understanding of the diversity of socio-cultural contexts which apparently shape country-specific capabilities.

In a recent paper, Dunning (1995) suggests that in order to understand properly the form, content and consequences of the emerging globalization of economic activity, the role of culture needs to be much more explicitly considered in economic analysis. This chapter aims to situate the discussion of national technological capability and the formation of international technology agreements within an understanding of the socio-cultural dynamics underlying such phenomena. In order to do this, it is constructed in three parts. The first section briefly reviews the literature which emphasizes the role of nation-specific factors in technological development. The second section then illustrates how such perspectives are consistent with the institutional approach to culture and the anthropological tradition of functional historicism. In doing so, it suggests an analytical framework that allows for more explicit integration of cultural elements with our understanding of national innovation systems and international technological agreements. Section 3 then illustrates the application of this framework by surfacing some of the historically embedded cultural patterns which underlie different institutional arrangements supporting innovation in the USA and Japan, the correspondingly different national technological trajectories in biotechnology, and the complementarities of these nation-specific trajectories which underpin the biotechnology R&D agreements between the two countries.

NATION-SPECIFIC ASPECTS OF TECHNOLOGICAL DEVELOPMENT AND INNOVATION: A BRIEF REVIEW

The importance of nation-specific factors in shaping technological development is central in a number of recent streams of literature, including work labelled as technological accumulation theory (for example, Pavitt, 1987; Cantwell, 1989), evolutionary theory of the multinational corporation (for example, Kogut, 1995), the resource-based view of strategy (for example, Porter, 1990), work on country patterns of organization (for example, Kogut, 1993; Westney, 1993), studies of national innovation systems (for example, Lundvall, 1992; Nelson, 1993), strategic trade theory (for example, Krugman, 1986), and comparative industrial policy research (for example, Ergas, 1987). The contributions of this literature are now briefly considered.

Building on earlier work in evolutionary economics (see, for example, Nelson and Winter, 1977, 1982), technological accumulation theory presents technological development as an evolutionary, cumulative process, differentiated across firms and locations (see, for example, Dosi, 1984; Pavitt, 1987; Cantwell, 1989). Technology is considered to accumulate in nations along a 'natural trajectory' of development and is shaped by location-specific elements; 'it is dependent upon the type of innovations previously established there, the skills developed by indigenous workers, the characteristics of the local education system, and the nature of linkages that exist between firms in the industry and with local suppliers and customers' (Cantwell, 1989: p. 139).

Drawing on the traditions of evolutionary economics and technological accumulation is an approach in the international management literature which Kogut (1995) labels the evolutionary theory of the multinational corporation. Kogut (1995) notes that this perspective has also been influenced by the body of work produced by a number of Japanese scholars (for example, Kagono *et al.*, 1985). This perspective suggests a view of international competition, 'as an evolutionary process, which begins with firms investing in organisational and technological resources which correspond to the cultural and demand characteristics of the immediate local environment' (Kogut, 1987, p. 317). The investments which firms make accumulate over time into, 'organisational routines and skills which are characteristic of the country, much like the genetic pool of a population' (Kogut, 1987, p. 317).

In the field of strategy, this perspective is referred to as the resource-based view of the firm (Barney, 1986; Dierickx and Cool, 1989). Resource-based theory has been translated across units of analysis from nation states (that is, Porter, 1990) to industries to firms (that is, Collis, 1991). At the national level, this perspective maintains that there are very diverse portfolios of resources and capabilities developed by companies which are nurtured in different economic, political and social environments (Bartlett and Ghoshal, 1991). For example, organizational learning and innovation depend in large part upon the dissemination and diffusion of information throughout the firm, and between the firm and different sources of knowledge and technology, such as other firms, research institutions and universities. Such patterns for communication and cooperation between firms, or between firms and other institutions, vary cross-nationally in accordance with different national institutional structures and norms (see, for example, Hamel *et al.*, 1989; Hampden-Turner and Trompenaars, 1993; Hill, 1995).

Similarly, in examining the persistent competitive differences among countries over long periods of time, Kogut (1991) highlights the role of institutional structures in influencing the learning and innovation patterns of different societies: 'learning is localized because knowledge is institutionally structured in on-going and enduring relationships' (Kogut, 1991, p. 40). Matthews (1986) and Lazonick (1990) also argue that national characteristics are a likely influence on the institutional arrangements within firms (Francis, 1992). A range of empirical studies on the underlying organizing principles of technology and work in different countries provides further evidence to support the view of technology as embedded in a wider set of institutional relationships. Such work presents, 'the common theme that country location matters, that organizing principles are difficult to change, and that historical patterns persist' (Kogut, 1993, p. 3).

Institutional organization may thus be seen as setting the context for technological organization (see, for example, Freeman, 1989; Dosi *et al.*, 1990; Ostry, 1990; Kogut, 1991; Dunning, 1992; Lenway and Murtha, 1994). As Porter (1990, p. 19) states: 'competitive advantage is created and sustained through a highly localized process. Differences in national values, culture, economic structures, institutions, and histories all contribute to competitive success'. While Porter also includes national factor conditions and national patterns of demand in his model of national competitive advantage, their importance lies not in their individual explanatory power (as in neoclassical economics), but in their functioning as part of a larger societal *system* of innovation. The concept of national systems of innovation has been developed further by Lundvall (1992) and Nelson (1993); however, as Freeman (1995) observes, the intellectual lineage of national systems may be traced back to the work of Friedrich List (1841). National innovation systems may

be defined as the societal institutions and mechanisms which support technical innovation (Nelson and Rosenberg, 1993). They span such features as,
'the allocation of R&D activity and the sources of its funding, the characteristics of firms ... the roles of universities, and government policies expressly
aimed to spur and mold industrial innovation' (Nelson and Rosenberg, 1993,
p. 19). Each nation state may thus be considered to have 'its own set of
institutions that function interdependently as a system, and each national
institutional system is characterized by differentiated but interdependent institutions' (Brahm, 1994, p. 43). Comparative empirical studies reveal both
substantial cross-national variance in institutional arrangements, and considerable 'institutional continuity' in national innovation systems (Nelson, 1993,
p. 509; see also Lundvall, 1992).

A critical element of national innovation systems is the role of government
in industrial and technological development. The call for a greater role for
government as a direct participant in industry has emerged in the so-called
'new international trade theory' or 'strategic trade theory' (see, for example,
Brander and Spencer, 1983, 1985; Ostry, 1990). This, 'reconceptualization of
government intervention serves as an important step toward appropriate rep-
resentation of firms' institutional environments' (Brahm, 1994, pp. 41–2).
Ostry (1990) cites developments in the nature of the international trading
environment, as well as changes in the economics discipline itself, as giving
rise to this new climate of ideas. In practice, the changing role of governments into more direct competitive participants within industries (Lessard,
1995) is reflected in the emergence of a new policy term in the OECD
countries – innovation policy:

> It is important to emphasize that innovation policy is not a given: it is a policy, or
> more precisely, a policy set, in the making, focused on the promotion and adop-
> tion of new technology (that is, the commercial development of the fruits of basic
> research). Thus, however much the policy mix and institutional structure of indus-
> try vary from country to country, the government–corporate interface is an essen-
> tial component (Ostry, 1990, p. 53).

Ergas (1987, p. 231) analyses the role of national innovation policy in explaining national differences in innovative performance, concluding that, 'the
dominant feature of national technological systems is *diversity*' (emphasis in
original). An important contribution of Ergas's analysis is the recognition that
individual national policies *per se* cannot be compared in terms of their
effectiveness; rather, national technology policy must be assessed in terms of
its relationship to the broader set of national institutional features which
affect innovation, such as the national tradition of scientific education, the
functioning of capital and labour markets, and the behavioural patterns of
firms themselves.[1] This view is consistent with Murakami (1982) that, 'the

competitive behaviour of a nation's firms and the policy decisions of its governmental agencies are inseparably intertwined in the nation's socio-institutional system' (Brahm, 1994, p. 42).

In summary, while the scope and approach of these streams of literature vary, two central themes are evident from their findings. The first of these themes is the key role which national institutional context plays in influencing industrial innovative capability. This body of literature highlights two ways in which institutional context explains cross-national differences in technological performance. First, the societal institutions which support industrial innovation vary cross-nationally. For example, the policies and practices of a nation's universities and government research institutes are shaped to a large extent by the nation's singular historical development (for example, see Mowery and Rosenberg, 1993; Odagiri and Goto, 1993; Swann, 1988; and Westney, 1993 among others). As firms in technology-driven industries often draw on universities and research institutes for knowledge and human capital, the technological performance of a country's firms may be influenced by the features of these institutions. Secondly, national context influences the institutional arrangements and behavioural patterns of firms themselves. For example, the organization of work and patterns of communication within and between firms, or between firms and universities, reflect broader societal characteristics which have been imprinted on firms and institutionalized over time (for example, see Brossard and Maurice, 1976; Hampden-Turner and Trompenaais, 1993; among others). Such national institutional arrangements seem particularly important determinants of innovative performance in contemporary high technology industries because when new technologies emerge, the relative success of different countries depends largely on the successful coordination between the infrastructure of scientific research and industrial capabilities (Dosi, et al., 1990).

The second key theme of this body of work is the historical consistency of such national institutional arrangements. The institutional continuity of national innovation systems suggests an explanation for the historical stability of national patterns of technological advantage which have been quantitatively verified in the technological accumulation literature. However, our understanding of this institutional continuity may be further enhanced through a more explicit recognition of the deep-rooted cultural values which infuse meaning into a society's particular institutional arrangements. The following section positions this literature (which shall be henceforth referred to collectively as the 'national innovation system literature') with respect to specific conceptualizations of cultural context in the field of anthropology. In doing so, it outlines an analytical approach which would allow for greater integration of cultural elements with the concepts of national innovation systems and technological trajectories.

INTEGRATING THE CULTURE CONCEPT INTO TECHNOLOGICAL DEVELOPMENT AND INNOVATION

The danger in evoking the concept of culture without rigorous conceptualization is that it can be 'overplayed to the point of meaninglessness' (Dunning, 1995) and reduced to a catch-all contingency factor for all unexplained variance. It is critical, therefore, to be explicit about the particular concept of culture we are using; there exist, 'well demarcated schools of thought on culture and adopting a particular definition of culture is a commitment to specific conceptual assumptions and ways of studying culture' (Allaire and Firsirotu, 1984, p. 195). In order to position the national innovation systems literature with respect to the broader cultural literature, three clarifications are required: (1) the conceptual distinction between 'institutional' and 'ideational' approaches to societal context; (2) the specification of the underlying causal structure of the national innovation systems literature in relation to cultural theories; and (3) the distinction between the levels of analysis of 'nation state' and 'culture'. Each of these issues is now discussed.

'Cultural context', in its broadest sense, encompasses the man-made part of the environment (Herskovits, 1955). A first distinction to be made within this broad concept is between *institutional* aspects of culture and *ideational* aspects of culture (Child and Tayeb, 1983; see also Keesing, 1974). Institutional aspects of culture include the systemic and structural components of social organization, such as educational and political systems. By contrast, ideational aspects of culture comprise the underlying values, attitudes and cognitive categories shared by a group of people.

The view of technological development as an evolutionary, location-specific phenomenon shares the same intellectual lineage as a tradition of scholarship in sociology and anthropology concerned with social systems and processes of institutionalization (for example, Gouldner, 1954; Selznick, 1957; Stinchcombe, 1959; 1968; Parsons, 1960; Crozier, 1964; Johnson, 1966; Musgrove, 1969). As discussed above, the national innovation systems literature which emerged in the early 1990s has placed considerable emphasis on the role of national institutional context in shaping technological trajectories. This focus is similar to anthropological and sociological studies which take an institutional approach to the study of culture:

> The institutional approach draws attention to institutions as the tangible manifestations of cultural distinctiveness. The cultural relevance of ideational systems is not denied, though the nature of a society's institutions is regarded as the expression of its dominant value orientation. In this view, institutions reflect the choices that have been made within societies among alternative structural arrangements to cope with problems such as the maintenance of social order, the promotion of economic and technical development, the allocation of people to productive

activity, and the distribution of material benefits in relation to services performed and personal need. (Child and Tayeb, 1983, p. 46)

Institutional approaches take account of the internal and external social forces which act upon organizations and, 'emphasize the *adaptive* change and evolution of organizational forms and practices' (Selznick, 1957, p. 12). These adaptive patterns of organizations are in turn embedded in the historical specificity of the society in which they evolve (Crozier, 1964; Brossard and Maurice, 1976).

Whether institutional context determines the ideational system of a society, or whether the shared ideational system determines a society's institutional context, has long been a matter of debate in cultural and social theory. Some theorists maintain the primacy of infrastructural and structural determinism, arguing that the prevalent social structures and systems determine the values and beliefs of society members (for example, Harris, 1979). By contrast, others maintain that social structures are the product of idea systems or cultural mindsets (for example, Weber, 1970). The underlying causal structure implicit in the national innovation systems literature is consistent with a tradition in sociological and anthropological analysis known as 'functional historicism' (Stinchcombe, 1968, pp. 101–30).[2] The functional school of thought suggests that the more critical factor in understanding societies is not which comes first, idea systems or institutions, but rather the *synchronization* or *balance* between these different components of society (for example, Parsons, 1960; Johnson, 1966). While nations may share certain basic needs for social organization, different functional alternatives to meeting these needs may be present in different societies. A number of assumptions about sociocultural systems are implicit in this perspective (Hagedorn, 1983, pp. 12–13). First, each part of society, both structures and idea systems, is considered to make a contribution to the whole. Secondly, the various parts of society are integrated with each other, each part supporting other parts as well as the whole. In other words, the ideational and the structural components, 'are integrated into a *sociocultural system*, postulating harmony, consonance and isomorphism between these two realms' (Allaire and Firsirotu, 1984, p. 195). Thirdly, the balance between these forces keeps societies relatively stable over time. This does not mean that societies do not change, but rather that the socio-cultural system seeks to remain in balance. A change in any one of the system's components thus usually leads to a change in the others (Harris, 1979, p. 71).

In addition to encompassing a functional perspective, the national innovation systems literature may be considered to be grounded in the causal structure of historicist explanations.[3] Historicist explanations are those, 'in which an *effect* created by causes at some previous period *becomes a cause of that same effect* in succeeding periods' (Stinchcombe, 1968, p. 103). In explaining cross-national differences in institutional arrangements, the historicist explanation turns to the singularity of each nation's historical development: 'which of a set of functional alternatives is found in a particular society is generally determined by historical events. But once a functional alternative becomes established, it tends to eliminate the causes of the other alternatives and thus to regenerate itself' (Stinchcombe, 1968, p. 105). In other words, certain forms or practices established for historical reasons will persist through time in a self-replicating causal loop, even after the disappearance of the factor which caused the initial selection of the particular form or practice.

In summary, the national innovation systems literature may be considered to be compatible with functional-historicist analysis, and shares a common empirical focus with studies which take an institutional approach to culture. Figure 3.1 positions the dominant focus of this work with respect to the functional-historicist conceptualization of socio-cultural systems. As illustrated in Figure 3.1, the national innovation systems literature has focused on the institutional elements of socio-cultural systems and their relationship to technological trajectories. The functional-historicist paradigm emphasizes the integration and intertwining of the institutional and ideational realms of

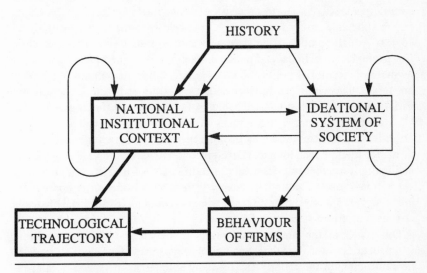

━━━━ = empirical focus of national systems of innovation literature.
──── = underlying causal structure of functional-historicist explanations.

*Figure 3.1   The focus of the national systems of innovation literature in
             relation to functional-historicist approaches to socio-cultural
             systems*

society. A significant literature exists on fundamental differences in ideational systems across national contexts which could be integrated with the national innovation systems literature within a functional-historicist perspective. The integration of knowledge about deep-rooted ideational elements of society which are isomorphic to prevailing institutional arrangements would add what we believe to be a much-needed anchor to the argument on the societal embeddedness and continuing diversity of national technological capabilities.

Before illustrating the outline of such an analysis, a final note should be added concerning the distinction between 'culture' and 'nation state'. The terms 'cultural context' and 'national context' have been used almost interchangeably within the international management literature, and clearly a greater analytical distinction is necessary between these levels of analysis in order to increase the conceptual rigour of research in the field (Boyacigiller and Adler, 1995). While a nation state is defined by its territorial and political borders, culture, when approached from an ideational definition, may encompass a group which is smaller than a nation (for example, French Canadian culture) which is identical to the nation (for example, in relatively homogeneous cultures such as Japanese culture), or which transcends national borders (for example, Jewish or Chinese culture). Research from a purely ideational cultural perspective thus runs the risk of conceptual ambiguity by using the nation state as a proxy for culture in research. In comparison, institutional context, which comprises the structures and systems of social organization (for example, educational and political systems), is defined to a larger extent by the *same* territorial-political borders which define the nation state. This is not to say that within the broader national institutional context there is not variation in regional institutional contexts. For example, different states in the USA or different *Länder* in Germany do vary in terms of their government priorities and policies, and may institute their own programmes and mechanisms for fuelling technological development. However, the very existence of national government implies a certain codification of institutional context at the national level. The nation state may thus be considered an appropriate unit or level of analysis for research which focuses on institutional elements of socio-cultural systems (see Freeman, 1995).

Our focus in the present analysis is to understand the socio-cultural embeddedness of national technological trajectories. Our unit of analysis here thus remains the nation state. In taking a functional perspective, our goal is to *integrate* knowledge of the diversity of national institutional systems with knowledge of the diversity of cultural ideational systems. It is important to point out, however, that in empirically comparing ideational systems across countries, we are always comparing national *norms* (that is, means) of a given dimension of values; by no means does this negate the diversity of values and attitudes that exists within nations (that is, variance and distribution).

In order to build cumulative knowledge in any field, a synthesis of existing findings is required (Noblit and Hare, 1988). By articulating a specific approach to culture which is compatible with the underlying assumptions of the national innovation systems literature, we suggest a conceptual framework which we hope will allow for greater integration of findings from the technological and cultural literature, and thus build more cumulative knowledge about the societal embeddedness of technological development. The central premises of this framework, as illustrated in Figure 3.1, may be summarized as follows:

1. National institutional systems supporting innovation are distinct and exhibit historical continuity.
2. Differences in deep-rooted ideational systems are integral to this diversity of national institutional arrangements.
3. National technological trajectories are reflective of the nation's sociocultural system (that is, both institutional and ideational elements).
4. Firms are driven to exploit these societally embedded capabilities in forming international technology agreements.

We now illustrate the application of this framework by surfacing some of the historically embedded cultural patterns which underlie the different systems of innovation in the USA and Japan, their correspondingly different technological trajectories in biotechnology, and the complementarities of these nation-specific trajectories which underpin the biotechnology R&D agreements between the two countries.

ILLUSTRATION OF SOCIO-CULTURAL EMBEDDEDNESS OF TECHNOLOGICAL DEVELOPMENT AND INTERNATIONAL TECHNOLOGY AGREEMENTS

The first part of this section presents the findings that distinct national trajectories of biotechnology have evolved in the USA and Japan, building on the respective country-specific capabilities, and that these different capabilities are a motivation for the technology agreements formed between Japan and the USA. We then discuss the historical embeddedness of some of the institutional arrangements which have shaped such country-specific trajectories and relate these to the literature on country differences in underlying cultural values.

The literature on technological accumulation and national innovation systems argues that both the particular characteristics of the technology and the institutional context in which it develops shape the emergence of successful innovation strategies. The particular technological trajectories which are pursued in a country, and which of these are successful, depends upon the extent to which the capabilities and resources embedded in the national system of innovation correspond to the requirements imposed by the particular technology. Building on this literature, Collins (1994) tests this premise on the development of biotechnology in the USA and Japan. Biotechnology is considered a distinct 'technological regime' and therefore has certain 'natural trajectories' resulting from its high dependence on basic science (primarily molecular biology) and its potential application across a wide range of industrial sectors (Collins, 1994). In the USA, R&D has been focused on applications in human pharmaceuticals, and the USA has emerged as the global technological leader in this sector (see, for example, Fortune, 1986; Euromonitor, 1988; UNCTC, 1988; Miller and Young, 1989; US Congressional Office of Technology Assessment, 1991). Country-specific factors shaping this particular trajectory include a proximity to the world's premier medical research institutions, more liberal regulations for new drug development and patenting, and an abundance of venture capital for new start-up firms (venture capitalists are particularly inclined to back start-up biotechnology firms focusing on pharmaceutical applications, as this is where the highest and most immediate profits are currently to be made in the biotechnology sector) (Kenney, 1986; Miller and Young, 1989; Collins, 1994). By contrast, a much wider approach to technological development in biotechnology has been pursued in Japan, with a relative lag in biopharmaceutical innovations. This particular trajectory is attributed to Japan's long tradition of fermentation technology, its comparative weakness in basic scientific research, and the dominance of large, diversified companies in R&D (Japanese Working Group on Biotechnology, 1985; Saxonhouse, 1986; Brock, 1989; Collins, 1994).

Shan and Hamilton (1991) cite similar country-specific factors as the basis of the technological gap in biopharmaceuticals between the USA and Japan. In a study of the cooperative agreements in the biotechnology sector, they empirically test the hypothesis that such country-specific capabilities are a motivation for the formation of international technological relationships. Their results confirm that Japanese firms cooperate significantly more with US firms in biopharmaceutical-related areas than they do with other Japanese firms or firms from other countries. Serapio and Dalton (1993) also present evidence that foreign firms are motivated to locate their biotechnology R&D in the USA as a means to access the US strength in biopharmaceutical innovations. These studies support the proposition that firms are driven to exploit the diversity of national innovation systems; in other words firms use international technological agreements as a means of strategically tapping country-specific technological capabilities (Cantwell, 1989; Porter, 1990; Archibugi and Michie, 1995b).

The conceptual framework presented earlier suggests that these country-specific technological trajectories are historically embedded in a nation's institutional context, and are shaped and reinforced by the dominant ideational system of the society's members. The dimensions of national institutional context which underpin national innovation systems are vast, spanning such features as, 'the allocation of R&D activity and the sources of its funding, the characteristics of firms ... the roles of universities, and government policies expressly aimed to spur and mold industrial innovation' (Nelson and Rosenberg, 1993, p. 19). It is beyond the scope of this chapter to discuss all such dimensions; the historical roots of a broader range of country-specific institutional elements and their links to biotechnology innovation are examined in detail elsewhere (Bartholomew, 1996). To illustrate our argument here, we shall consider only two dimensions of national innovation systems on which Japan and the USA vary, and which the previously mentioned studies have identified as key factors in shaping each country's distinct technological trajectory in biotechnology: (1) the greater strength in basic scientific research in the USA in comparison with Japan; and (2) the prevalence of small, start-up firms engaged in biotechnology R&D in the USA in comparison with the dominance of large, established firms in biotechnology R&D in Japan.

The weakness of basic science in Japan relative to the USA has been documented at length and has been traced to the foundation of contemporary education in Japan which was laid predominantly in the Meiji era (1868–1911) (see, for example, Saxonhouse, 1986; Bartholomew, 1989; Brock, 1989; Sun, 1989; Porter, 1990; Odagiri and Goto, 1993; Westney, 1993).[4] With the beginning of a non-feudal central government following the Meiji restoration of 1868, the government focused efforts on the development of engineering education in order to foster economic growth. Indeed, 'the Japanese government emphasized engineering education at the time when the more developed countries regarded pure science as superior to engineering' (Odagiri and Goto, 1993, p. 80).

By contrast, education in the USA was highly influenced by the German model which placed great emphasis on science (Swann, 1988; Porter, 1990). A significant number of American scientists trained in Germany during the late 1800s, returning to America inspired by German idealism and dedicated to building the American university in a similar spirit (see, for example, Veysey, 1965). In addition, substantial numbers of German scientists came to America during and after the Second World War, bringing with them their orientation to scientific research. This foundation, coupled with a tradition of heavy federal investment in basic research which began after the Second

World War, fostered a substantial accumulation of knowledge in the life sciences in the USA, with the universities emerging as the major centres of research (Mowery and Rosenberg, 1993).

Based on these historical contingencies, the Japanese and US educational systems have evolved with different levels of emphasis on basic scientific research; biases which are reflected today in the enrolment levels of engineers versus research-oriented academics:

> In engineering in 1986, for example, Japan produced 73,316 bachelor's graduates in engineering, compared to the United States' 77,061; however, it produced only 588 doctoral graduates of university courses, compared to the 3,376 in the United States. (Westney, 1993, p. 43, based on data from the National Science Foundation, 1988)

Similarly, Odagiri and Goto (1993, p. 104) observe that:

> One notable feature of the Japanese research personnel is a relatively larger proportion of engineers (42% of the total research personnel in 1989) than scientists (16%). The same tendency exists for university degrees: the number of Ph.Ds granted was 860 in science and 1,404 in engineering in 1988. In contrast, these were 7,438 and 3,236 in the United States and 2,894 and 1,020 in Germany, respectively. The same can be said of the undergraduate students in Japan. In 1988, there were 368,000 students in the engineering departments in contrast to 62,000 in science departments.

The shortage of university-trained scientists in Japan is particularly evident in disciplines related to biotechnology. For example, 'the United States ... graduates thirty-six times the number of PhDs in biology and ten times the number of PhDs in chemistry' than does Japan (Saxonhouse, 1986, p. 127).[5] More specifically:

> There is a shortage of qualified Japanese molecular biologists graduating from the nation's universities. While in the 1960s and early 1970s, European universities hummed with the bustle of newly implemented molecular biology and genetics departments, Japan by 1986 had only about fifteen public universities holding simple lecture series in molecular biology. (Brock, 1989, p. 106)

This has direct implications for the supply of scientists upon which Japanese biotechnology firms have been able to draw:

> while a number of subsidized public universities including Tokyo, Kyoto, Osaka, and Kyushu have significant programs in biotechnology, the role of these programs as a source of advanced research personnel for Japan's industry is limited. More than 1,200 Ph.D. scientists and engineers work in U.S. biogenetic engineering according to a 1982 survey by the Office of Technology Assessment and National Academy of Sciences. In contrast, a Keidanren survey found only

161 Ph.D. scientists and engineers doing firm-based research and development work in biotechnology in Japan in 1982, including Japanese with Ph.D.s from American universities. (Saxonhouse, 1986, p. 126)

In addition to the smaller number of PhDs produced in Japan, the quality of the Japanese PhD degree is considered to be weaker than in the USA, and academic research to be below world-class (Lepkowski, 1992, p. 16). The low level of scientific discoveries in biotechnology originating in Japan has been linked to the institutionalized norms of the Japanese educational system, which values tradition and respect for senior academics over creativity and originality (Sun, 1989; Westney, 1993). As Michiyuki Uenohara, Senior Executive Vice President and Director of Research at the Nippon Electric Corporation states:

We have to increase money for basic research, but that's a secondary consideration. The primary goal should be how to motivate young researchers ... there's
been a suppression of new ideas ... [In Japan] the teacher is almighty. Japanese
researchers are rather shy to express novel ideas. They incubate ideas until they
are quite sure of them. We have to change that, especially in the primary school.
(as quoted in Sun, 1989, p. 1286)

The suppression of new ideas would also appear to be institutionalized in the Japanese system of basic research funding: 'Much of the government's re-search money is distributed according to seniority rather than merit ... This perpetuates mediocrity in basic research ... Some researchers complain that the system keeps inferior scientists on the payroll (Sun, 1989, p. 1285). For example, Kenichi Matsubara, Director of Osaka University's Institute for Molecular and Cellular Biology, states that in the USA, 'unproductive scientists usually don't get money whereas here, they can survive' (as quoted in Sun, 1989, p. 1286; see also US Congressional Office of Technology Assessment, 1991, p. 243). Funding in US universities is tied much more to the performance and contribution of the individual researcher (Kenney, 1986). Renowned university scientists may also seek substantial funding from industry, a practice traditionally discouraged in Japanese universities (Brock, 1989).

The different structures and norms of universities and research institutions in the USA and Japan may be further understood through more explicit consideration of differences in underlying cultural values. A range of literature has documented fundamental differences between the USA and Japan on a number of value dimensions; for the purposes of this discussion, we will consider these differences with respect to three dimensions of cultural values defined by Hofstede (1980, 1983): individualism/collectivism, power distance and uncertainty avoidance. Hofstede's initial framework[6] was based on research conducted between 1967 and 1978 on comparable samples of IBM employees across 50 countries. We have selected Hofstede's framework, and these particular dimensions within it, for several reasons:

1. These dimensions correspond to core concepts in the anthropological and sociological literature.
2. There is substantial agreement among leading anthropologists and sociologists that these dimensions are central to understanding organized life.
3. Hofstede's data allowed for systematic cross-national comparison of measures of these dimensions.
4. As Hofstede's framework has been the most utilized cultural framework in management literature, the integration of the national innovation systems literature with the cross-cultural management literature is best achieved by retaining a common framework of terminology and concepts.

The first of Hofstede's (1980) values, individualism/collectivism, refers to the degree of integration between members of society and the relative value of individual over collective needs. In collectivist societies, identity is defined in relation to an 'in group', and group interests supersede individual interests. In individualistic societies, ties between individuals are loose, with greater emphasis on individual identity and self-sufficiency.

Power distance refers to the degree to which an unequal distribution of power is accepted in society. In large power distance societies there is greater acceptance of an unequal distribution of power and a high degree of dependence of subordinates on superiors. In small power distance societies there is more emphasis on equality of status and limited dependence of subordinates on superiors.

Uncertainty avoidance refers to the degree to which a society tolerates ambiguity or uncertainty. Societies with strong uncertainty avoidance seek to minimize uncertainty by establishing strict codes of conduct and having minimal tolerance for deviance from these social rules. Societies characterized by weak uncertainty avoidance have greater tolerance of risk and ambiguity, less strict social codes and greater tolerance for deviance from social norms.

Hofstede's results for Japan and the USA are summarized in Table 3.1 in terms of their relative position to each other on these three dimensions. The institutional norms and structures underpinning the different capabilities in basic scientific research in Japan and the USA are reinforced by the pattern of these underlying values in each country. New advances in scientific research often require challenging existing scientific paradigms and approaches (Kuhn,

Table 3.1   *Comparison of Japanese and US cultural values according to*
            Hofstede

Japan	United States
More collectivistic	More individualistic
Higher power distance	Lower power distance
Stronger uncertainty avoidance	Weaker uncertainty avoidance

1970). The tendency to suppress new ideas which, as discussed earlier, appears to be institutionalized in the Japanese educational system, reflects the pattern of values outlined above. The higher power distance in Japan reinforces the great hesitancy of young researchers to challenge authority figures such as professors and teachers. Collectivism and strong uncertainty avoidance discourage individuals from raising new ideas, as is reflected in the Japanese saying, 'the nail that sticks out will be hammered down'.

Hill (1995) links the origins of this collectivist and high power distance orientation to the values and norms evident in the Tokugawa era which preceded the Meiji restoration. These values are derived from two traditions: (1) the blend of Confucian, Buddhist and Shinto religious and ethical thought, also known as neo-Confucianism; and (2) the traditional agrarian village life based on rice production (Hill, 1995; see also Bellah, 1957; Smith, 1959). Hill (1995, p. 122) stresses that the values of Tokugawa Japan emphasized the importance of integration with a particular in-group: 'In Japan it is the particular group or collective of which one is a member which counts, whether it be family, village, fief (*han*), or Japan as a whole'. Group membership was vital to economic survival, as more than 80 per cent of the population was living in rural areas in this period; economic development was built around rice production, the nature of which requires collective work (Hill, 1995; see also Smith, 1959). In addition: 'Pressures towards group identification and group conformity were further reinforced by the wide acceptance of the ethic of loyalty to superordinates. In neo-Confucian ideology loyalty to one's superiors was regarded as a sacred duty' (Hill, 1995, p. 123).

By contrast, the dominant cultural values in the USA emphasize individualism, equality of status (low power distance) and greater tolerance of ambiguity (weak uncertainty avoidance). This particular pattern of values conforms more to the requirements for scientific discovery. For example, Hampden-Turner and Trompenaars (1993, p. 66) draw a link between the 'inner-directedness' of Americans and this orientation of the USA towards basic research and initial discovery: 'The person who creates is steered from within, by the new connections formed in the mind's eye. Here Americans easily out-distance their rivals'. The inner-directed individualism of American society has its roots in Puritan ethics and became entrenched with the emigration from Europe to the New World. In America:

> There was an extended trek westward, with a frontier the length of the whole continent. The United States was thinly populated by native Americans, so that in many essentials the land was for the taking. The opportunities available to individuals, soon to be followed by wave upon wave of new immigrants, is probably unprecedented in the history of the world and is unlikely to ever be repeated. (Hampden-Turner and Trompenaars, 1993, p. 50)

The different historical contingencies and dominant ideologies shaping the respective development of Japanese and Amercian society can thus be seen to underpin profoundly different capabilities; whereas Japan excels at applied research and development and complex manufacture, functions requiring integration and cooperation (Hampden-Turner and Trompenaars, 1993, p. 183), the USA excels at basic research and initial discovery, functions enhanced by a spirit of inner-directed individualism. Indeed, biopharmaceutical innovation in the USA is largely considered to be driven by individual scientists searching for fame and fortune through the discovery of the 'magic bullet' (Kenney, 1986; Swann, 1988).

A second institutional variation between the USA and Japan which is central to the different technological trajectories in biotechnology concerns the characteristics of firms in the industry. The USA is marked by a prevalence of small start-up firms specializing in biotechnology R&D; by contrast, biotechnology R&D in Japan is dominated by large, established, diversified firms. This difference in industrial structure also reflects the pattern of underlying values presented above. In the USA, the large universities, 'served as important "incubators" for the development of innovations that "walked out the door" with individuals who established firms to commercialize them' (Mowery and Rosenberg, 1993, p. 49). Such university 'spin-offs' have been established largely in the San Francisco and Boston areas by scientists from America's most prominent research universities. These start-up biotechnology firms, founded by 'entrepreneurial academics', have been hailed as a distinctly American phenomenon, reflecting the combination in American society of an individualistic, entrepreneurial culture, and the availability of risk capital to fund such ventures (see, among others, Canadian Office of Industrial Innovation, 1985; Kenney, 1986; Sharp, 1989; US Congressional Office of Technology Assessment, 1991; Hampden-Turner and Trompenaars, 1993). The US venture capital market is much more developed than in most other nations (Porter, 1990) and may be regarded as the institutionalization of the pattern of values described earlier, 'a vote of confidence in the creative capacities of the entrepreneurs involved' (Hampden-Turner and Trompenaars,

1993, p. 66). The American cultural hero of the 'self-made man' is typified by the risk-taking entrepreneur, characteristics which reflect values related to individualism, weak uncertainty avoidance (greater acceptance of risk) and low power distance (belief in equal opportunity to all).

By contrast, the availability of venture capital to fund start-up biotechnology firms is substantially lower in Japan than in the USA (US Congressional Office of Technology Assessment, 1991). The relative conservatism of the Japanese venture capital market and the related absence of start-up firms may be considered an institutional reflection of the societal orientation towards collectivism, high power distance and strong uncertainty avoidance:

> ...not a single entrepreneur or research scientist in Japan has been willing to give up permanent status at an existing firm and assume the risks of starting a new biotechnology firm. In consequence, entirely unlike the U.S. case, almost no new firms have come into existence to exploit this special new opportunity. (Saxonhouse, 1986, p. 122)

Similarly, Brock (1989, p. 112) observes that: 'It is almost unthinkable for a Japanese professor or lecturer to leave his job in a rigid hierarchical academic system for the financial and career risks of a company such as an NBF [new biotechnology firm]'. Biotechnology R&D in Japan is thus dominated by large, established, diversified firms which have long had preferential access to government-coordinated R&D and technology development programmes (Westney, 1993). Technological development in biotechnology in Japan has thus been more broadly based than in the USA, with greater emphasis on developments in applications which potentially benefit a wide range of industries (such as pollution control applications). This stands in sharp contrast to the trajectory in the USA, where biotechnology R&D has been highly specialized in application in human pharmaceuticals, the sector where individual firms and investors stand to make the greatest and most immediate profit.

In summary, national technological trajectories may be seen to be shaped by country-specific capabilities which are deeply embedded in the socio-cultural system. Cross-national differences in country-specific capabilities are in turn a motivation for firms to form international technological agreements, as reflected in the large number of R&D agreements related to biopharmaceuticals which Japanese firms form with US firms. In addition to the motivation of gaining access to particular technological developments, firms may enter foreign alliances to learn about the underlying patterns of organization that lead to particular advantages in other countries. This motivation is typified in the biotechnology R&D relationship formed between Kirin Brewery Co. of Tokyo and Amgen Inc. of Thousand Oaks, California (as reported in Gibbons, 1992). In early 1984, Kirin put up $12 million, and Amgen invested $4 million and the fundamental technology to make erythropoiten, a protein which stimulates red blood cells and may be used to treat patients who are anaemic because of kidney failure or treatment for AIDS:

> Kirin's main intent was not to harvest valuable research but rather to use the joint venture to learn how Americans translate research into biotech products ... It also hoped to learn something about the American style of research, says Koichiro Aramaki, vice president of the pharmaceuticals division in Tokyo. (Gibbons, 1992, pp. 1431–2)

Thus international technological cooperation may be seen as a means not only to gain access to country-specific technological capabilities, but also to tap into the more tacit knowledge embedded in a particular socio-cultural system.

CONCLUSION

The aim of this chapter has been to increase awareness of the socio-cultural dynamics which shape distinct national technological trajectories, and of how the *diversity* of different cultural systems is a motive for international technological cooperation. International competition generates a force of mimetic isomorphism, a pressure to adopt patterns recognized in the industry as 'state of the art' (DiMaggio and Powell, 1983), and firms are increasingly entering cross-border technological alliances to tap into country-specific capabilities. However, if these capabilities *are* so deeply embedded in the particular society in which they have evolved, to what extent, then, can they be successfully absorbed by firms from other countries? More importantly, does the adoption of 'best practices' which have evolved under a different set of socio-historical conditions pose a threat to the fundamental balance of a national innovation system? Such questions are difficult to answer because, as Dosi and Kogut (1993, p. 260) note: 'The causality between action and outcome is [itself] highly dependent on institutional context'. We believe, therefore, that one of the most fruitful avenues for future research in international management will be this complex interplay between the effects of societal culture on national technological trajectories, and the effects of cross-border technological relationships on the internal coherence of socio-cultural systems. Such a research agenda will provide an opportunity for – in fact will require – greater integration of perspectives from anthropology and sociology with evolutionary theories of economic and technological change.

NOTES

1. For further analysis of specific patterns of synchronization or discontinuity between institutional, economic and technological variables, see Aglietta (1976), Boyer and Mistral (1983), Dosi (1984), Dosi and Orsenigo (1988) and Perez (1983) among others.
2. For a seminal review of different explanatory approaches to culture and social systems, see Keesing (1974). For a discussion of the relationship between the organizational literature and different concepts of culture, see Allaire and Firsirotu (1984).
3. Interestingly, when functional analysis was first explicitly introduced into anthropological theory, it was presented as an alternative to historicist explanations (see, for example, Radcliffe-Brown, 1963, pp. 32–48). Stinchcombe (1968, p. 104), however, demonstrates that, 'a functional process will give rise to infinite self-replicating causal loops. Far from being an alternative, a functional causal structure generally *implies* a historicist structure' (emphasis in original).
4. The successful introduction of a broad-based public education system in Japan in the Meiji era, however, was also due to the broadly based educational background established in the Tokugawa era (1603–1868). For example, the percentage of children attending school during the Tokugawa era, 'suggests that the literacy rate in Japan in the seventeenth and eighteenth century was likely higher than in Europe and America' (Odagiri and Goto, 1993, p. 78).
5. This figure may overestimate the American strength in these disciplines since a large proportion of those pursuing doctoral degrees at American universities are in fact foreign students, many of whom are Asian. However, a recent study on science in Asia in *Science* (Vol. 262, 15 October 1993, pp. 345–50) shows that an exceedingly small proportion of Asian doctoral recipients from US universities are Japanese. Furthermore, the number of Japanese students seeking US PhDs in the natural sciences has increased only marginally between 1980 and the present, whereas the number of Taiwanese students has more than doubled, and the number of students from South Korea, and more recently from China, has more than quadrupled.
6. Hofstede's initial framework included a fourth dimension, masculinity/femininity; in addition, a fifth dimension, Confucian dynamism, was articulated in subsequent work (see Hofstede and Bond, 1988).

BIBLIOGRAPHY

Adler, N.J. and Bartholomew, S. (1992), 'Managing Globally Competent People', *Academy of Management Executive*, **6**(3), 52–65.

Aglietta, M. (1976), *Regulation et Crise du Capitalisme*, Paris: Calmann-Levy.

Allaire, Y. and Firsirotu, M. (1984), 'Theories of Organizational Culture', *Organization Studies*, **5**(3), 193–236.

Archibugi, D. and Michie, J. (1995a), 'Technology and Innovation: An Introduction', *Cambridge Journal of Economics*, **19**(1), 1–4.

Archibugi, D. and Michie, J. (1995b), 'The globalization of technology: a new taxonomy', *Cambridge Journal of Economics*, **19**(1), 121–40.

Barney, J. (1986), 'Strategic Factor Markets: Expectations, Luck and Business Strategy', *Management Science*, **32**, 1231–41.

Bartholomew, J. (1989), *The Formation of Science in Japan*, New Haven, Conn.: Yale University Press.

Bartholomew, S. (1996), 'The Institutional Basis of National Advantage in Biotechnology', PhD thesis, McGill University, Montreal, Canada.

Bartlett, C. and Ghoshal, S. (1989), *Managing Across Borders: The Transnational Solution*, Boston: Harvard Business School Press.

Bartlett, C. and Ghoshal, S. (1991), 'Global Strategic Management: Impact on the New Frontiers of Strategy Research', *Strategic Management Journal*, **12**, 5–16.

Beck, N. (1992), *Shifting Gears*, Toronto: Harper Collins.

Bellah, R. (1957), *Tokugawa Religion: The Cultural Roots of Modern Japan*, New York: Free Press.

Boyacigiller, N. and Adler, N.J. (1995), 'Insiders and Outsiders: Bridging the Worlds of Organizational Behaviour and International Management', in B. Toyne and D. Nigh (eds), *International Business Inquiry: An Emerging Vision*, Columbia, South Carolina: University of South Carolina Press.

Boyer, R. and Mistral, J. (1983), *Accumulation, Inflation, Crises*, second edition, Paris: PUF.

Brahm, R. (1994), 'The Institutional Embeddedness of International Business Strategy: Implications for US Firms', *Journal of Management Inquiry*, **3**(1), 40–50.

Brander, J.A. and Spencer, B. (1983), 'International R&D Rivalry and Industrial Strategy', *Review of Economic Studies*, **50**, 707–22.

Brander, J.A. and Spencer, B. (1985), 'Export Subsidies and International Market Share Rivalry', *Journal of International Economics*, **18**, 83–100.

Brock, M.V. (1989), *Biotechnology in Japan*, London: Routledge.

Brossard, M. and Maurice, M. (1976), 'Is there a Universal Model of Organizational Structure?', *International Studies of Management and Organization*, **6**(3), 11–45.

Canadian Office of Industrial Innovation (1985), *Technology Transfer Mechanisms in Biotechnology in the US, UK, Japan and Canada: Review by Country and Recommendations for Canada*, Ottawa: Office of Industrial Innovation, Department of Regional Industrial Expansion.

Cantwell, J. (1989), *Technological Innovation and Multinational Corporations*, Oxford: Basil Blackwell.

Child, J. (1981), 'Culture, Contingency, and Capitalism in the Cross-National Study of Organizations', in L.L. Cummings and B. Staw (eds), *Research in Organizational Behaviour, Vol. 3*, Greenwich, Conn.: JAI Press.

Child, J. and Tayeb, M. (1983), 'Theoretical Perspectives in Cross-National Organizational Research', *International Studies of Management and Organization*, **12**(4), Winter, 1982–3, 23–70.

Cohen, S.D., Teece, D., Tyson, L. and Zysman, J. (1984), 'Global Competition: The New Reality', Working Paper of the President's Commission on Industrial Competitiveness, University of California at Berkeley.

Collins, S.W. (1994), 'Genes, Markets, and the State: The Emergence of Commercial Biotechnology in the United States and Japan', PhD thesis, University of Virginia.

Collis, D.J. (1991), 'A Resource-Based Analysis of Global Competition: The Case of the Bearings Industry', *Strategic Management Journal*, special issue, **12**, 49–68.

Crozier, M. (1964), *The Bureaucratic Phenomenon*, London: Tavistock Publications.

Dierickx, I. and Cool, K. (1989), 'Asset Stock Accumulation and Sustainability of Competitive Advantage', *Management Science*, **33**, 1504–13.

DiMaggio, P.J. and Powell, W.W. (1983), 'The Iron Cage Revisited: Institutional Isomorphism and Collective Rationality in Organizational Fields', *American Sociological Review*, **48**(2): 147–60.

Dosi, G. (1984), *Technical Change and Industrial Transformation*, London: Macmillan.

Dosi, G. and Kogut, B. (1993), 'National Specificities and the Context of Change: The Coevolution of Organization and Technology', in Bruce Kogut (ed.), *Country*

Competitiveness: Technology and the Organizing of Work, New York: Oxford University Press.

Dosi, G. and Orsenigo, L. (1988), 'Coordination and Transformation: An Overview of Structures, Behaviours and Change in Evolutionary Environments', in G. Dosi *et al.* (eds), *Technical Change and Economic Theory*, London: Pinter Publishers.

Dosi, G., Pavitt, K. and Soete, L. (1990), *The Economics of Technical Change and International Trade*, New York: New York University Press.

Dunning, J.H. (1992), *Multinational Enterprises and the Global Economy*, Reading, Mass: Addison-Wesley.

Dunning, J.H. (1995), 'Micro and Macro Organizational Aspects of MNEs and MNE Activity', in B. Toyne and D. Nigh (eds), *International Business Inquiry: An Emerging Vision*, Columbia, South Carolina: University of South Carolina Press.

Ergas, H. (1987), 'Does Technology Policy Matter?', in B.R. Guile and H. Brooks (eds), *Technology and Global Industry: Companies and Nations in the World Economy*, Washington, DC: National Academy Press.

Euromonitor (1988), 'The Biotechnology Industry in Western Europe', in *The International Biotechnology Handbook*, London: Euromonitor Publications.

Fortune (1986), 'Life Sciences,' *Fortune*, 13 October, 32–4.

Francis, A. (1992), 'The Process of National Industrial Regeneration and Competitiveness', *Strategic Management Journal*, **13**, 61–78.

Freeman, J.R. (1989), *Democracy and Markets: The Politics of Mixed Economies*, Ithaca: Cornell University Press.

Freeman, C. (1995), 'The "National System of Innovation" in Historical Perspective', *Cambridge Journal of Economics*, **19**(1), 5–24.

Gibbons, A. (1992), 'In Biotechnology, Japanese Yen for American Expertise', *Science*, **258**, 1431–3.

Gouldner, A.W. (1954), *Patterns of Industrial Bureaucracy: A Case Study of Modern Factory Administration*, New York: Free Press.

Hagedorn, R. (1983), *Sociology*, second edition, Toronto: Holt, Rinehart, and Winston of Canada.

Hamel, G., Doz, Y. and Prahalad, C.K. (1989), 'Collaborate with your Competitors – and Win', *Harvard Business Review*, **67**(1), 133–9.

Hampden-Turner, C. and Trompenaars, F. (1993), *The Seven Cultures of Capitalism*, New York: Doubleday.

Harris, M. (1979), *Cultural Materialism: The Struggle for a Science of Culture*, New York: Random House.

Herskovits, M.J. (1955), *Cultural Anthropology*, New York: Knopf.

Hill, C. (1995), 'National Institutional Structures, Transaction Cost Economizing and Competitive Advantage', *Organization Science*, **6**(1), 119–31.

Hofstede, G. (1980), *Culture's Consequence: International Differences in Work-Related Values*, London: Sage.

Hofstede, G. (1983), 'The Cultural Relativity of Organizational Practices and Theories', *Journal of International Business Studies*, **4**(2), 75–89.

Hofstede, G. and Bond, M.H. (1988), 'The Confucious Connection: From Cultural Roots to Economic Growth', *Organizational Dynamics*, **16**, 4–21.

Japanese Working Group on Biotechnology (1985), 'Japanese R&D Situation with Regard to Biotechnology', paper presented at the First US–Japan Conference on High Technology and the International Environment, Santa Barbara, CA, (1985).

Johnson, C. (1966), *Revolutionary Change*, Boston: Little Brown.

Kagono, T., Nonaka, I., Sakakibara, K. and Okumura, A. (1985), *Strategic versus*

Evolutionary Management: A US–Japan Comparison of Strategy and Organization, Amsterdam: North-Holland Press.

Keesing, R. (1974), 'Theories of culture', *Annual Review of Anthropology*, 3, 73–97.

Kennedy, P.M. (1987), *The Rise and Fall of the Great Powers: Economic Change and Military Conflict from 1500 to 2000*, New York: Random House.

Kenney, M. (1986), *Biotechnology: The University–Industrial Complex*, New Haven: Yale University Press.

Keohayne, R.D. and Nye, J.S. Jr (eds) (1973), *Transnational Relations and World Politics*, Cambridge, Mass.: Harvard University Press.

Kindleberger, C. (1975), 'Size of Firm and Size of Nation', in J.H. Dunning (ed.), *Economic Analysis and the Multinational Enterprise*, New York: Praeger.

Kobrin, S.J. (1995), 'Transnational Integration, National Markets, and Nation-States', in B. Toyne and D. Nigh (eds), *International Business Inquiry: An Emerging Vision*, Columbia, South Carolina: University of South Carolina Press.

Kogut, B. (1987), 'Country Patterns in International Competition: Appropriability and Oligopolistic Agreement', in N. Hood and J.E. Vahlne (eds), *Strategies in Global Competition*, London: Croom Helm.

Kogut, B. (1991), 'Country Capabilities and the Permeability of Borders', *Strategic Management Journal*, 12, 33–47.

Kogut, B. (1993), 'Introduction', in B. Kogut (ed.), *Country Competitiveness: Technology and the Organizing of Work*, New York: Oxford University Press.

Kogut, B. (1995), 'The Evolutionary Theory of the MNC: Within and Across Country Options', in B. Toyne and D. Nigh (eds), *International Business Inquiry: An Emerging Vision*, Columbia, South Carolina: University of South Carolina Press.

Krugman, P.R. (ed.) (1986), *Strategic Trade Policy and the New International Economics*, Cambridge, Mass.: MIT Press.

Kuhn, T. (1970), *The Structure of Scientific Revolutions*, second edition, Chicago: University of Chicago Press.

Laurent, A. (1983), 'The Cultural Diversity of Western Conceptions of Management', *International Studies of Management and Organization*, 13(1–2), 75–96.

Lazonick, W. (1990), *Competitive Advantage on the Shop Floor*, Cambridge, Mass.: Harvard University Press.

Lenway, S.A. and Murtha, T.P. (1994), 'The State as Strategist in International Business Research Literature', *Journal of International Business Studies*, 25(3), 513–36.

Lepkowski, W. (1992), 'Japan Issues New Science, Technology Goals', *Chemical & Engineering News*, 70(24), 16.

Lessard, D.R. (1995), 'Finance and International Business', in B. Toyne and D. Nigh (eds), *International Business Inquiry: An Emerging Vision*, Columbia, South Carolina: University of South Carolina Press.

List, F. (1841), *The National System of Political Economy*, English edition (1904), London: Longman.

Lundvall, B.-A. (1992), *National Systems of Innovation: Towards a Theory of Innovation and Interactive Learning*, London: Pinter.

Matthews, R.C.O. (1986), 'The Economics of Institutions and the Sources of Growth', *The Economic Journal*, December, 903–18.

Miller, H.I. and Young, F.E. (1989), 'Japanese Pharmaceutical Biotechnology: Potent but not a Threat', working paper, US Food and Drug Administration.

Mowery, D.C. and Rosenberg, N. (1993), 'The US National Innovation System', in R.R. Nelson (ed.), *National Innovation Systems: A Comparative Analysis*, New York and Oxford: Oxford University Press.

Murakami, Y. (1982), 'Toward a Socio-institutional Explanation of Japan's Economic Performance', in K. Yamamura (ed.), *Policy and Trade Issues of the Japanese Economy*, Seattle: University of Washington Press, 3–46.

National Science Foundation (1988), *International Science and Technology Update 1980* (rept. no. NSF 89–307), Washington, DC: National Science Foundation.

Nelson, R.R. (ed.) (1993), *National Innovation Systems: A Comparative Analysis*, New York and Oxford: Oxford University Press.

Nelson, R.R. and Rosenberg, N. (1993), 'Technical Innovation and National Systems', in R.R. Nelson (ed.), *National Innovation Systems: A Comparative Analysis*, New York and Oxford: Oxford University Press.

Nelson, R.R. and Winter, S.G. (1977), 'In Search of a Useful Theory of Innovation', *Research Policy*, 5(1), 36–76.

Nelson, R.R. and Winter, S.G. (1982), *An Evolutionary Theory of Economic Change*, Cambridge, Mass.: Harvard University Press.

Noblit, G.W. and Hare, R.D. (1988), *Meta-Ethnography: Synthesizing Qualitative Studies*, Beverly Hills, CA: Sage.

Odagiri, H. and Goto, A. (1993), 'The Japanese System of Innovation: Past, Present, and Future', in R.R. Nelson (ed.), *National Innovation Systems: A Comparative Analysis*, New York and Oxford: Oxford University Press.

Ohmae, K. (1990), *The Borderless World*, New York: Harper.

Ostry, S. (1990), *Governments and Corporations in a Shrinking World: Trade and Innovation Policies in the United States, Europe and Japan*, London and New York: Council on Foreign Relations Press.

Parsons, T. (1960), *Structure and Process in Modern Societies*, Glencoe: Free Press.

Pavitt, K. (1987), 'International Patterns of Technological Accumulation', in N. Hood and J.E. Vahne (eds), *Strategies in Global Competition*, London: Croom Helm.

Perez, C. (1983), 'Structural Change and the Assimilation of New Technologies in the Economic and Social System', *Futures*, 15(4), 357–75.

Porter, M. (1990), *The Competitive Advantage of Nations*, New York: The Free Press.

Prahalad, C.K. and Doz, Y. (1987), *The Multinational Mission – Balancing Local Demands and Global Vision*, New York: Free Press.

Radcliffe-Brown, A.R. (1963), *Structure and Function in Primitive Society: Essays and Addresses*, New York: Free Press.

Saxonhouse, G. (1986), 'Industrial Policy and Factor Markets: Biotechnology in Japan and the United States', in Hugh Patrick (ed.), *Japan's High Technology Industries*, Seattle: University of Washington Press.

Scott, R.S. and Lodge, G.C. (1984), *US Competitiveness in the World Economy*, Boston: Harvard Business School Press.

Selznick D. (1957), *Leadership in Administration: A Sociological Interpretation*, Evanston, Ill.: Row Peterson.

Serapio, M.G. Jr. and Dalton, D.H. (1993), 'Foreign R&D facilities in the United States', *Research and Technology Management*, 36(6), 33–9.

Shan, W. and Hamilton, W. (1991), 'Country-Specific Advantage and International Cooperation', *Strategic Management Journal*, 12, 419–32.

Sharp, M. (1989), 'The Management and Coordination of Biotechnology in the UK 1980–1988', *Philosophical Transactions of the Royal Society of London*, 324, Series B, 509–23.

Smith, T. (1959), *The Agrarian Origin of Modern Japan*, Stanford, CA: Stanford University Press.

Stinchcombe, A.L. (1959), 'Bureaucratic and Craft Administration of Production: A Comparative Study', *Administrative Science Quarterly*, **4**, 168–87.

Stinchcombe, A.L. (1968), *Constructing Social Theories*, New York: Harcourt, Brace and World.

Sun, M. (1989), 'Japan Faces Big Task in Improving Basic Science', *Science*, **243** (March 10), 1205–7.

Swann, J.P. (1988), *Academic Scientists and the Pharmaceutical Industry: Cooperative Research in Twentieth-Century America*, Baltimore: Johns Hopkins University Press.

United Nations Centre on Transnational Corporations (UNCTC) (1988), *Transnational Corporations in Biotechnology*, New York: United Nations.

US Congressional Office of Technology Assessment (1991), *Biotechnology in a Global Economy*, Washington, DC: Congress of the US Office of Technology Assessment.

Veysey, L.R. (1965), *The Emergence of the American University*, Chicago: University of Chicago Press.

Weber, M. (1970), *Max Weber: The Interpretation of Social Reality*, London: Joseph.

Westney, D.E. (1993), 'Country Patterns in R&D Organization: The United States and Japan', in B. Kogut (ed.), *Country Competitiveness: Technology and the Organizing of Work*, New York: Oxford University Press.

PART II

The Globalization of Technological Activity

4. Pooling the technology base: the globalization of European research and technology organizations

Michael F. Kluth and Jørn B. Andersen[1]

INTRODUCTION

The structural crisis of the European economies which became apparent with the first oil shock is commonly considered the crisis of Fordism. While Fordism, and increasingly *post*-Fordism, are widely associated with certain production paradigms – which have received extensive academic attention – less effort has been made to probe another and equally important facet of post-Fordism, namely the institutional aspect.

The institutional aspect of post-Fordism is intrinsically linked to the globalization of the economy. Taking the institutional angle, globalization denotes the process whereby key national institutions are subject to increased external pressures for change and adaptation. As such, globalization represents a qualitatively different process than internationalization, which merely implies an increase in international transactions.

Rather than looking at concerted action, coordinated demand management strategies or other macro phenomena at regional or global levels, this study will be directed towards the changes and adaptation of micro-oriented institutions when assessing the impact of globalization and with it the institutional ramifications of post-Fordism.

This chapter will investigate the process of change and adaptation in national research and technology organizations (RTOs) across Europe. The process will be analysed with reference to variations in formal institutions and institutional infrastructures (Soskice, 1991). Three case countries – Britain, Germany and France – are examined. Variations between national systems with regards to adaptation strategies will be assessed for each of the countries.

GLOBALIZATION AND INSTITUTIONAL CHANGE

The term 'globalization' was established as one of the 'buzz words' of social science in the course of the 1980s, with numerous connotations across and even within disciplines. In the literature on institutional political-economy the term is used to denote both what was previously simply considered internationalization, and qualitative new dynamics in relation to institutional development. Globalization thus seems to be interpreted as both a quantitative and a qualitative phenomenon.

Particular attention has been devoted to grasping the character and implications of globalization within technological development. Attempts at conceptual clarification have been made by Archibugi and Michie as they distinguish between three categories of 'techno-globalism' (Archibugi and Michie, 1995). These are:

- the global *exploitation* of technology;
- global technological *collaboration*;
- the global *generation* of technology.

Exploitation of technology is a world-wide phenomenon, with diminishing lead times between the market of origin and other markets. While virtually all countries maintain systems underpinning this aspect of globalization, such as patent laws, some countries have adopted a deliberate strategy of enhancing the absorption capacity of national industry in incorporating international technological advances in production processes and products. This is particularly true of some of the Asian economies, but Denmark, Norway and Italy also provide examples of national successes relying on the application of externally generated technology. The observed escalation with regard to this aspect of techno-globalism is thus mainly numerical.

Firms increasingly embark on cross-border *collaboration*, not least with respect to R&D. However, as Archibugi and Michie (1995) point out, the phenomenon may not be as recent as often believed, and the growth which can be recorded in the area, 'is confined to a very few, although crucial, fields'.

Multinationals are relying on information technology in their effort to create synergy between several national innovation facilities in connection with the *generation* of new technology. If a hierarchy, or a measurement of 'matureness', was to be constructed, this aspect of Archibugi and Michie's taxonomy can be said to constitute the epitome of what is identified as the globalization process within technology. It is, however, also the aspect which exhibits the most modest growth rates!

Following Archibugi and Michie, techno-globalism is very much measured and conceptualized in quantitative terms, and as such it is viewed as a 'natu-

ral' extension of the internationalization of the economy witnessed throughout the post-war era. The taxonomy thus emphasizes the operational manifes-
tation of the internationalization of technology at the inter- and intra-firm
level.

The taxonomy summarizes the various usages of techno-globalism within
mainstream economic literature. As such it offers a substantial contribution to
a much-needed conceptual clarification. In approaching the question from a
political science angle, it is, however, evident that a dimension needs to be
added in order to grasp fully the globalization process in relation to technology. The globalization of technology thus contains a distinct qualitative – or
institutional – element.

Viewed from an institutional angle, globalization can be interpreted as a
continuation of the internationalization debate of the 1970s. Although this
debate has been reflected in a rather heterogeneous body of literature, a logic
can be identified which holds that a process of institutional convergence is
underway as market pressures force an adaptation of national institutions
towards a best fit which will optimally serve all capitalist economies. The
logic of this argument itself leans rather heavily on the basic theoretical
outlook of traditional abstract economics, which makes a similar claim with
regards to the universal application of its assumptions and causality.

The logic implied in the convergence thesis can be linked to that of classical political economists such as Smith and Ricardo, who were mainly preoccupied with the distortive mechanisms of private and public regulatory regimes
as based on the state and the guild system. In the works of Friedrich List,
focus was on the possible positive effects on national economic performance
of enhancing and re-engineering the properties of institutions deemed 'ob-
structive' by the liberalists, and employing them in the quest for industrialization (Kluth and Andersen, 1994).

Today institutional political economists seem to have rediscovered the
insights of List's 1841 publication entitled *The National Systems of Political
Economy* in which it is implied that, contrary to liberalist beliefs, there are
several paths to national economic success – we indeed live in a pluralist
world where multiple capitalisms thrive (see Freeman, 1987).

National economic performance varies from country to country beyond
what can be merely attributed to differences in factor endowments. This
difference reflects corresponding variations in the character of the dynamics
of national and regional market-places. Thus different patterns in the quality,
sophistication and adaptation of the goods and services demanded and supplied can be observed between, for instance, the UK and Japan.

Key national institutions define the character of national political economies, which even within the traditional Western economic bloc vary considerably. Examples of key national institutions are foremost the financial regime,

the labour market and core elements of the national innovation system, such as technological services performed by RTOs.

Institutions are historically rooted and culturally embedded, consequently their impact on national economic operations extends beyond macro-level economic policy. Institutions can be altered but the direction of the alteration cannot be fully determined in advance, and generally institutional properties exhibit a vast element of rigidity. Globalization denotes the process whereby key national institutions are subject to increased external pressures for change and adaptation. As such, globalization represents a qualitatively different process than internationalization, which merely implies an increase in international transactions.

Changes in international banking practices and regulation illustrate the globalization process well. National banking systems have been subject to an immense pressure due to the deregulation process and the prominence of the free capital movement discourse. The effects of this on individual financial systems have varied as national institutional infrastructures have influenced the character of the adaptation process. German banking will consequently not completely resemble American or British banking as an outcome of globalization, even though the dominant discourse associated with the globalization of banking is biased towards a British- or American-styled system.

Financial systems were the first key set of institutions subject to globalization. This event has additionally accelerated and shaped the process, as it prompted a re-orientation in economic thinking from the macro to the micro level. As a consequence the second round of substantial globalization will take place at levels directly related to the firm. It is likely to influence the organization of firms and the innovation, application and diffusion of new technologies.

The globalization of the economy is prompted by a dramatic increase in international transactions. Besides an expansion in the volume of traditional international transactions, the thrust of globalization is additionally boosted by the growing diversity of transactions. The latter phenomenon is illustrated by Archibugi and Michie as they draw a parallel between traditional transactions such as collaborative R&D and foreign direct investment.

In short the quantitative aspects of globalization amount to internationalization. They constitute a vital aspect of globalization but fail to grasp fully the character and complexity of the phenomenon. Yet the categories listed by Archibugi and Michie (1995) contain elements which point to institutional impacts.

To the extent that real growth can be detected in international collaborative R&D for example, this development is likely to exert qualitative globalization pressures on national institutions. Implied in this line of thinking is the assertion that an upsurge in collaborative R&D is likely to undermine the *raison d'être* of customized national institutions erected with the sole purpose of disseminating competences now acquired directly from collaborative partners.

A comprehensive analysis of the globalization of technology thus needs to consider the adaptation processes in national systems of innovation prompted by global pressures. We believe that this supplementary analysis must include comparative qualitative studies of the changes in key components of national systems of innovation.

RTOs: TASKS AND RATIONALE

Virtually all OECD countries have RTOs. Germany boasts the world-renowned Fraunhofer Gesellschaft (FhG); the Dutch similarly operate a nation-wide system in the TNO; the British system displays a series of mutually independent operators established on the basis of sectors (for example, British Maritime Technology, ERA Technology Limited and the Leatherhead Food Research Organization); Denmark has the so-called GTS system; France has ANVAR; and so on. Several of these organizations have been in operation since the first half of the century. RTOs have increasingly been subject to political attention within OECD countries because of their crucial role as major agents in the process of diffusing new R&D results and technology to potential users/firms and thereby enhancing the innovation capacity of firms. This intermediary role performed by RTOs is often referred to as 'technology transfer', which plays a key role in the distribution power of national systems of innovation.

A number of national organizations perform bridging functions. In order to avoid confusion this study has adopted the definitions employed by the European Commission. Hence establishments conforming to the RTO label encompass organizations supporting R&D activities of client firms, organizations engaged in the dissemination of new technologies, and organizations whose activities include more than one of the following:

- applied research;
- certification, testing, measurement and standards;
- information, consultation and training.

This definition excludes universities and public research centres, which concentrate on research rather than technology transfer. Similarly, entirely private businesses such as contract research companies are not regarded as RTOs (Kandel, 1994). Yet differences in national practices make it difficult to adhere strictly to standard definitions; we consequently also consider organizations that in a national context are regarded as RTOs – for example, by law or history.

Within the context of technology policies implemented by European governments the promotion of technology transfer has common characteristics. First, the public sector is encouraged to share and distribute research results generated by government R&D laboratories and officially commissioned research. Secondly, R&D-intensive firms are assisted by reducing constraints on the availability of finance (especially venture capital).

Thus at the surface there are a number of similar elements among technology transfer initiatives and among RTOs and governments in different nations, but diverse political, economic, legal and educational systems within countries result in different strategies for the development of RTOs.

Consequently, the globalization of RTOs cannot simply be understood as a function of their customers' (that is, firms') globalization strategies and the globalization of technology. The pace, character and direction of RTOs' globalization will just as much be driven by the underpinnings of the distinct national social and institutional community from which they originate.

The world of RTOs is far from homogeneous. So even if questions regarding globalization are the same, the answers are different. Greater demand for speed in the field of innovation places a considerable strain on the expenditure of RTOs in terms of renewing equipment, providing staff with continuous training, and marketing campaigns, and this at a time when public funding is drying up, clients are less faithful and more demanding, and competition is fierce. Choosing a strategy under these circumstances is of course an essential, but not an easy, task. How far should RTOs go in maintaining their own R&D capacity so as to be able to assimilate technology from elsewhere? Should they give up the idea of having their own R&D capacity and make do with using the results of R&D carried out elsewhere? Or should they follow their innate desire for national independence and maintain R&D capacity/ expenditure, which is all the more expensive for the fact that their R&D investment capacity is limited and the R&D seldom has an immediate relevance to their economy?

To choose between commercial activities and 'public service' activities is an especially difficult task for many RTOs. There are pros and cons for each strategy. RTOs are placed somewhere between basic research institutions and 100 per cent commercial business consultancy firms. They thus have a dual role – on the one hand to operate as a firm among firms (that is, when they sell their technology services to other firms on market conditions) and, on the other, to be engaged in a certain level of R&D. This bridging function is what makes them unique in relation to university laboratories and consultantcy firms.

Yet the service they sell on a commercial basis is essentially an outcome of their R&D activities. These activities to a large extent are financed by 'core grants' from governments. This make RTOs vulnerable to cuts in government spending, and suggests that RTOs with origins in nations which traditionally adhere to free market principles will adopt a globalization strategy which brings them closer to private consultancy firms; eventually they may give up their longer-term R&D activities and close relationship to their national government. Similarly, it can be expected that RTOs originating in more interventionist states will remain bridging institutions with substantial in-house R&D, and be supported financially by their respective government in the process of globalization.

RTOs and National Systems of Innovation

Continued generation and exploitation of new technology is a key factor for creating competitive advantage among nations, regions and firms. Efficient employment of technical advances thus influences the level and distribution of economic growth. Most users of technology are forced to acquire the technology from the originators, intermediaries or other users.

The development of research and technology policies over the past two decades has been characterized by the increasing application of measures to enhance collaborative research, joint technological projects and the transfer of technology. From the mid 1970s to the early 1980s European governments became more concerned over the lack of university–industry linkages. Both the general ills of Eurosclerosis and the apparent backwardness within the information technology sector were seen partly as a result of this missing linkage. However, it was not until the mid 1980s that technology policies gained momentum, involving national technology programmes and collaborative pre-competitive research projects, focusing on high technology-based firms. In combination with this, the internationalization of industrial activities has called into question the efficacy of national RTOs, particularly with a view to their roles as 'bridging institutions' and facilitators of international R&D results for domestic users.

All industrialized nations have policies for strengthening the innovativeness of their companies. There are several reasons for this. The activities and investments for becoming the leader in the introduction of a new product or process and those associated with staying near the head of the pack, or catching up, are much less sharply distinguishable than is commonly presumed. Moreover, the strict Schumpeterian innovator, the first firm to bring a new product to market, is frequently not the firm that ultimately captures most of the economic rents associated with the innovation. International experience shows the crucial importance of high quality technical services that are widely and easily available to all firms, and especially to small and medium-sized enterprises (SMEs). Autarky is impossible in science and technology: all firms need external sources of advice, information and technical collaboration. They also need access to specialized testing and measurement services and other advanced equipment and instruments.

For all these reasons, technology policies in most OECD countries have recently given far greater emphasis to the role of intermediary organizations such as RTOs. The provision of techno-economic framework conditions that enables companies to be at the forefront technology-wise, and thereby to remain competitive in increasingly fierce international competition, is thus becoming a core component of industrial policy.

This change of focus should in particular be seen in relation to the general set of theories derived from the new evolutionary line of thought which have had wide implications for the way innovation and economic growth are perceived today. 'Technology trajectories', 'creative destruction' and 'imperfect competition' have thus become key words within the new vocabulary of national innovation policies. And today evolutionary economic thought stands out as an alternative basis for economic policy-making. The major breakthrough on the policy level was the Technology and Economic Programme – known as the TEP Report – carried out by the OECD in 1992 (OECD, 1992).

A company's innovative capacity is not only determined by its investments in R&D. Access to the right sources of knowledge is essential. A nation's technological capacity is determined by its capacity to produce technological knowledge and its ability to transfer this knowledge to potential users. In short, a country's national system of innovation should be assessed on its production and distributive efficiency. It is within this context that the role assigned to RTOs should be assessed and understood.

Strengthening framework conditions for industry has become the new policy paradigm in OECD countries. It is forthcoming, explicitly or implicitly, in the policies and actions of an increasing number of governments. It succeeds, and in certain respects complements, the structural adjustment (liberalization, deregulation and competition) policies of the 1980s. The future success of the adjustment reforms initiated in the 1980s may depend on the efficacy of accompanying policies to strengthen framework conditions for industry.

A critical point here is that the understanding of RTOs – like technological knowledge – cannot be exogenous to arguments about growth and trade. The argument presented here is thus close to that of Paul Romer, described by Zysman as follows:

> at the core of the growth process are ideas, not simply the accumulation of physical or financial capital. The ideas are not just a matter of training of workers in existing procedures, or of education that transmits codified knowledge. Rather, economic growth springs from better recipes not just from more cooking ... economic growth occurs whenever people take resources and rearrange them in ways that are more valuable. (Zysman, 1994)

RTOs belong to the category of institutions within national systems of innovation that import, modify, translate and diffuse new technology. As such, RTOs can be seen as 'cooks' who bring new recipes to national firms. As there are different technology trajectories, the pace and direction of development is a matter of decision. In this sense 'innovation policies matter', because they influence the future technology trajectories within countries and firms. Zysman compares this:

> to the covering of the table at the roulette wheel. The multiple bets that technological development requires will not be evenly placed around the table. The bet 'placer', be it a company or a nation, will put its bets according to past practise and the needs to which technology is being applied, which will be different for each national community, and so the tasks addressed will vary from firm to firm and country to country. (Zysman, 1994)

As there are different organizing principles for RTOs from country to country (for example, access to knowledge may be based on the firms' willingness or ability to pay the market price for the information or the access to information may be heavily government-subsidized), this will affect the firms' strategies for getting access to information. Institutionally RTOs thus play an important part in what Soskice labels the National Framework of Incentives and Constraints (NFICs) (Soskice, 1991). Soskice advocates that NFICs create distinctive national Product Market and Innovation Strategies for firms. Or, to use the words of Dosi and Orsengio:

> social rules, inherited norms and attitudes, the laws of organization of the linkages between and within various groups of economic agents do matter in determining the set of admissible strategies and behaviours, and of observed innovative performances. The specification of the institutional rules constraining individual behaviour becomes therefore a crucial task in the analysis of the patterns of technical change, which accounts for the observed differences across countries within the same technologies. (Dosi and Orsengio, 1988)

We argue that the same logic should be applied in analysing RTOs' strategies for globalization – as specific interactions between actors within national systems of innovation, the role of governments and the character of the company base produce distinct strategies.

GLOBALIZATION AND NATIONAL RTOs

Different national industrial policies in general, and different degrees of adherence to the 'invisible hand's' ability to spur growth and technological development, have created national systems of innovation which look quite different from country to country. The proposition is that distinct national culture, economic development, technology trajectories and the role of government have not only shaped national RTOs, they will also have shaped the global architecture of technology service, as the RTOs increasingly expand their activities to this level.

In all countries governments play, or have played, a prominent role as regards the steering of RTOs. National governments' role in steering RTOs is additionally reflected in the strategies that RTOs prefer or follow in relation to globalization. The aim of the following section is to contribute to the understanding of the workings of national systems of innovation in relation to globalization, by analysing the role of bridging institutions and how they interact with governments.

Germany's Regional *Nationaloekonomie*

Germany has often been held up as the model case of 'liberal-corporatism', exhibiting a political-economic regime emphasizing direct negotiations between labour, business and government, and producing a political climate positive to complex and long-reaching bargains. The underpinning institutions of the German system are perhaps best described within the framework of the so-called 'negotiated economy' school (Nielsen and Petersen, 1989), and their origins are often attributed to the specific historical circumstances of German nation-state-building and industrialization.

In comparison with other European states, Germany was a latecomer, both in political and in economic terms. As is the case in relatively late industrialized countries such as Sweden and Japan, the government had from the beginning a key role in the country's industrial development. The theoretical understanding of Germany's RTOs and the general role played by the government in relation to, for example, the globalization of technology service, may essentially be explained with reference to the works of Friedrich List and Joseph A. Schumpeter. In opposition to the classical political economy of Smith and Ricardo, List and Schumpeter advocated an evolutionary perspective focusing on the long-term development of productive forces and on the relationship between entrepreneurship, innovation and growth (see Reinert, 1994; Michie and Prendergast, Chapter 8, this volume).

The German adherence to these two scholars is not only relevant from a theoretical point of view, but also when it comes to explaining why, for example, the German RTO, Fraunhofer Gesellschaft (FhG), adopts a totally different globalization strategy to, for example, British RTOs.

In later writings Schumpeter stressed that the entrepreneurial function need not be embodied in a physical person and in particular in a single physical person. The role of entrepreneur may be, and often is, filled cooperatively. Even the state can be an entrepreneur and Schumpeter referred to how the US Department of Agriculture many times had revolutionized the practice of farmers by introducing new methods of cultivation (see Swedeberg, 1991).

Combining this line of thought with that of List, holds to a large extent the key for understanding the German national system of innovation. List asserted that English economists failed to distinguish between national and global interests. Their political economy was a cosmo-political economy, but nations needed to build a national system of political economy (see Reinert, 1994).

The institutional arrangements that characterize the national system of innovation in Germany have two distinct features. First, there is the German model of education that places great emphasis on combining formal education with practical work experience through apprenticeships. The second feature is the existence of a number of semi-public 'bridging institutions', of which the institutions of (FhG) are the most important at the national level, and Steinbeis Stiftung in Baden-Württemberg the most important at the *Länder* level.

FhG was founded in 1949 and specifically designed to secure German industry a strong position internationally. It is the biggest European RTO, consisting of 46 institutions with 7700 employees and has an annual budget of 1 billion Deutsch Mark. Financially FhG receives one-third of its income from the federal government and the *Länder* governments. Another third of FhG funds comes from public contract research projects and a final third comes from performing contract research for industry. Each of the FhG institutes has close ties with both the academic world and industry. The mechanisms that ensure close links with universities include: a shared infrastructure of FhG institutes and their complementary university institutes (measurement and testing equipment); FhG employs students as research candidates who often take the opportunity to write their diploma thesis under the guidance of FhG, and university faculties appoint FhG researchers to complement their teaching programmes by lecturing on their experience in applied research and in new industrial applications. FhG engages university staff members as consultants for its research projects.

Close links with industry are established by: the deployment of researchers from industry to FhG, partly with the support of a federal programme and partly at the cost of individual firms; representatives from industry play a major role in the supervisory board, which monitors the work and results of FhG; and FhG serves as a stepping stone to an industrial career for many engineers, with around 50 per cent leaving the organization after 3–5 years to take up positions in industry.

As opposed to countries like France, Britain and the USA, which are mission-oriented systems, Germany's national system of innovation is predominantly a distribution-oriented system (Ergas, 1986). Technological co-operation among firms is encouraged by the government but the government is not an active match-maker.

As the commercial use of R&D results has become more important to firms' international competitiveness, several countries have looked over the fence to the German model. At present, FhG is the role model for countries such as Malaysia, Poland, Spain and Hungary; all countries where FhG helps to establish RTOs that resemble FhG. FhG has established an office in the US to survey technological developments there, and it is currently negotiating with several states about setting up FhG institutes on a joint basis.

The UK's Opening of the Technology Market

Britain has come to be seen as Europe's most salient advocate of market reform since the coming into power of Margaret Thatcher. While the former premier has been a symbol and inspirator for free-marketeers all over the world, her governments' policies conformed with vital institutional features of the country's political economy.

In the post-war era, the 1960s and 1980s stand out as the decades in which the most determined and coherent efforts were made to halt the British decline. However, the approaches taken could hardly have been more different (Walker, 1993). During the 1960s, the guiding assumption was that the market economy could no longer be left to its own devices. The state had an important role to play in order to ensure that inventions turned into successful innovations. This decade resembles what could be labelled Schumpeterianism, with the focus on managing and strengthening the British system of innovation by means of allocating more resources to R&D, education and technological activity.

During the 1980s and onwards Britain has undergone a development heavily biased towards the belief that the market economy must be left to its own devices, and that Britain's economic problems stem from excessive state protection of individuals and firms. The aim has been to restore the 'spirit of free enterprise' and individual responsibility. A guiding assumption was that the government's support for innovation should be constrained in expenditure terms. The strategy adopted by British RTOs during the 1980s thus became focused on short-term gains, and to trading in, rather than developing, R&D competences for longer-term strategic use (Walker, 1993).

The case of ERA Technology Limited is illustrative in highlighting why it can be expected that British RTOs compared with, for example, German RTOs will pursue a strategy of adaptation stressing internationalization with special emphasis on market orientation and independence of government support.

ERA Technology Limited dates back to 1910, when technical directors of UK electrical manufacturing companies began to meet monthly to discuss pre-competitive collaborative research. In 1919 the government offered 50 per cent funding to industry research associations, and the aforementioned committee set up the Electrical Research Association to qualify for public funds. In 1969 it was recommended that 25 per cent funding support to various research associations should be withdrawn over a period of three years. As a result, ERA became a company limited by guarantee in 1974. Today, single client business provides 80 per cent of ERA Technology Limited's income. Moreover, income from public contracts is expected to decrease, leaving private contracts as the major source of income.

The main strategic issue for ERA is the disappearance of the domestic customer base, and hence the imperative to expand to overseas business. This need to reposition is reinforced by the decline of UK public contracts. This has forced ERA to forget the Department of Trade and Industry as a source of UK public funding. ERA looks at the world as its market, not just Europe. It has set up an office in Singapore and is considering setting up an office in Houston, USA (SPRINT EIMS, 1994).

British Maritime Technology (BMT) is another case which supports the view that the decreases in public funding and arm's-lengths relationships between British RTOs and central government have made it an imperative to move from R&D to more customer-driven activities. In short, BMT continued to benefit from funding until 1990 since when it has received no direct government grants. Strategically, BMT is keen to operate more as a high-tech consultancy than a traditional RTO. There is a need to operate as a commercial organization, and as a result most strategic issues are fundamentally financial ones. BMT has increasing international activities and has offices in Bangkok, Poland, the USA and Hong Kong. Finally, it is noteworthy that BMT considers lack of political support and a declining infrastructure as a strategic market issue. Consequently it has stated that it favours a European system in which RTOs are subsidized purely on the basis of turnover gained competitively in the market-place – on a 50:50 funding basis – to support the regeneration of the technology base (SPRINT EIMS, 1994).

UK government policies towards technology service organizations have remained more pragmatic in practice than rhetoric suggests. An example of this pragmatism is the regional technology transfer initiative known as 'One-Stop-Shops' or Business Links, which are set up to provide business support services. Business Link is initiated by the Department of Trade and Industry and is inspired by the German Steinbeis model and the Danish Technology Information Centres. As such, the networking component plays a significant role in this initiative. Yet the British government has set up an assessment panel which has to judge each proposal for setting up a

Business Link, and the guiding principle is that of franchising – that is, local industrial policy networks which get the right to call themselves Business Links will benefit from state support (Department of Trade and Industry, 1994).

In general the Business Link model has many similarities with the German and Danish network models and resembles an orientation towards a more diffusion-oriented technology service system. However, the franchise model clearly pulls this initiative more towards a market model than can be seen in Denmark's TICs or comparable local organizations such as the Innovation Centres in Holland. In other words, the franchise component of Business Links fits well with the 'British flavour' and ideological adherence to free market competition.

Until the late 1980s, the majority of European RTOs did not traditionally export their services and most of their clients tended to be national. Although RTOs such as Holland's TNO, the Danish Technological Institute and certain FhG institutes can show comparable or higher incomes from foreign clients today, the British RTOs were the first to go international. Generally, international comparative studies of bridging technology service organizations seem to support the view that the UK adheres more to the market model than most other countries and has developed a market-oriented profile at a faster pace than most other countries' RTOs. Finally, the UK experience should partly be seen as a result of the substantial reduction in the state's role in the national system of innovation during the 1980s.

Keeping the French State In

France is frequently cited as the textbook example of a centralized state-management system. The state occupies centre stage in both economics and politics. Policy initiatives are often formulated as 'grand projects' informed by ethereal visions held by the learned elite holding the decisive offices of the state.

Accordingly the country's national system of innovation is one of the clearest examples of a 'mission-oriented' innovation system. Big is seen as beautiful and priority has traditionally been given to large, technology-intensive systems (military, electrical power and electrical transport) or to products that are inherently systemic (such as aircraft or space-products). The market demand for these products has traditionally been created via politically dictated public procurement and sold abroad through the involvement of the French state in political deals.

Major parts of French technology policy have therefore been biased towards France's biggest companies, her biggest R&D institutions and 'grand projects'. France's technology service is at the national level especially centred around 'Agence Nationale del la Valorisation de la Reserche' (ANVAR), which belongs to the Ministry of Industry and Economic Development and the Ministry for Education and R&D. Its legal status is comparable to that of the SNCF – the French railway system.

The French state contributes 66 per cent of ANVAR's annual budget and the rest comes from clients and contract research. Like most other countries' RTOs, ANVAR was created to strengthen the commercial exploitation of public R&D results, but has in later years broadened its scope to other areas of activity. For example, ANVAR gives financial support to SMEs and tries to enhance network cooperation between SMEs in France.

ANVAR's interplay with other private and public R&D institutions is guaranteed by its status as financee for commercial R&D. This financing is mainly channelled through 'high risk' loans for the development of new products or technologies and through technology transfer. As regards financing of innovation in SMEs, Levy argues that the attempts made to reform the French banking system in the 1980s did not solve some of the problems of financing for French SMEs (Levy, 1994). Hence the French state has created a privileged state lending pool working through ANVAR, which offers a failsafe source of cheap credit.

Another illustrative example of a French RTO and the role of government in its development is CSTB, which was founded in 1947 and given the status 'Public Establishment'. The main reason to create CSTB was the need for the ministry in charge of reconstruction after the war to get technical assistance for the evaluation of the reconstruction project. At the beginning CSTB was almost exclusively financed by state funds and had very little commercial activity. Later, in the 1970s and 1980s, it was urged to work more on a demand-pull basis than on a technology-push basis.

As a result the share of basic state funds in the budget of CSTB was about 50 per cent in 1980. Nevertheless, it did not expand its commercial activities at a pace which satisfied the French government, which put pressure on CSTB to reorganize and to set up a special management department within its organization.

CSTB has had international activity since its creation – primarily at the European level. In recent years its international strategy has especially been focused on the European Community. In this context it has played a role on the European stage with regards to harmonization of standards, codification for building products and improvement of European cooperation research. It has been very active in penetrating EU R&D programmes such as BRITE-EURAM, ESPRIT, SPRINT, and so on.

In spite of the efforts made to 'commercialize' CSTB, it is still today a governmental public organization and plays a role as a regulatory body between government, industry and final users.

Compared with other countries' RTOs it is clear that the French case reveals that the role of government has been decisive. Take, for instance, the original creation of different RTOs. In countries such as Britain, Germany or, for that matter, a smaller country such as Denmark, RTOs were originally the result of initiatives made by industrialists (sometimes in concert with the authorities) during the first half of the 20th century. The role of government has never taken the same symbiotic character in Germany, Denmark and Britain as in France. This is also reflected in relation to the current globalization process. British RTOs were among the first to go international. The strategy has been to distance themselves from public funding, and they rely less on public contracts, be they domestic or European. In stark contrast, French RTOs seem to follow a strategy of expanding internationally by approaching the EU in the same way as they have traditionally interacted with the French state. Indeed, French officials have earlier turned to European institutions to 'support' emerging industries such as high definition television and semiconductors. French authorities have to a larger extent than most other EU countries looked to Europe to drive French industry in a manner that the French state no longer could. As such Europe may provide the relay to exhausted national *dirigisté* prescriptions (Levy, 1994).

In spite of the moves made towards a more market-oriented approach the French are basically following a technology-push strategy, as opposed to the British market-pull strategy. Germany, Holland and Denmark are placed somewhere in between these two extremes. RTO strategies devised to cater for new market and/or political demands are thus embedded in overall national institutional configurations. In the following section the national patterns of institutional adaptation will be sought, paired with theoretical reflections on the political economy of societal change.

NATIONAL PATTERNS OF INSTITUTIONAL ADAPTATION

In this study RTOs from various European countries have been examined. Table 4.1 attempts to group RTOs according to institutional affiliation and level of operation.

In France the state plays a leading and often decisive role. French RTOs have the status of state agencies and their services are delivered to other state agencies and individual firms upon request. A major proportion of French RTO funding stems from government or EU-financed research programmes. Hence ANVAR and CSTB, the two French RTOs considered in this study, are placed under the 'state' label, while at the same time being seen as operating at the firm level.

Table 4.1   RTOs according to institutional affiliation and level of operation

	State	Network	Market
National level			BMT
			ERA Research Ltd (UK)
Sector level	(FhG)	Steinbeis Stiftung (Baden Württemberg)	TNO (Netherlands) GTS system (Denmark)
Firm level	CSTB ANVAR (France)	ERVET CNA (Italy)	

In Germany there are two development models. At the state level Baden-Württemberg's Steinbeis Stiftung is a dominant actor and has established strong networks with state government, banks, industry and unions. At the national level the federal government plays a more prominent role, but still with a strong 'networking' component, in relation to, for example, FhG.

The UK shows the clearest example of a market-oriented model, where the role of government was reduced dramatically during the 1980s. The two smaller countries, the Netherlands and Denmark, resemble a model which can be said to be situated somewhere between Germany and the UK. In both countries there are strong similarities with the German institutionalist model; on the other hand both the TNO and the Danish GTS system are more market-oriented than FhG.

The globalization of R&D and other technology-related fields have prompted some to call the notion of specific national institutional and technology trajectories into question. Yet, as demonstrated above, national patterns of institutional design are replicated in the adaptation strategies of RTOs.

Tampering with national innovation systems is certain to produce strong societal responses, as changes may upset established power relations. The evolutionary terminology of the national systems of innovation approach is deceptive in that it suggests given paths of national development are charted by means of social selection mechanisms determined by cordial learning processes. As shall be illustrated in what follows, institutional import will inevitably produce fierce political struggles which plot the course of national trajectories. Institutionalized bias ensures some degree of order and predictability in national adaptation strategies in the face of globalization. However, political analysis is essential in order to assess the course of development.

The Political Economy of National Innovation Systems

As argued initially, adaptation strategies in the face of pressures for globalization follow distinct national trajectories. Trajectories of institutional development can by and large be attributed to institutional rigidity which in turn is caused by social embeddedness. But institutions may be subject to changes, and in any case are to be considered as frameworks of action for economic and political actors rather than the sole source of development (Kluth, 1997).

Early contributions on the institutional shaping of market dynamics took as a point of departure the role of the state. The dichotomy strong state–weak state was first introduced in academic writings by Stephen Krasner (see Katzenstein, 1977). Strong states had allegedly developed their strong capacity for industrial intervention due to their late industrialization. Kenneth Dyson probed yet deeper into the issue of historically rooted institutional foundations for government action, as he contended that differences in state capacity for industrial restructuring essentially are constrained by the industrial culture of the society in which the state has to operate and recruit its staff. Popular notions of public authority are centre stage when determining a given society's 'industrial culture' (Dyson and Wilks, 1983).

Andrew Shonfield's comparative study expanded the focus from the state to institutions such as social partners and the financial system (Shonfield, 1965). John Zysman's study of governments, markets and growth from 1983 – which explicitly adhered to the approach pioneered by Shonfield – argued that the institutional arrangements of the market and the public administration define the settings in which political fights about the economy occur. They structure the political conflicts over industrial change and economic policy; 'The institutions, both economic and political, in which those fights occur articulate how groups must organise to achieve their objectives, often who their allies will be, usually what their tactics must be, and certainly what can be obtained from them' (Zysman, 1983).

The arena where battles over French politics are fought seems to be the state apparatus itself. The main actors in the process are the executive branch of government and the highly skilled central bureaucracy recruited on the basis of an extremely elitist yet transparent set of rules (Allum, 1995).

In Italy the state apparatus also assumes a critical role in political battles. In the Italian model case of 'clientalism', public enterprises have had a dominant position in industrial and labour market policies. Interest groups do not, to the extent as occurs in, for example, northern Europe, constitute permanent and stable power centres in their own right (LaPalombara, 1987).

In a sense both the French and the Italian systems are essentially 'Etatist'. But while the French state is a highly autonomous actor in its own right,

Italian politics is characterized by being focused on controlling various branches and levels of government.

France can thus be seen as a proponent of a centralized state-management system. Industries have worked directly through government rather than through a 'civilian' interest group. Policy outcomes have often been monumental, although not always entirely relevant to the problems for which solutions were sought. The private nature of interests accessed to the policy arena has often resolved in solutions of a 'favouritist nature'. Instead of attempting jointly adopted and implemented structural solutions to, for example, the problems of unemployment and limited economic growth, the above policy environment has opted for solutions favouring picked winners, which benefit from massive loans, excessive public procurement and generous research grants.

Consequently the French approach to RTO design places the state at centre stage. The operation of ANVAR and CSTB is thus directly aimed at individual firms as the country's industrial policy tradition prescribes. With regard to internal organization both agencies submit to their legacy of state bureaucracy.

Italy's RTOs share certain elements with their French counterparts. Notable differences, however, greatly overshadow these common features. First and foremost the political culture of clientelism is paralleled by an economic culture featuring strong communal elements most manifest in the operation of rather close networks between firms. This is reflected in the design of Italy's ERVAT, which, although geared towards firm-level operation, is placed in the network category of the typology presented in Table 4.1.

The United States and Britain in turn can be viewed as examples of decentralized market-managed systems. Governments have preferred to intervene as little as possible in the economic sphere, giving little incentive to the rise of nation-wide interest groups. As a rule groups tend to be more fragmented, issue specific and directly aimed at tangible benefit aggregation than is the case with their northern European counterparts. This has spurred the development of a political system dominated by pluralism (Allum, 1995).

Both American and British economic culture features a dynamic competitive ideal of firm behaviour. In line with this, British RTOs operate according to a market rationale and display little of the bureaucratic features inherent in ANVAR and CSTB.

Finally, Germany, Scandinavia and Holland have operated a system emphasizing direct negotiations between labour, business and government. This has produced a political climate positive to complex and long-reaching bargains.

The northern European systems are perhaps best described within the framework of the so-called 'negotiated economy' school (Nielsen and Petersen,

1989). The negotiated approach constitutes a departure from the preoccupation with formal institutions. Various segments of institutions are thus grouped under functional headings according to their role in the discourse formation process.

Emphasis is on the making of a common understanding of key societal issues and how to deal with these problems. This is achieved via direct interaction between key actors as well as through the media. By focusing on the Gramscian notion of discourse formation, the proponents of the negotiated approach shifted attention from the closing of specific corporatist bargains to the forming of the overall 'regime' within which these deals were to be struck (Kluth and Andersen, 1994).

David Soskice draws attention to the operation of 'institutional infrastructures' which predispose societies towards specific modes of policy-making. Soskice points to the duration of, and level of trust in, relationships between societal actors and the state as being particularly important in shaping the general political environment (Soskice, 1991).

In polities with advanced institutional infrastructures no formal institutions are necessarily needed in order to achieve an effective system of private–public sector interaction. The demise of high salience institutional configurations, as found in the neo-corporatist settings of north-western Europe in the mid 1970s, has not resulted in competitive-pluralism but rather a decentralized yet negotiated polity designated by Soskice as a flexibly coordinated system.

Hence both formal and informal institutional features determine the operation of national political-economic regimes. These regimes in turn contain embedded preferences on institutional design which ensure a measurement of replication whenever core components of national innovation systems respond to either internally or externally generated challenges. Table 4.2 summarizes the basic characteristics of national political economies. Following Zysman, the overall institutional properties of national polities frame decisions on future developments of national systems of innovation. Formal institutional structures denote mainly the character of the state and the efficiency and operational transparency of other political-economic pillars such as business associations and trade unions. Institutional infrastructures denote the character of relationships between actors – such as firms, government agencies and trade unions – in national political economies. Institutional infrastructures to a large extent determine the development of formal structures, consequently institutional infrastructures are more firmly socially and culturally embedded than are formal structures. In essence Table 4.2 thus illustrates the framework within which national adaptation processes will take place.

Table 4.2 National political economies

	Weak formal institutional structures	Strong formal institutional structures
Simple institutional infrastructures	Pluralism Competing elite's sectorized governance	Etatism Centralized 'dirigist' governance
Advanced institutional infrastructures	Clientalism Segmented patron governance	Networking Post-corporatist discourse governance

CONCLUSION

Distinct national approaches to the production, diffusion and application of technology can be identified. This is well illustrated by pointing to the German, British and French models. Differences are reflected in the design and operation of national RTOs and in their response to pressures for globalization. In the above we have illustrated the differences between national RTOs in relation to institutional dynamics and design.

In order to assess the patterns of adaptation among RTOs, it must be taken into account that pressure for change is channelled through the distinct community of actors in which these organizations are embedded. Additionally, the responses of RTOs dealt with here should be seen in relation to two sets of developments. The first of these is the pressure sparked off by global changes. This refers to forces outside the control of each RTO and nation. The second is the development stemming from internal national responses and pressures signified by political choices made in the course of changes. In this respect RTOs' communities are national in the same sense as it has been shown that there are distinct national technology trajectories, technological networks and communities.

Following this argument, British RTOs and companies will most likely adopt a market-oriented approach when going global, whereas the French case will be one of tight cooperation with governments and public authorities at home and abroad. The German and, with some variations, the Danish and Dutch models will be institutionalist in the sense that the free market approach of the

British is basically seen as sound but needs – at least initially – a guiding hand. Finally, the fact that French RTOs are less engaged internationally is mainly due to the historical 'tutelage' of the French government. But if and when the French adopt a more global strategy it can be expected that the government will try to establish similar scale advances for its RTOs as has been the case in other fields of industrial development strategies in France.

Yet the globalization of RTOs also complicates the 'national hypothesis'. In particular the adaptation strategies of FhG and British RTOs may serve to blur central features of national systems of innovation. German- and British-based RTOs may assume a role of bridging government laboratories, universities, manufacturers and labour force educators *across* countries. Likewise the French way of conducting business within the EU could essentially be interpreted as a way of expanding the French national system of innovation to a European level. If successful the implication would be that 'only' the remaining EU members would have to converge to a new model.

The aims of this contribution have been three-fold. First, we have aspired to add an explicit institutional element to the notion of 'techno-globalism'. Secondly, we have sought to demonstrate different responses of national RTOs – constituting core elements of national systems of innovation – in the face of globalization. Finally we have attempted to construct a platform for refined analysis of national systems of innovation more explicitly taking the political dimension into account. While the final aim has been given the least elaborate treatment in the present text, it is possibly our most important point.

NOTE

1. At the time of writing Michael Kluth was Assistant Professor, Roskilde University and Jøorn Andersen was Head of Section, Ministry of Industry, both in Denmark. Michael Kluth received financial support for his research from Danish SSRC Grant No. 14-6329. A first draft of this chapter was presented at the Euro-conference on the Globalization of Technology in Cambridge, 21–24 June 1995. The authors wish to thank conference delegates and the organizers for valuable comments.

BIBLIOGRAPHY

Allum, P. (1995), *State and Society in Western Europe*, Cambridge: Cambridge University Press.

Archibugi, D. and Michie, J. (1995), 'The Globalization of Technology: A New Taxonomy', *Cambridge Journal of Economics*, **19**, 121–140.

Chesnais, F. (1993), 'The French National System of Innovation', in R. Nelson (ed.), *National Innovation Systems – A Comparative Analysis*, Oxford: Oxford University Press.

Clement, K. (1994), *Regional Policy and Technology Transfer: A Cross National Perspective*, Glasgow: European Research Centre, University of Strathclyde.

Department of Trade and Industry (1994), *Business Link – Prospectus for One Stop Shops for Business*, London: Department of Trade and Industry.

Dosi, G. and Orsengio, L. (1988), 'Industrial Structure and Technical Change', in A. Heertje (ed.), *Innovation, Technology, and Finance*, Oxford: Oxford University Press.

Dyson, K. and Wilks, S. (eds) (1983), *Industrial Crises – A Comparative Study of State and Industry*, London.

Ergas, H. (1986), 'Does Technology Policy Matter?', CEPS Paper no. 29, Centre for European Policy Studies, Brussels.

Freeman, C. (1987), *Technology Policy and Economic Performance: Lessons from Japan*, London: Frances Pinter.

Kandel, N. (1994), 'RTO Infrastructure in Europe: Analytical Survey', in J.R. Tiscar (ed.), *The Future of Research and Technology Organisations in Europe*, Luxembourg: European Commission.

Katzenstein, P. (ed.) (1977), *Between Power and Plenty*, Itacha, NY: Ithaca.

Katzenstein, P. (1985), *Small States in World Markets*, Ithaca, NY: Ithaca.

Kluth, M. (1995), 'Why a Social Dimension?', PhD-afhandlinger., Roskilde.

Kluth, M. (1997), *The Political Economy of the Social Dimension*.

Kluth, M.F. and Andersen, J.B. (1994), Creating Institutional Infrastructures for Structural Change: The Case of the Danish 'Resource Area Analyses', paper presented at Annual EAEPE Conference, Copenhagen (November).

LaPalombara, J. (1987), *Democracy Italian Style*, New Haven, Conn.

Lehmbruch, G. (1977), 'Liberal Corporatism and Party Government', *Comparative Political Studies*, 10.

Levy, J. (1994), 'After Etatisme: Dilemmas of Institutional Reform in Post-Dirigiste France', in J. Levy (ed.), *Toqueville's Revenge: Dilemmas of Institution Building in Post-Dirigiste France*, University of California, Berkeley.

List, F. (1841), *The National System of Political Economy*, English Edition (1904), London: Longman.

Lundvall, B.-Å. (ed.) (1992), National Systems of Innovation: Towards a Theory of Innovation and Interactive Learning, London: Pinter.

Ministry of Business and Industry/Danish Agency for Development of Trade and Industry (1995), *Teknologisk service*, Copenhagen: Ministry of Business and Industry/Danish Agency for Development of Trade and Industry.

Nelson R. (ed.) (1993), *National Innovation Systems – A Comparative Analysis*, Oxford: Oxford University Press.

NGL Consulting Ltd (1991), *Canada's Science and Technology Relations with Europe – A Review Prepared for Industry, Science and Technology*, Ontario: NGL Consulting Ltd.

Nielsen, K. and Pedersen, O.K. (1989), *Forhandlingsøkonomi i Norden*, Copenhagen.

OECD (1992), *TEP – The Technology Economy Programme – Technology and The Economy: The Key Relationships*, Paris: OECD.

Reinert, E. (1994), 'Competitiveness and its Precedessors – a 500 Year Cross National Perspective, paper presented at the Nordic Innovation Network Conference, Copenhagen (1994).

Shonfield, A. (1965), *Modern Capitalism*, London: Oxford University Press.

Soskice, D. (1991), 'The Institutional Infrastructure for International Competitiveness: A Comparative Analysis of the UK and Germany', unpublished paper, Berlin.

SPRINT/EIMS (1994), *Research and Technology Organizations Study to Support Evaluation, Auditing and Benchmarking Leading to Strategy Development*, Copenhagen: Danish Technological Institute.

Swedeberg, R. (1991), Joseph A. Schumpeter – His Life and Work, Cambridge: Cambridge University Press.

Tiscar, J.R. (ed.) (1994), *The Future of Research and Technology Organizations in Europe*, Brussels: European Commission.

Walker, W. (1993), 'National Innovation Systems – Britain', in R. Nelson (ed.), *National Innovation Systems – A Comparative Perspective*, Oxford: Oxford University Press.

Zysman, J. (1983), *Governments, Markets and Growth*, Ithaca, NY.

Zysman, J. (1994), *How Institutions Create Historically Rooted Trajectories*, Oxford: Oxford University Press.

5.   Globalization of innovative capacity in the chemical and related products industry

Vivien Walsh

INTRODUCTION

This chapter is not a report of a finished piece of research with an analysis of the data that have been assembled. It is a preliminary discussion of some thoughts on the globalization of the chemical industry, written at the outset of a research project on this topic.[1] It surveys the background to the programme of research, discusses the research questions that seem to be important, and considers the kind of data that are available and the methodological approach that will be taken.

WHAT IS GLOBALIZATION?

There has been much hype about globalization (Dicken, 1992), and different views of what the term actually means, but the OECD (1992) has taken the view that it nevertheless reflects a real phenomenon: the emergence of a new set of processes and relationships, representing a new phase in internationalization which differs significantly from earlier phases. If we define internationalization rather generally as the process of increasing interrelationship and economic interdependence of previously fairly separate national economies (via trade, foreign direct investment (FDI) and sourcing of inputs, see Table 5.1), then globalization is the latest phase of this process, encompassing the following trends:

1.   The increased rate of FDI from the mid 1980s.
2.   The wave of international mergers and acquisitions over the past 5–10 years, leading to more concentrated supply structures and more powerful global oligopolies.
3.   The growth of intra-firm trade within multinational enterprises.[2]

4. The much faster rate of growth of FDI compared with world trade since 1985[3] and the particular predominance of the former over the latter in services (Chesnais 1994, p. 44).
5. The complex international networks of inter-firm and inter-organizational cooperative alliances, joint ventures and technological agreements.

Table 5.1   Factors included in internationalization

---

1. International trade in goods and services
2. Foreign direct investment – the internationalization of production
3. International financing and transfer of capital
4. Transborder sourcing of inputs such as:
    Skilled personnel
    Information
    Raw materials and energy sources
    Embodied and disembodied technology

Thus an increasing proportion of value and wealth is produced and distributed world-wide through a system of interlinking private networks, at the centre of which are multinational enterprises, whose strategies dominate the globalization process. These concentrated world supply structures take advantage of financial globalization, while information technology facilitates the management of global businesses with different elements operating in different time zones, and (where electronic signals have replaced pieces of paper as money) enables international financial transactions to be carried out more easily (see Antonelli, 1984).

Figure 5.1 shows a similar rate of growth of international trade, of internal investment (gross fixed capital formation), and of the national economies in the OECD area (gross domestic product). However, it shows the rate of growth of international production (FDI) to be three times as high as these three indicators after 1985.

This has been accompanied by a number of structural changes: Japan's share of the overseas investment of the OECD countries, for example, more than quadrupled during the 1980s (OECD, 1990). From a position in the 1960s and 1970s when outward investment from the USA dominated the internationalization process (46.4 per cent of OECD flows 1971–80), the USA has become a major location for *inward* investment, mainly from Japan and Europe (51.4 per cent of OECD flows in 1988–89) (OECD, 1990). European share of outward investment did not change a great deal during the 1970s and 1980s, although inward investment went down from nearly two-thirds of OECD flows to under half. There was also more than a four-fold

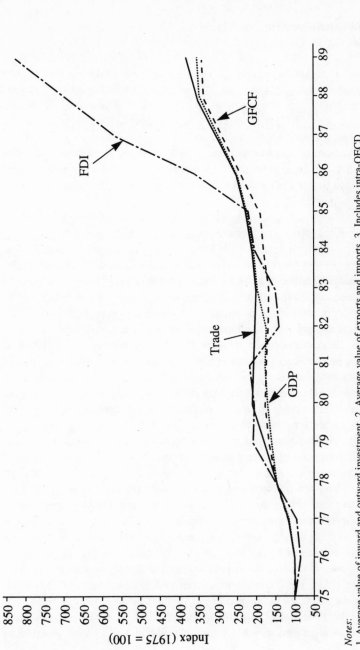

Index (1975 = 100)

850
800
750
700
650
600
550
500
450
400
350
300
250
200
150
100
50
75 76 77 78 79 80 81 82 83 84 85 86 87 88 89

FDI

Trade

GDP

GFCF

Notes:
1. Average value of inward and outward investment. 2. Average value of exports and imports. 3. Includes intra-OECD.
Source: OECD (1992).

Figure 5.1   Trends in foreign direct investment,[1,3] gross domestic product[2,3] total trade and gross fixed capital formation in the OECD area, current prices

increase in mergers and acquisitions by the 1000 largest firms in the EU from 1982 to 1989 (OECD, 1992).

Alternative Definitions of Globalization

In contrast, or in addition, to the definition I have adopted above, the term 'globalization' might suggest the idea that, whereas internationalization could involve transactions across only one or two national borders, today's international transactions are the result of global strategies involving the whole world. Petrella (1990), for example, speaks of the economic exploitation of material and non-material means of production organized *on a global basis*. Thus international trade becomes an activity planned by a firm which has either designed a 'global product' or which has planned from the outset a product range to suit the spectrum of cultural variations in pattern of demand in the global market.

Richards (1993) uses a definition of globalization similar to the first of these but distinguishes it from the second, which he calls internationalization. In his approach, firms which operate *globally* seek to market relatively standardized products world-wide simultaneously, requiring world-wide production facilities; *internationalization* is a market-based strategy in which the firm seeks to promote products that have been adapted to local conditions but which originate in the home country. Thus Richards's definition of globalization is based on FDI while his definition of internationalization is based on trade.

There is little evidence to support the idea that globalization in the sense of world-wide production of standard products is taking place in any significant way. In the food industry, one of the sectors most concerned with local variations in taste and cultural patterns of consumption, there is clearly a far wider variety of 'foreign' products available in most countries (to the consumers who can afford them) than was the case 40 or 50 years ago. This is far from there being standardized global products or global consumers. In fact even where products are quite standardized, most so-called 'global products' vary to a greater or lesser extent with different tastes in different markets. Moreover, globalization in the sense of firms carrying out operations all over the globe to more or less the same extent or at more or less the same time is rare. On the contrary, international investment flows, cross-border mergers and acquisitions (UNCTC, 1991) and international inter-firm agreements (for example, Freeman and Hagedoorn, 1995)[4] are heavily concentrated in just a few of the world's economies: those within the triad of North America, Europe and Japan. Less than 20 per cent of OECD countries' FDI was going to developing countries by the end of the 1980s (Chesnais 1994, p. 49).

In Porter's (1986) terms, a global industry is one in which a firm's competitive position in one country is significantly affected by its position in another; high levels of coordination among business units and subsidiaries and with corporate headquarters produce a global strategy. This implies among other things a world-wide *intra-firm* division of labour, according to van Tulder and Ruigrok (1993). They contrast the idea of *glocalization*, or *global localization*, as an alternative strategy to that of globalization, based on their study of the car industry. In their view globalization strategies mean that firms produce strategic inputs themselves and locate production according to the comparative advantage and economies of scale of certain sites.

According to this definition, van Tulder and Ruigrok argue that globalization is largely a matter of ideology and hype, and that *glocalization* is more like the strategy they have observed in practice. This involves a geographically concentrated *inter-firm* division of labour in which firms develop an integrated supply, production and distribution chain, interacting closely with independent suppliers and dealers, locating production in or close to their major markets (concentrated in the triad), and aiming to be accepted as part of the local communities in which they are located.[5]

I have adopted the OECD's definition of globalization rather than the narrower ones discussed above, restricted to criteria based on global products or a world-wide intra-firm division of labour in production, though these may be features of globalization. In addition I would emphasize globalization as a *process* rather than the *outcome* of that process, capturing the idea that it is more advanced in some industries and in some countries than in others, and may take place more rapidly (or decline) in some periods than in others. In that sense of the term, then, globalization seems to be generally accepted as a real phenomenon in the case of production and trade.[6] The rest of this chapter is concerned with the globalization of technology or, more particularly the globalization of innovative capacity, about which there is more debate and no consensus in the literature.

GLOBALIZATION OF TECHNOLOGY AND OF INNOVATIVE CAPACITY

Archibugi and Michie (1995) distinguish between global *exploitation* of technology, global *generation* of technology and global technological *collaboration*. Howells (this volume, Chapter 2) proposes a model of globalization of technology which distinguishes between *sources, flows* (inter- and intra-firm) and *sinks* (consumption or uses) of technology. These are useful distinctions to consider when gathering information about trends in the globalization of technology. Within this framework, I am more concerned in this chapter with the sources or generation and the flows of technology; that is to say it focuses on the globalization of *innovative capacity*.

Global Location of R&D

Howells and Wood (1993, p. 23) show that foreign company-financed industrial R&D in the USA grew from 4.8 per cent of total company-financed
R&D in 1977 to 11.26 per cent in 1988. Wortmann's (1990) study of German
multinationals showed that 17 per cent of their R&D staff were based abroad.
Individual cases of firms and industries also provide data on overseas location of R&D. Howells and Wood (1993), for example, provide maps of the
world with the locations of selected firms' R&D centres. They have also
discussed in some detail the strategic thinking behind overseas location of
R&D.

Pearce and Singh (1992a) carried out a survey of 914 parent and overseas
subsidiary laboratories of 500 of the largest industrial enterprises listed by
Fortune (Table 5.2). Only 12 countries were involved and, as Richards (1993)
says, 'large global firms carry out research ... in each others' backyards'. The
authors have further elaborated the reasons for overseas location of R&D (see
also Pearce and Singh (1992b) and Casson *et al.* (1992a)). Casson *et al.*
(1992b) have provided a more detailed breakdown of the foreign locations of
R&D by the *Fortune* 500 largest firms (see Table 5.3). This shows that over
50 per cent of the UK, German, Italian, Dutch and Swiss firms' laboratories
in the sample were located outside the home country, while over 50 per cent
of the laboratories in the sample located in Canada, Britain, Italy, the Netherlands and 'other European countries' are foreign-owned. Japan is exceptional
in that it has by far the smallest proportion of foreign-owned industrial
laboratories (3 per cent), while Japanese firms have easily the smallest share
of their laboratories located abroad (8 per cent).

*Table 5.2 International distribution of laboratories owned by 500 leading
firms listed by* Fortune

Ownership	Parent R&D	Overseas R&D
US/Canada	303	126
UK	55	81
EU	64	98
Europe (other)	28	40
Japan	96	8
Australia	4	0
Rest of world	11	0
Total	561	353

Source:　Pearce and Singh (1992a).

Table 5.3 International distribution of the laboratories owned by 500 major firms

Ownership	Location												Total		Int. ratio
	USA	Can.	UK	Fr.	Ger.	Italy	Neth.	Swe.	Swtz.	Oth. Euro.	Jap.	Rest of World	Total overseas	Total	
USA	282	17	41	12	14	7	3	1	6	11	1	11	124	406	31
Canada		11	1								1		2	13	15
UK	68	1	55	1	3		2		1	1		4	81	136	60
France	12		1	25		1						1	15	40	37
Germany	50		4		29					2		1	57	86	66
Italy	3		1			5		1					5	10	50
Netherlands	12		4	2	2		5		1				21	26	81
Sweden	1						1	11					2	13	15
Switzerland	26		2	1	3			1	10	1	1	1	36	46	78
Other Europe	2									7			2	9	22
Japan	7		1								96		8	104	8
Rest world												15	0	15	0
Tot. overseas	181	18	55	16	22	8	6	3	8	15	3	18	353		
Grand Total	463	29	110	41	51	13	11	14	18	22	99	33		904	
Foreign dependence ratio	39	62	50	39	43	62	55	21	44	68	3	107			

Source: Casson *et al.* (1992b), p. 181.

The industries which spend more than 10 per cent of their R&D expenditure abroad are food products, pharmaceuticals, transport equipment of all kinds, coal and petroleum products and professional and scientific instruments. Clearly, firms have not yet started doing *a majority* of their research abroad, or anything like it: but they are certainly locating an increasing proportion of R&D abroad, especially in certain industries.

The key questions are: how significant is overseas R&D in the technology strategy of the firm, is this likely to continue to grow, and what sort of R&D is carried out abroad? For example, is it basic, applied, near market, fundamental or adaptation to local markets and regulatory environments? What are the consequences for national systems of innovation and national government policies towards industry and technology? What are the implications for strategic management of technology, of innovation and of other operations by the firm?

Where Patents are Taken Out

Patel and Pavitt (for example, 1992) have used patent statistics to argue that innovation is still largely produced at home. There are, of course, many arguments for and against the use of patent data as proxy measures for trends in innovative behaviour. These are now very familiar and will not be dealt with here. The authors' study of the patenting activity of 686 of the world's largest firms is used to argue that they are responsible for 60 per cent of the technology (patents) produced by firms. These large firms' share of world patenting is greater than their share of world production.

The authors show that Japanese-owned large firms in Japan produce 62.5 per cent of patents taken out in the USA by Japan-based firms. Only 1.2 per cent are from foreign-owned large firms in Japan and 0.6 per cent come from the overseas operations of large Japanese firms. The remaining 35.7 per cent of patents are taken out by smaller Japanese-owned firms.

Only Belgium and Canada have a larger share of US patents from foreign-owned large firms operating in those countries than from Belgian or Canadian-owned ones. As far as large firms operating outside their home base are concerned, the largest share of patents are those from Dutch firms outside the Netherlands, which account for 82 per cent of Dutch firms' patents. The next largest in this category is Switzerland with 28 per cent. From these data Patel and Pavitt argue very strongly that technological activities are still concentrated in the home country of the large multinational, even though their other activities may be highly international; and that therefore the national system of innovation is still a major influence on the innovative behaviour of large firms.

However, the Patel and Pavitt patent data (like the R&D investment data) show that there is a difference in internationalized generation of technology according to industrial sector. For example, internationalized R&D is high in pharmaceuticals and food processing and low in aerospace. The top 50 firms with the largest share of US patents outside their home country (1985–90) are given in Table 5.4.

Table 5.4   Fifty large firms with the biggest share of US patents outside their home country, 1985–90

Building materials (Hanson, Pilkington, Redland, American Standard, Saint Gobain)
Drink and tobacco (Molson, Grand Met, BAT)
Mining and Petroleum (Nova, RTZ, Shell, Labofina, BP)
Textiles (Coats Viyella)
Paper and wood (Esselte, Universal Match)
Vehicles and parts (GKN Engineering)
Machinery (FKI Babcock, IMI, SKF, Gillette, TI, Northern Engineering, Hawker Siddeley, BTR, Black & Decker)
Chemicals (Akzo, BOC, Solvay, ICI, Ciba-Geigy, Hoechst, Norsk Hydro, Dai Nippon)
Food (Unilever, Nestlé, Reckitt & Colman, Sara Lee)
Metals (Inco, Alcan, Elkem, Metallurgie Hoboken-Overpelt)
Electrical (Racal, ITT, ABB, Electrolux, Philips)
Pharmaceuticals (Wellcome, Hoffman La Roche, Sandoz)

Cantwell, meanwhile, (for example, 1995) has assembled a large collection of patent data over a considerable period of time and uses it to argue a different case from that of Patel and Pavitt. One of his aims has been to challenge the two hypotheses of the Vernon product-cycle theory, one of which is that innovation is nearly always located in the home country of the parent company, and usually close to the site of the corporate technological headquarters. Cantwell found that the share of foreign research in the total corporate technological activity of the largest US and European firms averaged about 8 per cent in the periods 1920–39 and 1945–68, before rising significantly to an average of about 14.5 per cent in 1969–90. As one might expect there were different trends to be found in different countries and different industries. The proportion of foreign research in the share of the largest chemical firms' patents doubled between the periods 1945–68 and 1969–90.

The advantages of being located in certain foreign countries rather than staying at home have been discussed at some length elsewhere (for example, Caves, 1982; Lundvall, 1985; Dunning, 1993; Howells and Wood, 1993) but may be summarized as follows:

1. Access to the host country's science base or market.
2. Availability of high quality R&D staff (perhaps with skills not available at home, or cheaper to employ).
3. Interaction with sophisticated lead users, who can provide useful feedback on innovative products and services.
4. A favourable regulatory environment, or the need to carry out R&D activities locally in order to comply with local regulations.
5. Existence of other favourable government policies providing tax breaks, incentives, advice or support.

The balance between the influence of the national system of innovation of the firm's home country and factors such as those in the above list will vary between industrial sectors and with different home and host countries, so the pattern of globalization will also vary between sectors and countries. Lundvall's work on innovation supplier–user interaction, for example, discusses the balance between some of these factors, notably the tension between the need for interaction with lead users and the existence of other tendencies which might exist towards increasing footlooseness (see Lundvall, 1985, 1988, 1992).

International Sourcing of Technology

Overseas R&D activity accounts for a small proportion of a multinational firm's total R&D (around 11 per cent on average), though this is more significant in some industries and in some countries than others and appears to be a growing trend. Similarly, overseas R&D activity generates a small proportion of a firm's patents, again with exceptions among firms in some countries and some industries, and again is an increasing trend. The interesting thing, however, is whether this is a key strategy for the future in firms and whether it is likely to increase substantially. This information can be inferred from historical trends but is likely to be obtainable mainly by surveys and interviews.

Overseas location of R&D and overseas sources of patents are indicators of different activities. Investment in R&D is an input into the invention and innovation process, and there are other equally important inputs needed for innovation in the form of tangible and intangible investment, including investment over a period of time to allow the accumulation of competences of various kinds. Patents measure an output of the inventive process, and overseas patents in particular are used as a proxy for innovative output on the basis that they are likely to represent the intention of turning an invention into an innovation. However, many patents still do not become innovations, so this indicator can only be considered to be a measure of an intermediate output of the innovation process. The final output is the innovation itself, or possibly even its impacts (economic, social, environmental and other). The latter brings us back to Archibugi and Michie's category of exploitation of technology and Howells's category of technology sinks, which are outside the scope of this chapter.

From the point of view of getting a good indication of the globalization of innovative capacity, location of R&D spending and of inventions generating patents are important indicators, but do not tell the whole story. For example, an invention may be made as a result of a firm's R&D activities in its home country laboratories as a result of the investment of capital in buildings and equipment, and the expenditure of money on research materials, publications and the employment of skilled personnel and their subsequent training. A patent may then be granted to the firm giving that address. However, the invention may equally be the result of the firm's investment in several locations, some of which may be in the home country and some abroad. Howells and Wood (1993), for example, have illustrated the multiple locations of stages in the production of a drug by a pharmaceutical company. Furthermore, in order to generate that invention or innovation the firm may also have used other sources of knowledge, for example as a result of its collaborative R&D with another firm or public sector research institution; as a result of its use of sophisticated techniques, machinery and equipment and its purchase of intermediates, all embodying knowledge from elsewhere; as a result of its recruitment of skilled research technical and production staff, trained and experienced elsewhere; and as a result of its purchase of licences to use proprietary knowledge developed elsewhere. In each case 'elsewhere' could well be another country.

I have analysed in detail the inputs of all these kinds of knowledge from outside the innovating firm in the case of steroid drugs in the 1930s–60s (Walsh, 1997). This case shows that even before the recent take-off of inter-firm collaborative alliances (and the take-off of studies of such alliances) all these inputs, including collaborative research, played a very significant role in the innovative process in some sectors. The steroid case also gives an example of the extent to which the simple purchase of an intermediate product represents a substantial input of knowledge, skill and competences accumulated elsewhere. The synthesis of the compound diosgenin from the wild Mexican yam in the 1940s was scientifically interesting and drew on previous research carried out in a variety of other countries, but also had a commercial and political impact. It made the production of steroids commercially viable and made diosgenin an important intermediate in the process: previous routes to steroids were based on animal sources (pregnant mares' urine or bulls' testicles) and were too expensive for commercial production. The discovery also gave the Mexican government the opportunity (temporarily, until other sources were discovered) to encourage the development in Mexico of a pharmaceutical industry and of steroid expertise in the public research sector, by banning the export of yams, diosgenin and other intermediates. Thus the purchase of diosgenin as an intermediate by an innovating firm involved its acquisition of inputs which embodied the accumulated competences of many chemists, biologists and others from a range of public sector and private institutions in North America, Europe and Japan; and which represented the outcome of an array of political and economic processes concerning commercialization and the promotion of economic, scientific and technological development in a less advanced country.

Another example concerns the recent discovery of a route to the anticancer drug taxol (USA) and its analogue taxotère (France) from 10-deacetyl baccatin (10-DAB) obtainable from the (renewable) needles of the yew tree, *Taxus baccata* (see Walsh and Goodman, 1996). This route and its variants are the outcome of a research effort by up to 50 groups (some competing, some collaborating) of private and public sector chemists, biologists, biotechnologists and others in different countries and employing a variety of alternative approaches. The route makes 10-DAB an important intermediate for companies such as Bristol Myers Squibb and Rhône Poulenc (currently in dispute with each other over patent infringement). The previous source was the bark of the pacific yew, *T. brevifolia*, a non-renewable source using the normal methods of most of the firms collecting it. In the quantities being collected, it was also a source which threatened the continued existence of the *T. brevifolia* species, and that of the ecology of the American Pacific Northwest, even though resulting supplies of taxol were still limited and expensive. The intermediate 10-DAB embodies the accumulated competences of those who contributed to the programmes of work and the political and commercial pressures concerned with finding a manufacturing process, protecting the environment and developing treatments for cancer.

Today the contribution of alliances in research to innovative activity is greater than in the early days of research on steroids, especially in high-tech sectors (see, for example, Hagedoorn and Schakenraad, 1990, 1991), and where these alliances cross national borders they also contribute to the globalization of innovative capacity in a significant way. Thus the purchase of intermediates, equipment and licences to use patents; collaborative research; and recruitment are all sources of knowledge generated outside the firm and/ or outside the country (see Table 5.5). In analysing globalization of innovative capacity all these should be taken into account, although quantitative data are not necessarily available for all of the sourcing activities, and qualitative data obtained from interviews and case study material will need to be used with any statistics that can be assembled.

Table 5.5   Factors included in the globalization of innovative capacity

1. Licensing of technology produced abroad
2. Recruitment of foreign scientists and technologists
3. Merger and acquisition across national borders and involving R&D facilities
4. Overseas location of R&D
5. Patenting by firms outside their home base
6. Purchase of sophisticated machinery, equipment and intermediates, embodying knowledge produced abroad
7. Cross-border collaborative technological alliances with other firms and with public sector research organizations (formal and informal)

THE CHEMICAL AND RELATED PRODUCTS INDUSTRY

Even if the degree of internationalization or globalization is small, the key questions are: is this a trend, will it increase, and is it therefore significant as the beginning of a tendency for the future? In order to collect suitable data to provide indicators of the various elements of globalization (see Table 5.5) and to show trends over time, I decided to focus on one industrial sector at a time. This also permits the comparison of qualitative and quantitative data. Previous experience (for example, Walsh 1984) has shown that collecting both kinds of data gives a broader picture or two complementary pictures; and, indeed, that one kind of data alone can be quite misleading. I have chosen to look at the chemical and related products industry, to which this chapter now turns.

There are three main reasons for choosing this industry as a case study. First of all, to build on accumulated competences: I have worked on innovation, company strategy, restructuring, the challenge of new technology and changes in patterns of demand in the chemical industry for a number of years (for example, Walsh, 1984, 1993; Walsh and Galimberti, 1993). Secondly, because even those who argue against the phenomenon of globalization of the production of technology consider that the chemical and related products industry could be an exception: if globalization of innovative capacity is happening at all, evidence is likely to be found there. The generation of methods for identifying and analysing trends in globalization in the case of this industry may then be applied elsewhere in future studies. Thirdly, chemicals and related products constitute a sector or sectors where Europe has maintained over a substantial period of time its technological and market strength in the face of international competition. This raises interesting questions with regard to the accumulation of competences and market power versus the appearance of new technological and techno-economic paradigms, more successfully adopted by some national systems of innovation than others.

What is the Chemical and Related Products Industry?

I have chosen to define the sector I am studying as the complex of industries related to the exploitation of chemical knowledge or which have grown around a chemical base. Thus new materials, glass, food processing and waste treatment are based on flow processes and increasingly on chemical reactions. Some agrochemicals firms have moved into seeds (for example, Zeneca (starting when it was still part of ICI) and Sandoz (now part of Novartis)) and some pharmaceutical firms have moved into confectionary (for example, Warner Lambert bought Cachou Lajaunie while Finnish Huhtamaki bought Swedish Procordia's confectionary business while entering a pharmaceuticals joint venture with the same firm).

Table 5.4 listed the 50 firms with the largest share of patents coming from outside their home base country. Of these 50, eight are classified as chemicals, three as pharmaceuticals and four as food, which comes within the scope of our enquiry. In addition, some of the firms classified as building materials (for example, Pilkingtons Glass), mining and petroleum (for example, Shell and BP), drink and tobacco (for example, Grand Met), and metals (for example, Alcan) use flow and/or chemical processes, giving a total of 20 out of the 50 falling within the broad definition of chemicals and related products. Table 5.6 lists the products that might be considered to come within the scope of the industry in which I am interested.

Corporate boundaries are constantly shifting in the chemical industry, as a result of mergers (for example, Sandoz and Ciba to form Novartis in 1996), acquisitions, de-mergers (for example, ICI to form ICI and Zeneca in 1993), sell-offs, the movement out of low added value products, and 'swaps' whereby one firm will exchange an area of business that is marginal to its core competence for one which is more central, with another firm for whom the business it gains is closer to its core competences than the one relinquished.

Industry boundaries are also shifting: what now counts as the chemical industry? Of the list in Table 5.6, several categories would not at one time have been considered to be part of the chemical industry, although chemical firms have moved into these areas, and chemistry and chemical engineering are important aspects of their core competences. To illustrate this, Table 5.7 lists the major firms in plant research in 1991. Some of these are traditional seeds firms, while others have traditionally been chemical firms. The traditional seeds firms have concentrated on conventional areas of plant research, while the firms traditionally in the chemical industry have moved into plant

Table 5.6   The boundaries of the chemical industry and the chemical firm

---

Products and/or processes using flow engineering or chemistry

1. Bulk chemicals: raw materials, intermediates, catalysts, reagents
2. Paints and additives
3. Dyes, bleaches, textile additives
4. Detergents, shampoo, toothpaste, hair dye, household cleaning materials
5. Synthetic fibres including carbon fibre and additives
6. Synthetic rubber and additives
7. Explosives
8. Photographic chemicals
9. Human and veterinary medicines, prescription and over-the-counter drugs and disinfectants
10. Pregnancy and other diagnostic tests
11. Clean water and waste treatment
12. Paper processing and additives
13. Glass
14. Perfume
15. Foods, food processing, food additives
16. Agrochemicals
17. Plastics and plastics additives
18. Other new materials including advanced ceramics
19. Confectionary

---

research via their interest in crop protection (traditionally part of chemicals) and in biotechnology, as illustrated by the predominance of their spending on plant biotechnology. However, ICI (now Zeneca) and Sandoz and Ciba-Geigy (now Novartis) perform substantial amounts of both traditional plant research and plant biotechnology. They have made their strategic moves into the seeds business from a position of strength in crop protection, via their acquisition of seeds companies and of the latters' traditional competences (see Table 5.8). Table 5.9 shows the world's largest seeds firms and Table 5.10 the world's largest crop protection firms.

Globalization is a matter of shifting technological and competence boundaries as well as geographical ones. To map this process it is therefore important to look at mergers, acquisitions, de-mergers, divestments and technological alliances in terms of both changes in geographical location and in technical specialization.

The chemical industry has also faced a number of changes in its business, political and technological environment in recent years. In particular, three interacting factors are characteristic of the industry in the past 10–20 years: technological changes, changes in the competitive environment and organizational changes.

Table 5.7   Multinationals and plant research, 1991

Company	Estimated annual expenditure (US$ m)	
	Conventional breeding	Plant biotechnology
Sandoz	14	16
Pioneer	46	7
ICI	21	17
Upjohn	24	3
Ciba-Geigy	9	17
Limagrain	22	5
KWS	18	5
DeKalb	16	6
Shell	19	3
Du Pont	0	20
Monsanto	1	15
Enimont	0	15

Source: ICI.

Table 5.8   Acquisitions by ICI seeds

Year	Company
1985	Garst Seed Company
1986	Sinclair McGill
1987	SES
1987	Miln Marsters (asset purchase)
1987	Rohm & Haas (garnetocide technology)
1989	Contiseeds
1990	Agroplant
1990	Super Crost

Source: ICI.

Table 5.9   World's largest seeds companies by sales, 1990 and 1994

1990		1994	
Company	Sales (US$ m)	Company	Sales (SFr bn)
Pioneer	840	Pioneer	1.5
Sandoz/Hilleshog	473	Novartis	0.9
Limagrain	335	Limagrain	0.5
Upjohn	270	Seminis	0.5
ICI	250	Cargill	0.4
Cargill	240	KWS	0.3
DeKalb	205	DeKalb	0.3
Takii	157	Pau Group	0.3
KWS	153	Zeneca	0.2
Sakata	153	Van der Have	0.2

Source: ICI and *Financial Times*, 8.3.96, p. 28.

Table 5.10   Largest firms in crop protection by sales (bn SFr)

Company	Country	1994 sales
Novartis	Switzerland	5.0
AgrEvo	Germany	2.7
Du Pont	USA	2.7
Monsanto	USA	2.6
Zeneca	UK	2.6
Bayer	Germany	2.5
Rhône Poulenc	France	2.3
DowElanco	USA	2.1
American Home (Cyanamid)	USA	2.0
BASF	Germany	1.6

Source: *Financial Times*, 8.3.96, p. 28.

Technological changes facing the chemical industry

Biotechnology   Biotechnology is the basis for a number of different approaches in new product development. First, it represents a new technological paradigm in the search for new molecules, that is, a new paradigm in the R&D process. It can be used to target particular end uses, instead of the mass screening of randomly generated products known as 'molecular roulette'. The structure of the cell receptors which block or initiate biological activity suggests a structure for a molecule which can mimic that action or block it, and hence the possibility of generating 'designer' drugs, agrochemicals and other molecules; designed, that is, for a particular purpose rather than the previous hit or miss approach. These designed molecules are then manufactured using conventional chemical production processes.

Secondly, genetic engineering can be used to make products which in principle are available from other sources, but only available in small amounts or subject to ethical restrictions, for example, human insulin, interferon or human growth hormone. Biomass can be used to generate energy. Thirdly, genetic engineering can be used to make new products which did not exist before, genetically modified organisms such as the transgenic tomato or the food product Quorn (which is targeted at slimmers rather than vegetarians since it is designed to resemble chicken as closely as possible). Fourthly, biological *processes* can be used as the basis of a product, for example, pregnancy and diabetic tests and other diagnostic kits.

Table 5.11 lists some of the uses of biotechnology. Nowadays biotechnology is normally taken to mean technologies based on monoclonal antibodies, recombinant DNA techniques and other recent developments that have grown out of molecular biology. It could equally be taken more generally to mean the commercialization of biological processes, in which case it would include pre-capitalist activities such as brewing (otherwise known as first-generation biotechnology) and second-generation activities based on large-scale applications of microbiology, including the production of penicillin by fermentation. In that case 'modern' biotechnology would be known as 'third generation' biotechnology. Table 5.11 includes first-, second- and third-generation biotechnology: examples of third-generation biotechnology would be items 1, 2, 3 and 7; examples of first-generation biotechnology would be 4 and 6; while 5 is second-generation biotechnology.

In the early days there were high expectations about the potential of biotechnology as a source of new processes, new products, new raw materials and a new source of energy. However, technological problems of industrial scale-up were more serious than anticipated, while demand did not materialize on the scale that was originally expected. This was partly due to the time taken to obtain licences for new pharmaceutical products or because of ethical and regulatory concerns about the more novel products of biotechnology; partly due to costs relative to traditional products and processes; and partly just as a result of novelty (see Walsh (1993) for a more detailed discussion of these factors). Diagnostic kits were less strictly regu-

Table 5.11   Commerical uses of biotechnology

1. New products based on biotechnological process	Diagnostic kits
2. New products based on genetic modification of known products	Transgenic tomato
3. Naturally occurring products made in greater quantity by genetic engineering	Human insulin, interferon
4. Energy from biomass	Gasohol for cars
5. Semi-synthetic products: biological and chemical processes	Steroid drugs, penicillin
6. Raw materials for production	Alcohol by fermentation for chemical processes (or beverages)
7. Biotechnology used in R&D with conventional chemical production	Designer molecules

lated and quicker to reach the market. Pharmaceutical products take longer to gain regulatory approval but are usually fairly straightforward; the longest-term outputs were either those whose commercial success was dependent on a change in prices for conventional materials (notably petroleum), or those involving release of genetically modified organisms into the environment. Not only were the latter the subject of public concern, but no standard procedure had been established for dealing with them. One of the most successful applications of biotechnology turned out to be its use as a new tool in the search for new products which could then be made by conventional synthetic methods. This had the advantage of a less wide-ranging impact on the established firms' cultures, and was not so dependent on the successful creation of demand or the negotiation of regulatory requirements.

Other technological changes   Changes in other areas of technology with enormous impact on the chemical industry include advances in instrumentation, computerized process control, remote control of dangerous operations, computer-aided molecular design, computer-based prediction of toxic effects on humans and the environment, and the development of equipment for the detection of small amounts of a chemical, thus allowing for tighter regulations. The science of epidemiology links chemicals with diseases and other unwanted effects using statistical techniques and probability, where causality is otherwise difficult to establish.

Implications of technological changes   Biotechnology, information and communications technologies, and instrumentation technologies all affect the costs of R&D because they need investment in equipment and skills and add to the variety of competences required for R&D activities. They also change the nature of production and the skills required for it, and influence the structure, organization and location of R&D. Firms pose themselves questions such as, how do we acquire the new technology and the new competences necessary for using it effectively? Which technologies and competences is it necessary to acquire? They have to choose between developing the competences in-house, perhaps by training and/or strategic recruitment of staff; acquiring them by purchase of, or merger with, another firm by subcontracting; or by strategic alliances with firms and non-business organizations which possess the necessary capabilities. Some of these options involve organizational changes for the firm: merger and acquisition clearly involve reorganization, while collaborative R&D generates a different organizational form for the generation of innovation. Firms may consider it appropriate to locate their own R&D activities close to centres of scientific and technological excellence, as well as markets, abroad.

Increased knowledge of consequences for the environment and human health of exposure to the products of the chemical industry (including side effects of products developed for human consumption such as drugs and food additives) and methods of measuring small concentrations of chemical substances, both permit the implementation of tighter regulations concerning toxicity testing of new products before commercial launch, and generate political pressure to establish such regulations. Legislation in a particular country often requires that toxicity testing be carried out in that country, to take into account local conditions of climate, work practices, eating habits, average body weight and culturally specific patterns of behaviour in the assessment of risk, thus encouraging internationalization of some aspects of R&D. Local variations in procedures for satisfying regulatory bodies and obtaining licences to market new products also mean that firms wishing to sell their products in the markets concerned will not only need to carry out some R&D locally but also to establish links with the regulatory authorities in each case, which equally has organizational implications.

Similarly, market variations – the need for adaptation to local tastes, patterns of demand, patterns of working, and so on –require local R&D to be carried out wherever the firm wishes to market its products. This is particularly so for foodstuffs, but is also true for other products: in the case of drugs, for example, cultural differences in expectations of the delivery system (for example, suppositories in France or Spain where Anglo-Saxon consumers would demand medicine in the form of pills or liquid) require local development work in the area of formulation. An important question to investigate is the extent to which overseas R&D activity is concerned with incremental innovation in adapting products to local patterns of demand and regulatory conditions, and to what extent more radical innovations are generated, based, for example, on interaction with local scientific and technological capabilities that do not exist at home.

Regulations concerning the impact of new products on the environment and on human health may lead to firms' relocation to countries where regulations are less strict. Adverse public opinion may have the same effect: for example, both regulations and public concern about the environment in Germany have been a contributory factor in German chemical firms' decisions about the location of both biotechnology-based R&D and production. Reorganization and relocation of R&D and production may also result from the discovery of new raw materials and intermediates which cannot be exported legally or without difficulty or at an acceptable cost (as illustrated by the case of diosgenin in Mexico).

Changes in the chemical industry's competitive environment

Over the past 10–15 years the chemical industry has experienced market saturation, levelling off, or even a decline in its traditional markets, and changes in patterns of demand for its output. It has been faced with increased costs, especially in R&D, as a result of the demands of regulatory compliance and the increased cost of R&D (since there are now more fields in which to keep at the cutting edge and more sophisticated equipment). Figure 5.2 shows an escalation in R&D costs in pharmaceuticals, with a levelling off and decline in the number of new chemical entities marketed as drugs during the 1970s and 1980s. Chemical process innovation began to decline in the 1970s and the number of chemical product innovations fell even more dramatically (Freeman, 1990). Chemical firms have increasingly been moving out of bulk commodity chemicals and concentrating on high value added products, such as fine chemicals and drugs. Established firms have also been faced with increasing competition from new entrants.

New entrants: countries New entrants may appear in the form of new firms and firms from new geographical areas. In the world chemical market European firms are still dominant: in fact this is one of the few sectors where this is still true. US and European chemical firms have been more successful in facing competition from Japan and the newly industrializing countries than have firms in the electronics sector, for example. In 1987, 30 per cent of world production still came from Europe, 25 per cent from the USA, 17 per cent from Japan, 14 per cent from Eastern Europe[7] and 14 per cent from the rest of the world (Yoxen and Green, 1990). Table 5.12 shows the world's largest chemical firms (as defined by *Chemical and Engineering News*): half

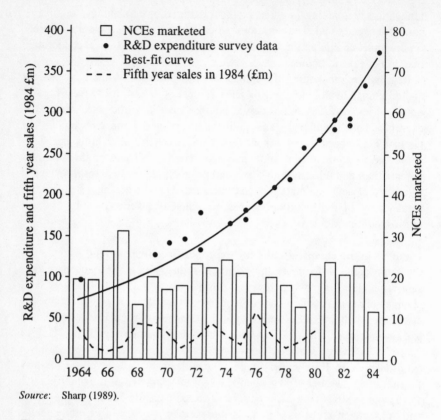

Source: Sharp (1989).

Figure 5.2   Return on R&D investment

the top 30 are European, eight are American and six are Japanese. Yoxen and Green (1990) also list the largest eight food processing firms in the world as Unilever (British/Dutch), Nestlé (Swiss), Grand Metropolitan (British) and five US firms (Philip Morris, Reynolds, Beatrice, Dart & Kraft and Sara Lee). In agrochemicals European and US firms are equally dominant in the world market (see Table 5.10).

The top 20 pharmaceutical companies world-wide are shown in Table 5.13. Of these firms, nine are European, seven are American, three are Japanese and one is jointly Swedish- and US-owned. In the case of Rhône Poulenc Rorer, the French group Rhône Poulenc acquired a majority share of the US firm Rorer and is listed as French, even though its headquarters (which represents only the pharmaceutical part of the Rhône Poulenc group) are now in the USA for strategic and market reasons. Table 5.13 also illustrates the

Table 5.12   World's largest chemical firms, 1994

Company	Country	Sales (US$ million)	R&D spending
Du Pont	USA	39 333	
Hoechst	Germany	30 640	2 080
BASF	Germany	28 744	1 183
Bayer	Germany	26 803	1 961
Dow Chemical	USA	20 015	1 261
Ciba	Switzerland	16 094	1 570
Rhône Poulenc	France	15 550	1 207
ICI	UK	14 072	369
Akzo Nobel	Netherlands	12 202	618
Roche Group	Switzerland	10 765	1 702
Norsk Hydro	Norway	10 122	86
Asahi Chemical	Japan	9 589	
Occidental Petroleum	USA	9 236	
Degussa	Germany	8 528	251
Mitsubishi Chemical	Japan	8 464	
Monsanto	USA	8 272	604
Solvay	Belgium	7 837	343
EniChem	Italy	7 134	123
L'Air Liquide	France	5 721	85
Sumitomo Chemical	Japan	5 481	
BOC International	UK	5 334	135
Toray Industries	Japan	5 137	
W.R.Grace	USA	5 093	132
DSM	Netherlands	4 932	192
Union Carbide	USA	4 865	136
Dai Nippon Ink & Chemicals	Japan	4 609	
Showa Denko	Japan	4 402	
Eastman Chemical	USA	4 329	
FMC	USA	4 011	

Source: *Chemical & Engineering News.*

Table 5.13   Top 20 pharmaceutical companies by prescription sales, 1994–95 (US$ million)

Company	Country	Pharm. sales	Pharm. sales (as % total)	Total R&D[a]
Glaxo Wellcome	UK	12 224	100	1 915
Merck & Co.	USA	9 416	63	1 231
Hoechst Marion Roussel	Germany	9 352	n/a	2 076
AHP (inc. Cyanamid)	USA	7 425	55	817
Bristol Myers Squibb	USA	6 970	58	1 108
Roche (inc. Syntex)	Switzerland	6 241	42	1 705
Pfizer	USA	5 811	70	1 139
Smith Kline Beecham	UK	5 532	60	951
Pharmacia & Upjohn	Sweden/USA	5 304	78	1 094[b]
Lilly	USA	5 248	92	839
Johnson & Johnson	USA	5 158	33	1 278
Takeda	Japan	4 857	64	657
Sandoz (now Novartis)	Switzerland	4 841	42	915
Ciba (now Novartis)	Switzerland	4 464	27	872
Rhône Poulenc Rorer inc. Fisons	France[c]	4 444	89	600
Bayer	Germany	4 274	16	1 958
Sankyo	Japan	3 909	72	463
Schering-Plough	USA	3 714	80	620
Shionogi	Japan	3 574	100	266
Astra	Sweden	3 567	98	509

Notes:
a.   All R&D, not just on prescription drugs.
b.   Pharmacia $487 million + Upjohn $607 million (they merged between the publication dates of the two sources of data for the table).
c.   The majority ownership is French but the corporate HQ is in the USA.

Source: Scrip's 1995 Pharmaceutical League Tables; R&D from *Scrip 2099*, 2.2.96, p. 8.

point about the blurring of boundaries in the chemical and related products industry. Only Glaxo and Shionogi are listed as having 100 per cent of their sales in pharmaceuticals. Five firms are in the top 20 pharmaceutical firms but nevertheless less than half their sales are of pharmaceutical products. Bayer, with only 16 per cent of its sales in pharmaceuticals, is primarily a chemical firm, as are Sandoz and Ciba (now Novartis), while Johnson & Johnson make personal care and baby products.

However, an increasing number of Japanese firms are appearing in lists of the world's leading chemical companies, and some newly industrializing countries have established successful chemical sectors. Table 5.14 shows that an increasing share of chemical patents is coming from Japanese firms, which may be reflected in their international competitive performance in the near future. Thus Japan's number of chemical US patents has doubled in ten years and its share of the world total has gone up by 7 per cent, twice the rate of French chemical patents taken out in the USA (the next highest growth rate).

Table 5.14   Chemical patents taken out in the USA by country of owner

Year	USA	Japan	Germany	France	UK	World total
1984	11 525	3 258	2 139	665	847	20 530
1989	13 847	5 447	2 798	946	1 010	27 033
1994	15 467	6 437	2 389	938	809	29 290
% change, 1984–94	3.0%	7.1%	1.1%	3.5%	–0.9%	3.6%

Source: *Chemical & Engineering News*, 28.8.95, p. 40.

New entrants: firms   As far as the challenge from new entrants in the form of new firms is concerned, traditionally this is a sector with high entry barriers due to the scale of production of many chemical products (for example, plastics), high R&D costs (especially in pharmaceuticals and fine chemicals) and the demands of regulatory compliance, which have tended to keep new entrants out. Nevertheless, biotechnology was first commercialized by new entrants. In principle they might have grown and formed the basis of a new industry, pushing out established firms, like the new firms in Silicon Valley and elsewhere did in the case of microelectronics. If biotechnology had generated gales of creative destruction, as described by Schumpeter, the old dominant firms would have been destroyed while a new industry was created on the basis of new dynamic firms taking their place and improving on it.

However, this did not happen in biotechnology. The large, established firms were influenced by the increased costs and risks they had experienced over the previous period, and the even greater ones posed by the new technology. A variety of technological knowledge is in any case required for the commercialization of one product. On top of that, firms were very uncertain about biotechnology – whether it would be commercially viable and, if so, which directions would be the most promising: drugs, food additives, seeds, agrochemicals, plants, waste treatment or something as yet undiscovered. At the same time, the dominant culture in the established firms was essentially a chemical one: even managers not directly concerned with production or R&D would typically have come from a chemical or chemical engineering background; chemical synthesis shaped the way they saw problems, what appeared to them as important, how they approached new business development and their strategies for the future (see Galimberti, 1993; Walsh and Galimberti, 1993). Biotechnology involved new people, different competences, different ways of working and different emphases on problems. In short, the established firms were locked in to the established paradigm (Chesnais and Walsh, 1994).

However, these firms were not pushed aside by the new entrants, for two reasons. In the first place, they were either sufficiently far-sighted or sufficiently cautious to want to keep abreast of the new developments while not committing themselves too heavily to a move into biotechnology. In the second place, the new entrants faced the kind of entry barriers mentioned above which had not been the case with the new electronics firms. Both established, large firms and new, small firms needed each other for reasons that have been thoroughly discussed in the literature (for example Walsh, 1993) and formed collaborative alliances. In summary, for the established firms it was a way of avoiding being swept aside by new entrants, and a low risk way of adopting the new technology, making use of their market power, resources and accumulated competences. The small firms had the technology but lacked management, finance and marketing knowledge and skills; production and distribution knowledge, facilities and networks; relationships with regulatory authorities and experience in how to get new product licences; and relationships with the intermediaries who test and recommend their products, such as doctors, agricultural experts or nutritionists.

Large firms' competences in this case were not therefore destroyed by a new paradigm. On the other hand, this was a temporary arrangement because they started to take over the small firms once they had established themselves in the technology and in the markets (I shall return to this point later). Moreover, new technology was adopted in such a way as best to adapt it to the established firms' existing skills and competences (for example, as a tool in R&D for searching for and designing new products (as mentioned above) rather than a new basis for production, although this was also related to the slow growth of demand, indeed the need to *create* demand (see Walsh, 1993).

Organizational changes

There has been an important trend in recent years towards organizational changes as a feature of corporate and R&D strategy, notably decentralization of multi-divisional firms, not just in the chemical industry but more generally (Rubenstein, 1989; Coombs & Richards 1993; Coombs, 1994). The advantage of a central R&D function is the ability to make the most of synergies, complementarities, economies of scale and scope, and spillover effects, and to take a long-term strategic view of the development of the technologies and core competences of the firm as a whole. The advantage of decentralized R&D close to the business units is that research staff are more able to be responsive to user needs and to keep in close touch with market demand.

At the same time, in the chemical industry the trend recently has been to re-focus on core competences, selling off more marginal areas of business (marginal both in relation to core competences and to profits). Where a firm has evolved into an organization based quite clearly on two or more distinct technological and market areas with different strategic emphases, they may carry this to the stage of de-merger into separate companies. Meanwhile other firms in the industry have maintained the earlier trend towards merger, acquisition, purchase of parts of other firms or purchase of equity in other firms with certain competences, in order to move into areas considered to be of strategic importance. Table 5.15 lists some mergers and acquisitions in the pharmaceutical industry apart from takeovers of biotechnology firms. In some cases there have been industrial swaps, where firms exchange activities marginal to them for business activities more central to their core competences with other firms whose focus is the other way round.

Strategic re-organization, whether merger or demerger, diversification, decentralization or refocusing on core competences, may be a response to changing competitive circumstances carried out in order to generate more favourable conditions for technological change and market success. Other organizational changes may be a response to, or consequence of, technological changes. The developments discussed above, including the establishment of networks of relationships with professional intermediaries and regulatory authorities which are necessary for a market to exist at all for some new products; location close to markets and sources of scientific and technological expertise and within the administrative area of regulatory bodies; collaborative alliances with other firms and public sector research; and acquisition of, or merger with, firms with complementary competences and assets, can all in some senses be both an organizational *response* to technological change, in order to deal with it in the least costly, least risky way; and a strategic move to secure a favourable position from which to *generate* future technological innovation. It is often difficult to distinguish cause from consequence.

Table 5.15 Examples of mergers and acquisitions in the pharmaceutical industry (excluding the purchase of biotechnology companies)

Company acquiring or partner 1 in merger	Acquired firm/ operation or partner 2 in merger	Vendor/notes	Date
Monsanto	GD Searle		1985
Eastman Kodak	Stirling Winthrop		1988
Bristol Myers	Squibb		1989
SmithKline Beckman	Beecham		1989
Novo	Nordisk		1989
Dow	Marion		1989
American Home Products	AH Robins		1989
Rhône Poulenc	Rorer		1990
Ciba Geigy	European otc section	ICI	1990
Johnson & Johnson	US otc section	ICI	1990
Feruzzi Group	Montedison		1990
Medeva	MD Pharmaceuticals		1991
China Synthetic Rubber	bulk penicillin mfg section	Glaxo	1991
Sterling Drug	Sanofi		1991
Hoffmann La Roche	Fisons healthcare		1992
Ivax	Waverley		1992
Pfizer	Koshin Medical		1992
Rhône Poulenc Rorer	Chugai		1993
Merck	Medco Containment Services		1993
Ethical Holdings	Gacell Holdings oral controlled release technology		1993
Sandoz	Veneziani		1993
American Home Products	Cyanamid		1994
Roche	Syntex		1994
Sanofi	Sterling pharmaceutical operations	Kodak	1994
SmithKline Beecham	Sterling Eur otc	Kodak	1994
Bayer	Sterling N.Am. otc	SKB	1994
BASF	ethical pharms operations	Boots	1994
Hoechst	Marion Merrell Dow	Dow Chem.	1995
Glaxo	Wellcome		1995
Ciba	Sandoz	now	1996
Upjohn	Pharmacia	called Novartis	1996

Notes:
mfg = manufacturing.
otc = over the counter.
tob = takeover bid.

Source: complied by author from various sources.

In the mid 1970s to early 1980s a great many established chemical firms entered into alliances with a variety of independent biotechnology firms as a way of gaining access to the new technologies and developing their own competences, as described earlier (see Figure 5.3). Some of these biotechnology fields turned out to have more potential for generating medium-term commercial output (for example, pharmaceuticals) than others (for example, agrofood products) which were a lot further from the market for reasons to do with cost and with public and governmental concern about the release of genetically modified organisms, as well as technical problems associated with moving from a laboratory to a commercial scale. In the late 1980s, established firms which had developed a competence in diagnostics, enzymes and reagents (products with short-term commercial potential) consolidated their position in biotechnology, as did firms which had developed pharmaceutical applications of biotechnology, such as human insulin, human growth hormone, interferon and interleukins, and/or which used biotechnology as an important tool for basic research in pharmaceuticals.

Firms which had pursued agrofood opportunities (for example, Bayer and Hoechst) reduced their biotechnology investments in what turned out to be a longer-term and more risky area, to keeping windows of opportunity open by maintaining some collaborative agreements but not building up significant in-house capabilities in biotechnology, and otherwise reinforced their positions in traditional agrochemicals. The ICI, Sandoz and, to some extent, Ciba agrochemicals businesses, however, had already diversified downstream into the seeds businesses, for example by acquiring seeds companies, and had developed competences in traditional plant breeding. They built up their in-house capabilities in plant biotechnology (Ciba being stronger in this area than in seeds). The centre of the world seeds business is in the USA for reasons of traditional comparative advantage: the corn belt is where corn grows well. In practice what happened with diversification, therefore, was decentralization and internationalization of the businesses (whose headquarters were in Britain and Switzerland) and decentralization of R&D to the business units, which were therefore also able to make linkages with the American infrastructure in bioscience and biotechnology. A significant share of basic bio-oriented research in these firms thereby came to be performed in the USA. But in other respects the two firms' organizational strategies have diverged sharply, with ICI de-merging in 1993 into Zeneca (mainly the biobusiness: agrochemicals, pharmaceuticals and specialities) and ICI (mainly commodity chemicals, paints and plastics), while Ciba and Sandoz merged in 1996 to form Novartis, now the world's largest firm in crop protection and second largest in seeds (see Tables 5.9 and 5.10), combining their complementary skills and achieving a dominant position in the world market.

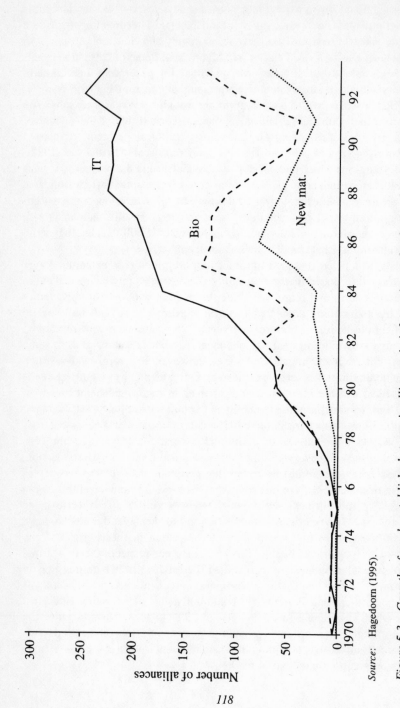

Number of alliances

Source: Hagedoorn (1995).

Figure 5.3   Growth of newly established strategic alliances in information technologies, biotechnology and new materials, 1970–93

The traditional ways of diversification were organic growth – building up in-house competence – or buying it from another firm. Now alliances, joint ventures and technological collaboration have formed a third category of organization which is neither hierarchy nor market. These organizations are not really new in the chemical industry, although they are now more widespread in industry generally and more widely studied. In steroid research in the 1930s Schering and Ciba, for example, collaborated with universities performing basic research such as the isolation and structure of hormones (Walsh, 1996). The firms had the resources to extract and prepare hormones for clinical research and for further biological and chemical research. In the 1950s Syntex, Searle and others also collaborated with universities on steroid research. The science and technology of steroids was further advanced by then, but it was new to the firms involved in the collaborating. When they had built up their experience sufficiently, they developed their own competences in-house.

This pattern has continued in the chemical industry, but more intensively. Established firms first responded to biotechnology by establishing inter-firm and firm–public sector research alliances, if necessary across national borders, as a strategy for gaining access to new technological areas and for learning how to make use of them. A major strategy of Japanese chemical firms was to move into biotechnology via alliances with US dedicated biotechnology firms (DBFs), building on their own strengths in fermentation and other earlier bio-industrial activities. When they had developed some experience in commercializing the new technology they invested more seriously in in-house capability where prospects were good; where they were still seen as having future potential only in the longer term, firms either reduced their commitment or simply continued with collaborative research. Some of the firms consolidated their positions in biotechnology by means of acquiring specialist biotechnology firms (sometimes the firms with which they had been collaborating). Many European firms established or bought small US DBFs to secure a US presence and for closeness to the US scientific and technological infrastructure, as well as to acquire the DBFs' technical knowledge. Figure 5.4 shows the relative increase in acquisitions and the relative decrease in alliances at the end of the 1980s.

Research on Globalization of Innovative Capacity in the Chemical Industry

So far this chapter has attempted to show the complex interactions between organizational change, technological change and globalization, with each partly a cause and partly a consequence of the other. The chapter has argued that the chemical industry is itself an entity with shifting boundaries, as

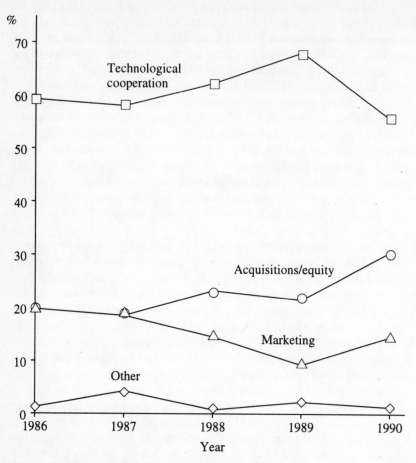

Sources: Bio/Technology, Dibner (1988), OTA (1988).

Figure 5.4   Types of biotechnology collaborations

chemical methods and processes become dominant in the production of products previously thought to belong in other categories, and as upstream and
downstream interests draw chemical firms into other activities. These shifting
technological boundaries have some overlap with shifting geographical ones.
I have also argued that globalization of innovative capacity is more than the
overseas location of R&D or the generation of patented inventions in overseas branches of a firm, though these are of course central features. It should
also include the global sourcing of the technological knowledge that contributes to innovative activity. Ideally this would include knowledge acquired

through collaborative research based on formal and informal agreements with other firms and with public sector research; patented knowledge produced outside the firm acquired by licence; purchase of sophisticated equipment and intermediates embodying knowledge produced elsewhere; and the recruitment of overseas scientists and technologists bringing with them knowledge and skills from abroad. Not all of this information is readily available.

The research project about to begin on the globalization of innovative capacity in the chemical and related products industry will assemble or collate data on mergers, acquisitions, R&D location and technological alliances in the industry in terms both of geographical location and technical specialization. This will capture both the extent of globalization and the shifting boundaries of the industry. Some of these data have already been assembled by researchers and will need to be collated with other data sets. For example, Figure 5.5 shows the trend in alliances in chemicals. Some of these data will need updating for the 1990s, which will be carried out using the same sources. Other series of data will be collected mainly from the financial and specialist trade press. This information will be compared with data on patents and on licensing in relevant fields. The statistical data will be compared with case study and other qualitative information obtained from

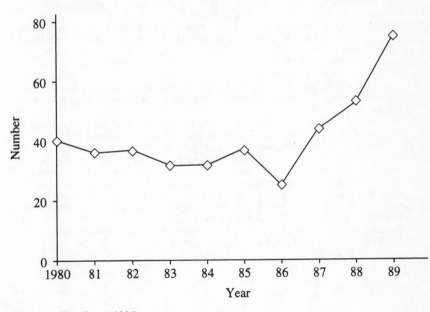

Source: Hagedoorn (1994).

Figure 5.5   Strategic technology alliances in chemicals

the literature and from interviews with the main firms concerned. Interviews will supply information on firms' strategies concerning their movements into certain geographical locations and into certain technological fields, about their organizational changes and about their perceptions of technological and competitive threats and opportunities. The type of R&D performed abroad and at home will also be obtained from interviews. Some information on recruitment and on inputs of equipment and intermediate products will also be obtained from trade journals, from scientific literature and from interviews.

NOTES

1. Funded by the UK Economic and Social Research Council, the support of which is gratefully acknowledged.
2. For example, intra-firm trade is nearly one-third of exports from, and 40 per cent of imports to, the USA (UNCTC, 1991).
3. In contrast, Soete (1991) argues that over the earlier period 1950–75, the prime motor of economic growth and international technology diffusion was international trade rather than FDI.
4. Although databases such as the MERIT one (on which this paper is based) must of necessity rely on reports in the financial and trade press, and are therefore somewhat biased towards agreements between organizations in the triad countries, they are more likely to be of interest to the readers of those source publications.
5. Clairmonte and Cavanagh (1981), however, argued 15 years ago that the international oligopolies had established a world-wide division of labour in the case of the textile and related products industry. Though some parts of the industry are characterized by large numbers of small producers based in local markets, their argument is that the web of a small number of interconnected multinationals has sufficient power to dominate production, distribution and employment throughout the chain of raw cotton production, yarn preparation, weaving, knitting, clothing production, wholesaling, retailing and textile machinery.
6. Note that Glyn and Sutcliffe (1992), for example, have put forward the view that capital flows and trade are no more internationalized than they were before the First World War (but using statistics up to the mid 1980s); and Glyn (1995) argues that, although FDI has grown since the beginning of the 1980s, it still represents a very small proportion of total investment. Chesnais (1994, p. 34) has also pointed out that British firms, for example, had achieved a degree of internationalization at the end of the 19th century similar to that in 1960–70; while 7.3 per cent of US investments in 1914 were overseas, a level reached again only in 1966. But his point is that a new wave of globalization, based on FDI rather than trade, took off in the 1980s, and in particular after 1985.
7. This was before unification of Germany, and various mergers that are reported elsewhere in this chapter, so the figures will have changed somewhat.

REFERENCES

Antonelli, C. (1984), *Cambiamento Tecnologico e Imprese Multinazionale: il Ruolo delle Reti Telematiche nelle Strategie Globali*, Milan: Franco Angeli, quoted by Chesnais (1994).

Archibugi, D. and Michie, J. (1995), 'The Globalization of Technology: A New Taxonomy', *Cambridge Journal of Economics*, **19**(1), 121–40.

Cantwell, J. (1995), 'The globalization of technology: what remains of the product cycle model?', *Cambridge Journal of Economics*.

Cantwell, J. and Hodson, C.(1990), *The Internationalization of Technological Activity and British Competitiveness*, W.P. Series B, Vol. III, Reading: University of Reading.

Casson, M., Pearce, R. and Singh, S. (1992a), 'Business Culture and International Technology: Research Managers' Perceptions of Recent Changes in Corporate R&D', in O. Grandstrand, L. Håkanson and S. Sjölander (eds), *Technology Management and International Business*, Chichester: Wiley.

Casson, M., Pearce, R. and Singh, S. (1992b), 'Global Integration through the Decentralisation of R&D', in M. Casson (ed.), *International Business and Global Integration*, Basingstoke: Macmillan.

Caves, R. (1982), *Multinational Enterprise & Economic Analysis*, Cambridge: Cambridge University Press.

Chesnais, F. (1994), *La Mondialisation du Capital*, Paris: Syros.

Chesnais, F. and Walsh, V. (1994), 'Biotechnology and the Chemical Industry: The Relevance of some Evolutionary Concepts', paper for the EUNETIC conference, 'Evolutionary Economics of Technical Change', European Parliament, Strasbourg, 6–8 October.

Clairmonte, F. and Cavanagh, J. (1981), *The World in their Web: The Dynamics of Textile Multinationals*, London: Zed Press.

Coombs, R. (1994), 'Technology and Business Strategy', in M. Dodgson and R. Rothwell (eds), *A Handbook of Industrial Innovation*, Aldershot: Edward Elgar.

Coombs, R. and Richards, A. (1993), 'Strategic Control of Technology in Diversified Companies', *Technology Analysis and Strategic Management*, **5**(4), 385–96.

Dibner, M., *Biotechnology Guide USA*, New York: Stockton Press.

Dicken, P. (1992), *Global Shift: The Internationalization of Economic Activity*, London: Paul Chapman.

Dunning, J. (1993), *The Globalisation of Business*, London: Routledge.

Freeman, C. (1990), 'Technical Innovation in the World Chemical Industry and Changes of Techno-economic Paradigm', in C. Freeman and L. Soete (eds), *New Explorations in the Economics of Technical Change*, London: Pinter Publishers.

Freeman, C. and Hagedoorn, J. (1995), 'Convergance and divergance in the internationalization of technology', in J. Hagedoorn (ed.), *Internationalization of Corporate Technology Strategies*, London: Elgar.

Galimberti, I. (1993), *Large Chemical Firms in Biotechnology: Case Studies on Learning in Radically New Technologies*, D. Phil. thesis, Science Policy Research Unit, Sussex University.

Glyn, A. (1995), 'Internal and External Constraints on Egalitarian Policies', paper presented at the Conference on Globalization and Progressive Economic Policy, Economic Policy Institute, Washington, DC, 27–29 October.

Glyn, A. and Sutcliffe, R. (1992), 'Global but Leaderless? The New Capitalist Order', in *The Socialist Register 1992*, London: The Merlin Press.

Grandstrand, O. and Sjölander, S. (1992), 'Internationalisation and Diversification of Multi-technology Corporations', in O. Grandstrand, L. Håkanson and S. Sjölander (eds), *Technology Management and International Business*, Chichester: Wiley.

Hagedoorn, J. (1994), 'Strategic Technology Partnering during the 1980s: Trends, Networks and International Patterns', paper presented at the conference on R&TD cooperation, Vienna, 5–6 December.

Hagedoorn, J. (1995), 'The Economics of Cooperation among High Tech Firms – Trends and Patterns in Strategic Partnering since the Early 1970s', paper presented at the Conference on the Economics of High Technology Competition and Cooperation in Global Markets, Hamburg, 2–3 February.

Hagedoorn, J. and Schakenraad, J. (1990), 'Inter-firm Partnerships and Co-operative Strategies in Core Technologies', in C. Freeman and L. Soete (eds), *New Explorations in the Economics of Technological Change*, London: Pinter.

Hagedoorn, J. and Schakenraad, J. (1991), 'The Role of Interfirm Cooperation Agreements in the Globalization of Economy and Technology', EU FAST/MONITOR Programme, Vol 8, Dossier on Globalization of Economy and Technology, FOP 280.

Howells, J. and Wood, M. (1993), *The Globalization of Production and Technology*, London: Belhaven Press.

Lundvall, B.-Å. (1985), *Product Innovation and User–Producer Interaction*, Aalborg: Aalborg University Press.

Lundvall, B.-Å. (1988), 'Innovation as an Interactive Process – From User Producer Interaction to National Systems of Innovation', in G. Dosi *et al.* (eds), *Technical Change and Economic Theory*, London: Pinter Publishers.

Lundvall, B.-Å. (1992), *National Systems of Innovation: Towards a Theory of Innovation and Interactive Learning*, London: Pinter Publishers.

OECD (1990), *Economic Outlook, No. 48*, Paris: Organization for Economic Cooperation and Development.

OECD (1992), *Technology and the Economy: The Key Relationships*, Paris: Organization for Economic Cooperation and Development.

Office of Technology Assessment, *New Developments in Biotechnology: US Investment in Biotechnology*, Washington, DC: Government Printing Office.

Patel, P. and Pavitt, K. (1991), 'Large Firms in the Production of the World's Technology: An Important Case of Non-globalisation', *Journal of International Business Studies*, **22**(1), 1–21. Also in O. Granstrand, L. Håkanson and S. Sjölander (eds) (1992), *Technology Management and International Business*, Chichester: Wiley.

Patel, P. and Pavitt, K. (1992), 'The innovative performance of the world's largest firms: some new evidence', *Economics of Innovation and New Technology*, **2**, pp. 91–102.

Patel, P. and Pavitt, K. (1994), 'Technological Competencies in the World's Largest Firms: Characteristics, Constraints and Scope for Managerial Choice', Science Policy Research Unit STEEP Discussion Paper No. 13.

Pearce, R. and Singh S. (1992a), *Globalising Research and Development*, Basingstoke: Macmillan.

Pearce, R. and Singh, S. (1992b), 'Internationalisation of Research and Development among the World's Leading Enterprises: Survey Analysis of Organisation and Motivation', in O. Grandstrand, L. Håkanson and S. Sjölander (eds), *Technology Management and International Business*, Chichester: Wiley.

Petrella, R. (1990), 'Technology and the Firm', *Technology Analysis and Strategic Management*, **2**(2), 99–110.

Porter, M. (1986), *Competition in Global Industries*, Boston, MA: Harvard Business School Press.

Richards, A. (1993), 'The Global Management of Technology', briefing paper for Technology Strategy Forum, May, CROMTEC, Manchester School of Management, UMIST (mimeo).

Rubenstein, A. (1989), *Managing Technology in the Decentralised Firm*, New York: Wiley.

Sharp, M. (1989), 'Collaboration in the Pharmaceutical Industry – Is It the Way Forward?', DRC Discussion Paper 71, Science Policy Research Unit, Sussex University (mimeo).

Soete, L. (1991), 'The Internationalization of Science and Technology: How do Nations Cope?', paper presented at the Conference at Centre de Recherche en Développement Industriel et Technologique, Université du Québec à Montréal, 7 November.

UNCTC (United Nations Centre on Transnational Corporations) (1991), *World Investment Report 1991: The Triad in Foreign Direct Investment*, New York: United Nations.

van Tulder, R. and Ruigrok, W. (1993), Regionalisation, Globalization or Glocalisation: The Case of the World Car Industry', in M. Humbert (ed.), *The Impact of Globalisation on Europe's Firms and Industries*, London: Pinter Publishers.

Walsh, V. (1984), 'Invention and Innovation in the Chemical Industry: Discovery Push or Demand Pull?', *Research Policy*, **13**, 211–34.

Walsh, V. (1993), 'Public Markets, Demand and Innovation: The Case of Biotechnology', *Science & Public Policy*, June, **20**, 138–156.

Walsh, V. (1997), 'Industrial R&D and its Influence on the Organisation and Management of the Production of Knowledge in the Public Sector', in J.-P. Gaudillière, I. Löwy and D. Pestre (eds), *The Invisible Industrialist: Manufactures and the Construction of Scientific Knowledge*, Basingstoke: Macmillan.

Walsh, V. and Galimberti, I. (1993), 'Firm Strategies, Globalisation and New Technological Paradigms: Biotechnology and the Pharmaceutical Industry', in M. Humbert (ed.), *The Impact of Globalisation on Europe's Firms and Industries*, London: Pinter Publishers.

Walsh, V. and Goodman, J. (1996), 'Yews and Scientists in the Struggle against Cancer', paper presented at the London School of Hygiene and Tropical Medicine Conference 'Science Speaks to Policy', 12–13 July.

Wortmann, M. (1990), 'Multinationals and the Internationalisation of R&D: New Developments in German Companies', *Research Policy*, **19**, 175–83.

Yoxen, E. and Green, K. (1990), *Scenarios for Biotechnology in Europe: A Research Agenda*, Luxembourg: Office for Official Publications of the European Communities (European Foundation for the Improvement of Living and Working Conditions).

6. The internationalization of technological activity: the French evidence in a comparative setting

John Cantwell and Usha Kotecha[1]

INTRODUCTION

Until the 1970s, it was often supposed (based mainly on American evidence) that almost all technological activity undertaken by multinational corporations (MNCs) was carried out at or near their headquarters in the parent country. This followed the traditional product cycle hypothesis, the central assumption of which was that the creation of new technology occurred at home; the country of origin of the MNC was the base of its new investments in technology. However, since that time, the role of internationally dispersed technological activity has become more apparent. It is now clear that many European companies have enjoyed quite a high degree of internationalization of their technological activity for some time, and even some US firms had a significant international dispersal of research facilities in the inter-war period (Cantwell and Hodson, 1991; Cantwell, 1995).

What has altered recently is that the use of international networks for innovation by the MNCs has become steadily more important (Bartlett and Ghoshal, 1989; Cantwell, 1993a, 1995). The internationalization of research is obviously affected by (and affects) the organizational form of the MNC. In the 1960s it was common to view the MNC as comprising a parent company and a system of affiliates which were largely independent of one another. In this event the degree of geographical dispersion of R&D depends upon the relative strength of competing centripetal and centrifugal forces (for a review see Pearce, 1989; Pearce and Singh, 1992).

The main centralizing forces are economies of scale in the innovation process, economies of agglomeration and the avoidance of duplication. The main decentralizing force is the need for adaptation: a capacity to respond to local demand-side opportunities as reflected in local markets and the low relative costs of technical professionals overseas. Faced with these conditions a typical choice would be to concentrate the bulk of basic or fundamental research in the parent company, while decentralizing adaptive research more widely. However, matters become rather more complicated once firms adopt strategies of technological specialization across affiliates, in the same way that they specialize in their productive operations (forming integrated global networks, see Hedlund, 1986; Dunning, 1992). The technological specialization of each firm within its industry is closely related to the pattern of its corporate technological competence (Cantwell, 1993b). Given its focus on particular branches of technological development, a company may choose to concentrate its efforts on each area of activity in certain international locations rather than others.

There are two reasons why MNCs may take such an internationally integrated approach to technological development. First, technological activity in any industry is locationally differentiated, as part of different national systems of innovation (Lundvall, 1988). The distinct characteristics of innovations in each country provide MNCs with an incentive to disperse research facilities to gain access to complementary paths of technological development, which they can then integrate at a corporate level. Secondly, it follows that the geographical dispersion of research to gain access to new lines of innovation may be related to technological diversification. It appears that in recent years there has been a growing interrelatedness between formerly separate technologies, and so to improve technological development even in its own immediate primary field of interest the firm may be obliged to broaden its technological activity through an international strategy. In what follows, data on the internationalization of technological activity by the world's largest industrial firms are related to evidence on the wider geographical composition of innovation in each major manufacturing industry. Particular attention is paid to the internationalization of technological activity by French firms, and to the significance of France as a research centre.

The chapter presents evidence on the internationalization of technological activity by the major French industrial firms, and by the largest foreign multinationals in France, by comparison with the equivalent evidence for other countries over the period 1969–90. It represents the extension of earlier such studies for the UK (Cantwell and Hodson, 1991; Cantwell, 1992). Using data on the US patenting of the world's largest firms, variations between industries in the extent of the internationalization of the technological activity are described and discussed. The French case is compared with the US, Japan, Germany and the UK. Changes between the early 1970s and the late 1980s are investigated.

We move from an examination of the overall state of the internationalization of technological activity in large industrial firms, to a steadily more detailed account of the French case from the aggregate to the company level. In section 1 we begin by describing the database and the evidence it provides on the internationalization of technological activity by different national groups of firms, by different industry groupings of companies and by types of technological activity. The specific position of French firms abroad, and of foreign firms in France, is then examined in greater detail in section 2, by comparison with the general picture outlined in the previous section. In section 3 we turn our attention to selected French industries, and relate the patterns of corporate technological specialisation to the internationalization of activity as discussed in the earlier sections. In section 4 we then proceed from the industry level to the company level, and investigate the technological specialization of three leading French companies in the context of their international strategies. We comment briefly on our findings and on prospects for the future in a concluding section.

Two industries are chosen for particular analysis in greater detail: chemicals and electrical equipment, in which the volume of science-related activity is most intense. In each industry particular attention is paid to the international specialization of corporate technological activity across locations, in which each location provides access to specific capabilities complementary to those found elsewhere. This is the major effect of the current re-organization of international research networks by the world's leading companies.

While countries have tended to narrow their technological specialization (becoming more focused on their areas of strength), as a result of the new multinational strategies the major firms have tended to broaden the extent of their technical specialization (drawing on a wider system of related technologies to support their core strengths) (Cantwell, 1989, 1992). These trends are explored for the leading French firms and other multinationals in the chemicals and electrical equipment industries. A distinction is drawn between the pattern of technological development of parent companies in their home country, and the composition of technological activity in their affiliates located abroad.

THE PATENT DATABASE AND AN OVERVIEW OF ITS EVIDENCE ON THE INTERNATIONALIZATION OF TECHNOLOGICAL ACTIVITY BY THE WORLD'S LARGEST INDUSTRIAL FIRMS

The Data

The data on technological activity presented here relate to patents granted in the USA between 1969 and 1990. These data are extremely valuable because of the variety of information provided on each patent granted. It is possible to identify separately the firm to which the patent has been granted, the location of the research facility originally responsible for the innovation, and a sectoral classification of the technological activity with which the patent is associated. It has also proved possible to establish the ultimate ownership of patents where they are granted to affiliates of MNCs.

A consolidation of the technological activity of international corporate groups has been carried out for the world's largest 792 industrial firms, derived from the listings in the *Fortune* 500. The data on this group of firms have been described by Dunning and Pearce (1985). Of these 792 companies, patenting activity was recorded for 730 firms during the period 1969–90. In addition, a further 40 of the world's largest firms which are not in the *Fortune* 500 listing are included, because they are among the most technologically important either historically or recently (for example, AT&T and RCA). In addition to the information just mentioned the nationality of the parent company and the industrial composition of the output of the corporate group are known. Together they account for over 47 per cent of all patents granted in the USA between 1969 and 1990. Patel and Pavitt (1989) discuss further the significance of US patenting by this group of firms relative to all firms.

Patents are a measure of inventions or advances in knowledge. They provide a proxy measure of technological activity, by which we mean all activity directed towards changes in the methods of production, involving either (and normally both) new and improved processes or products. The basis of technological activity is thus a continual process of learning and problem-solving within production, which leads to the creation of new productive capability supported by the generation of new scientific and engineering knowledge, which in turn is mainly the responsiblity of divisions for R&D, production engineering and similar specialized functions. It is very difficult to measure directly the creation of new productive capability itself since this is essentially tacit, but patents are a reasonable proxy for the new scientific and engineering knowledge that is strictly complementary to this capability, and hence they constitute a proxy for technological activity as a whole (Cantwell, 1993a).

Patents are often treated also as a proxy for the inventive output of corporate R&D. This is reasonable for large firms, since the creation of new scientific and engineering knowledge is principally the responsibility of in-house corporate R&D facilities in the large modern industrial firm. However, two qualifications are necessary in this respect. First, new patentable knowledge is also sometimes created by those responsible for production engineering and design, which play some role in all firms, even though they are relatively more important in smaller companies. Secondly, basic research is less likely to lead directly to patents than other R&D. With locational specialization within the MNC, basic research in one location may then feed into patentable improvements in productive know-how developed in R&D laboratories elsewhere that enjoy closer links with local production.

Consequently patents are not a very good proxy for basic research, especially where such research is carried out in specialized facilities and separated from subsequent development. However, on balance this is probably an advantage when (like here) using patents as a proxy for technological activity as a whole, and not simply for the creation of new knowledge as such. The R&D output which is picked up in patenting is that knowledge which is most closely allied with learning and problem-solving activities in production. It is usually knowledge that has been refined to the point where it is usable in production and provides part of the answer to problems that have been posed in the development of production. Hence patents capture mainly the generation of new knowledge that is associated with the establishment of tacit capability that makes such knowledge operational, or in other words that is associated with the forging of technological competence.

Despite the facts that knowledge creation is only one supporting element in technological activity, that some knowledge creation takes place outside formal R&D facilities, and that some basic research is locationally separated from the technological activity in which the knowledge it creates is eventually used; for the sake of convenience, and since we are dealing with the creation of capability in large firms (which is generally linked to R&D and to which most of their research is directly devoted), we often use the terms 'research' and 'technological activity' synonymously in what follows.

Patel and Pavitt (1989) also elaborate upon the strengths and weaknesses of the use of US patent data in the context of the technological efforts of large companies. Patent counts offer the best (and in many cases the only) source of information on the sectoral and geographical composition of innovative activity across firms. Other recent studies have also supported the suitability of patent data in cross-firm empirical investigations. Griliches *et al.* (1987) and Griliches (1990) argue that despite certain difficulties in using patents to describe time-series trends in innovation, patenting provides a good indicator of cross-firm variation in inventive activity, which is well correlated with R&D expenditure especially for large firms. Acs and Audretsch (1989) find that patenting varies across firms with R&D, skilled labour and size in the same manner as innovative activity when the latter is directly measured. Although there are differences in the relationship between patenting and measures of the appropriability of technology (such as concentration in the relevant industry) across firms, Acs and Audretsch conclude that overall patenting serves as a good proxy for innovative activity.

In another survey, Pavitt (1988) summarizes evidence in favour of using patenting in a third country when making international comparisons of technological activities, and particularly patenting in the USA which enforces common screening procedures that provide a standard for comparison, and in which (as the single largest national market) large firms generally patent first after their own home country. The measure is improved by virtue of the fact that patents extended to the USA by non-US firms are more likely to represent significant inventions than do purely domestic patents. Indeed the reliability of this indicator is reinforced by considering only the largest firms, since larger firms follow stricter screening procedures than do smaller firms or individual inventors prior to embarking upon patent applications (Schmookler, 1966).

It is well known that there are inter-industry differences in the propensity to patent (Scherer, 1983), inter-sectoral differences in the likelihood of patenting from various types of technological activity, and international differences in that US-based firms are more likely to patent in the USA than are non-US firms. In addition, the propensity to patent may vary over time, and changes in the efficiency with which the US Patent Office processes applications have also altered the length of lag from patent application to grant from time to time (Griliches, 1990). Thus problems exist when comparing absolute numbers of patents across industries, across types of technological activity, across different national groups of firms, or over time. The measures that we construct below from US patent statistics are in the form of shares and ratios that are deliberately designed to avoid most of the difficulties associated with absolute numbers.

To illustrate, as a measure of the degree of internationalization of technological activity we calculate the share of total patenting of some given group of firms that is attributable to research or other technological activity outside the home country of the parent company. Firms in different industries or originating from different home countries can then be compared with one another. The higher propensity to patent of, for example, pharmaceutical firms relative to shipbuilding companies does not affect matters, provided that pharmaceutical firms are equally more likely to patent from both their foreign and their home-located activity, which is a plausible assumption. There is just one qualification that may be needed when comparing different national groups of companies, and in particular when comparing US and non-US firms. Since there may be a higher propensity to patent in the USA from US-located inventions, it follows that the share of US patents attributable to inventions outside the home country of a parent company is likely to underestimate the degree of internationalization of technological activity of US-based firms. The effect for non-US firms is likely to be less marked, since, as remarked above, they are likely to patent in the USA only their most significant inventions, whatever their geographical origin.

A special case occurs where patents result from the cooperative research of two or more companies, sometimes as a result of international strategic alliances. Where patents have been assigned to joint ventures that are partially owned by two or more of the large firms in our database (Dow Corning is one of the best known and among the longest standing) we have included these patents under each of the corporate groups in question. The problems that might be created by double-counting in this way are, in fact, quite minimal, since the patents of joint ventures of this kind account for significantly less than 1 per cent of the total patents of all the large firms included in the study. Of course, technological cooperation between these major companies runs beyond such joint ventures. It often involves agreements over the cross-licensing of patents. Where exchange arrangements of this sort are important, each firm typically takes chief responsibility for patenting in the technological fields in which it has its greatest (relative) strength. Once again this suits our purposes when using patents as a proxy for the types of activity and the geographical origins of the underlying technological competence of each company.

There is, however, a drawback to the procedure used for consolidating the patents granted to corporate groups. This arises due to the regular changes in ownership of firms through mergers and acquisitions. To make the task manageable, it was necessary to identify corporate groups at a particular point in time, namely the year 1984. The patent data for the entire period 1969–90 were then consolidated on this basis. Consequently, changes in ownership links during the period were not directly allowed for when consolidating patents over related companies.

This is likely to create greater difficulties in the earlier part of the period than in the later part. Affiliates acquired between 1969 and 1984 are counted under their eventual corporate group for the entire period, thereby inflating the patenting of the group in question in the years prior to the acquisition. In contrast, patents due to the research of affiliates acquired after 1984 may still be correctly assigned to their new corporate group following the acquisition. This is because most firms centrally apply for patents on behalf of many of their affiliates for strategic reasons (Etemad and Séguin Delude, 1985). Centralized application procedures help to reduce the extent of any understatement of corporate group patenting associated with acquisitions after 1984.

It should be noted that the institutional form chosen by a corporate group in registering patent applications (whether or not the parent company or an agent acting on its behalf takes central responsibility for the application procedure for various affiliates), does not affect the information recorded in the patent database. In particular, the location of the inventor, to which we have attached some significance, must still be declared quite separately from the location of the specific company that registers the application, to which we attach no significance here. If the consolidation of patents to corporate groups were not carried out, then groups that adopted a more centralized application strategy would be better represented, but after consolidation all firms have their patenting fully represented irrespective of the extent of centralization of their application and assignment procedures.

The consolidation of patents to corporate groups in their 1984 form means that unfortunately it is difficult to assess the true extent of any trend over time towards the internationalization of technological activity. Any such trend is likely to be understated in the data on the patenting of the world's largest firms for two reasons. First, where this internationalization was achieved through acquisition before 1984, this is not recorded as a change in the geographical composition of the firm's technological development since the affiliate has been considered as part of the corporate group at both the beginning and the end of the period. A study of the foreign-located research of Swedish firms conducted by Håkanson suggested that around 60 per cent of the personnel they employed in foreign R&D facilities worked for affiliates which had been acquired by the parent firm. Secondly, where acquisitions have had motives other than the extension of research facilities (and there have been many of these), it may be expected that the new parent company would tend to wind down affiliate research. Any duplication with the existing research of the MNC may be eliminated, and other functions may be centralized in the technological headquarters. This would appear in the data as a move away from the internationalization of technological activity.

The Evidence on Internationalization

The evidence of Table 6.1 must be viewed in this light. Overall, it shows that the world's largest firms witnessed a mild trend towards the internationalization of technological activity over the 1969–90 period, even without properly allowing for the effects of acquisitions, although there was a decrease between the periods 1973–77 and 1978–82. The share of US patents granted to these firms attributable to research in foreign locations (outside the home country of the parent firm) rose from 10.4 per cent in 1969–72 to 11.2 per cent in 1987–90.

Comparing industrial groups of firms at each point in time provides a decomposition of this trend. Firms involved in the manufacture of food products, chemicals, pharmaceuticals, non-metallic mineral products (building materials), and coal and petroleum products were especially prone to international research strategies throughout the period. Of these, companies involved in the manufacture of food products and non-metallic mineral products experienced a clear trend towards the greater internationalization of technological activity during the period. A similar trend was observed in mechanical engineering, office equipment and other manufacturing. Furthermore, by the mid 1980s almost a quarter of the innovative activity of the major food product firms was located outside their home countries, although

Table 6.1   The share of US patents of the world's largest firms attributable to research in foreign locations (outside the home country of the parent company), organized by the industrial group of parent firms, 1969–90 (%)

	1969–72	1973–77	1978–82	1983–86	1987–90
Food products	16.85	20.72	23.43	24.73	23.70
Chemicals nes	12.37	13.46	13.47	13.78	14.38
Pharmaceuticals	16.88	19.14	17.25	16.38	18.24
Metals	10.92	9.20	10.88	9.79	11.54
Mechanical engineering	10.33	10.07	11.23	14.28	14.77
Electrical equipment nes	10.26	9.84	8.71	9.68	9.80
Office equipment	5.09	8.52	10.11	12.00	11.23
Motor vehicles	4.88	5.34	5.72	7.13	7.03
Aircraft	1.95	2.03	2.29	2.93	2.47
Other transport equipment	9.70	3.36	7.64	5.24	6.54
Textiles	6.45	8.49	7.10	4.31	3.10
Rubber and plastic products	7.02	7.44	6.70	6.02	8.47
Non-metallic mineral products	11.51	12.21	14.16	15.45	16.61
Coal and petroleum products	16.53	15.18	13.60	15.12	18.41
Professional and scientific instruments	6.22	4.00	2.93	2.69	1.86
Other manufacturing	5.07	7.68	10.05	12.31	14.03
Total	10.35	10.91	10.62	11.10	11.22

Note: nes = not elsewhere specified.

Source: The data on the geographical origins and industrial distribution of patents granted in the USA have been compiled at the University of Reading with the support of the US Patent and Trademark Office. The opinions expressed in this chapter are those of the authors, and do not necessarily reflect the views of the Patent and Trademark Office.

the trend towards decentralization of technological activity diminished slightly during the 1980s.

At the other extreme, technological activity is most geographically concentrated in the aircraft and aerospace sector and the professional and scientific instruments industry. In the aircraft and aerospace industry there has been a slight increase in the amount of overseas technological activity, although in the period 1987–90 this trend was reversed, with the share of US patents of these firms attributable to research (or other similar activity) in foreign locations falling from 2.9 per cent in 1983–86 to 2.5 per cent in 1987–90. A continuing strong trend towards the locational centralization of technological activity is evident in the professional and scientific instruments sector throughout the 22 year period. This is also the case in the textiles industry, in which the foreign located share of technological activity has fallen by over 50 per cent since 1982.

It is also possible to look at the same data classified by the sectoral composition of the technological activity itself, and this is done for comparative purposes in Table 6.2. As described above, branches of technological activity do not correspond to industries. As a rule, firms require a broader range of technological capability to support a narrower range of products (Pavitt *et al.*, 1989). For example, chemical firms all have a substantial involvement in the creation of new chemical equipment, which appears under mechanical rather than chemical technology. Pharmaceutical technology here includes biotechnology.

What emerges most clearly when comparing Tables 6.1 and 6.2 is that the strong internationalization of research by food product, non-metallic mineral product, and coal and petroleum product firms is not especially concentrated in those technological fields in which they are most immediately involved, but in other (presumably related) areas. This is due in part to the locational specialization that is associated with the growth of international networks of interrelated activity; MNCs based in the major centres of innovation are increasingly undertaking mutual intra-industry direct investment in accordance with the comparative advantage of local expertise in each of the other centres (Cantwell and Sanna-Randaccio, 1992). Where foreign technological strengths are in different areas to those being developed by the MNC at home, its foreign activity may then complement (in a new area) rather than simply replicate (in the same area) the core fields of technological creation undertaken in the parent company.

It is also clear that in general the trend towards internationalization of research by firms involved in a particular sector is not necessarily related to the trend in the technological field in which they are most interested. For example, the strong growth of internationalization of research by office equipment (mainly computing) firms is not matched by a corresponding increase in the internationalization of the creation of office equipment technology itself. Furthermore, although the major textile and instrument firms are not very highly internationalized in their overall technological development, textiles and professional and scientific instruments technologies themselves have been rather more subject to the international dispersion of research, even if the trend towards a still greater dispersion was reversed in the 1980s.

The comparison between Tables 6.1 and 6.2 already tells us a great deal about the relationship between corporate technological specialization and the internationalization of technological activity. For example, in a specialized capital goods sector such as scientific instruments, the specialized suppliers are not as internationalized in their activity as are their customers in some of the downstream industries that they supply. Through their international

Table 6.2   The share of US patents of the world's largest firms attributable to research in foreign locations (outside the home country of the parent company), classified by technological activity, 1969–90 (%)

	1969–72	1973–77	1978–82	1983–86	1987–90
Food products	12.35	15.60	14.90	16.80	12.34
Chemicals nes	11.98	12.33	11.81	11.38	13.50
Inorganic chemicals	9.44	9.46	9.05	11.33	11.21
Organic chemicals	13.01	13.38	12.70	11.57	14.71
Agricultural chemicals	11.46	10.28	10.04	10.36	11.24
Chemical processes	10.67	10.83	10.76	11.07	12.40
Bleaching and dyeing processes	8.31	9.76	12.44	14.92	13.49
Pharmaceuticals	16.17	18.24	19.06	20.27	21.80
Metals	9.04	10.01	10.24	11.59	10.94
Metallurgical processes	7.88	8.27	8.03	8.50	8.09
Other metal products	9.98	10.60	12.16	14.59	13.66
Mechanical engineering	11.19	11.89	12.07	13.13	13.31
Chemical equipment	11.47	12.12	10.63	11.97	14.05
Metal working equipment	8.73	9.59	12.91	13.12	12.50
Assembly equipment	11.66	11.76	12.23	10.82	10.80
Mining equipment	16.31	13.35	10.56	13.70	13.29
Specialized industrial equipment	14.12	15.15	16.23	15.94	15.13
General industrial equipment	8.40	10.11	10.53	13.10	12.91
Electrical equipment nes	9.24	9.07	8.13	9.61	9.47
Telecommunications	13.60	11.60	10.18	11.40	11.01
Image and sound equipment	9.06	7.50	7.73	9.33	8.58
Semiconductors	9.07	10.21	8.04	8.87	8.65
Electrical systems	8.19	8.54	7.41	10.01	10.11
General electrical equipment	7.72	7.82	7.80	8.00	7.80
Office equipment	7.39	8.75	7.68	7.35	7.73
Motor vehicles	6.71	5.01	4.06	7.28	5.79
Aircraft	4.65	1.87	2.40	2.67	2.37
Other transport equipment	7.72	7.74	12.94	15.01	10.07
Textiles	11.05	14.56	18.99	10.95	9.17
Rubber and plastic products	9.50	10.90	10.36	11.01	11.16
Non-metallic mineral products	7.59	8.41	9.32	8.83	9.87
Coal and petroleum products	10.22	10.22	7.48	9.11	10.21
Professional and scientific instruments	8.75	9.26	10.62	9.66	8.57
Photographic equipment	6.89	6.51	4.19	5.32	2.77
Other instruments	9.08	9.78	10.05	10.56	9.65
Other manufacturing	9.47	12.01	9.53	14.44	11.44
Total	10.35	10.91	10.62	11.10	11.22

Source: As for Table 6.1.

operations these customers then develop some of their instrument requirements abroad, perhaps in conjuction with other specialized suppliers with their own source of local expertise in other selected countries. Conversely, computer-based technologies are mainly the province of the computer companies themselves. While these computer or office equipment firms have now become quite internationalised in their strategies for technological development, they have tended to focus on computer work at home while specializing relatively more in other complementary technologies in their activities abroad. In general, the major science-based technologies (chemicals and electrical equipment including computers) tend to be chiefly the responsibility of firms in the relevant industry, while the development of other mechanical technologies is more widespread, as user companies in a broad range of industries strive to acquire some upstream capability in their creation (Patel and Pavitt, 1993).

Table 6.3 looks at the share of US patents of these large firms attributable to overseas research in terms of the nationality of the parent companies. What is clear is that France, as well as Italy, used to be in an unusual position

Table 6.3   The share of US patents of the world's largest firms attributable to research in foreign locations (outside the home country of the parent company), organized by the nationality of parent firms, 1969–90 (%)

	1969–72	1973–77	1978–82	1983–86	1987–90
USA	4.96	5.93	6.47	7.61	7.96
Japan	2.62	1.88	1.22	1.26	0.93
Germany	12.76	11.04	12.07	14.47	17.05
UK	45.37	43.93	41.08	47.86	49.18
Italy	13.39	16.03	13.85	12.59	11.14
France	8.19	7.74	7.19	9.20	15.87
Netherlands	50.40	47.37	47.65	53.99	53.91
Belgium	50.00	54.24	56.27	71.21	56.04
Switzerland	44.45	43.63	43.78	41.59	42.99
Sweden	18.01	19.51	25.19	28.82	28.34
Canada	41.19	39.30	39.49	35.82	40.12
Others[1]	16.58	19.92	22.38	35.82	17.39
Total	10.35	10.92	10.62	11.10	11.22

Note: 1.   Excluding companies registered in Panama.

Source: As for Table 6.1.

among the European countries in the sense that its technological activity had remained very centralized. This is consistent with the relatively late internationalization of French firms in terms of investments in the other major industrialized countries (Michalet and Delapierre, 1975; Savary, 1984). However, by the end of the 1980s, this had begun to change. The largest French firms witnessed a substantial increase in the internationalization of their technological activity in 1987–90, much greater than any other group of firms and bringing them on a par with the largest German industrial companies. In contrast, British firms have long been among the most multinational in their organization of technological activity, with almost half this activity being carried out abroad. This is also the case for firms based in the Netherlands and Belgium, where the proportion of international activity is over 50 per cent for both.

The figures for Belgium reveal that the dramatic increase in the early 1980s in the share of US patents attributable to research carried out abroad was not sustained in the late 1980s. There is also evidence of further centralization of technological activity in Japan. Japan's position among the major industrialized countries in terms of the centralization of its research is unique, especially when taking into account that the internationalization of technological activity by the largest US firms is probably understated by this measure (owing to their high propensity to patent in their own home market from domestically located research). In 1969–72, only 2.6 per cent of US patents of Japanese firms were attributable to research undertaken outside Japan. Since that time, this figure has steadily decreased, despite Japan's strong global position. In the period 1987–90, the figure had fallen to 0.9 per cent, far below that of any other country in this study. This is because of the tremendously rapid growth of technological activity in Japan itself, which has outstripped the still quite notable growth of activity in the foreign affiliates of Japanese MNCs.

Of course, this result may well relate more to the relative lack of the internationalization of technological capability in Japanese firms than to a lack of internationalization of the R&D function itself in those same companies. As noted earlier, where an R&D facility conducts basic research on a specialized basis in some centre of scientific expertise, but unrelated to any local production plants, the patent data may well not reflect the output of such laboratories. The results of such pure research may be incorporated instead into problem-solving efforts in production and R&D in the home country. There is indeed evidence that Japanese multinationals are more prone to carry out basic research in their foreign laboratories than they do in the equivalent R&D facilities in Japan (Papanastassiou and Pearce, 1993). Especially in the chemical industry, Japanese firms have set up fundamental research facilities in Europe, attracted by local scientific expertise, but as yet not very closely related to European-located production and the broader local development of technological capability.

Largely because of the size of technological activity of US and Japanese firms, and the significance of their home-based operations, the bulk of the research of the world's largest firms is concentrated in the USA and Japan. In 1978–90, 51.6 per cent of US patents granted to the largest firms were attributable to research facilities in the USA. Of those attributable to innovations in non-US locations, 49 per cent were from Japan, 22.2 per cent from Germany and 7.6 per cent from the UK. European locations collectively accounted for 48.2 per cent of innovative activity outside the USA.

This also illustrates the high degree of concentration of the technological activity of the largest firms in the industrial centres. Taking all patents granted in the USA in 1978–90 (not just to this group of firms), of those due to research outside the USA 38.4 per cent were attributable to Japan, 20.9 per cent to Germany, 8.0 per cent to the UK and 49.7 per cent to the European countries as a group. This left 11.9 per cent due to research outside Europe or Japan, as opposed to 2.7 per cent of patents granted to the biggest firms.

THE CONSEQUENCES FOR FRENCH FIRMS AND INDUSTRIES

French Firms Abroad

It is important to examine how and to what degree the internationalization of technological activity has impinged upon French firms and industries. Table 6.4 shows the share of US patents of French firms attributable to research or related activity undertaken outside France. What is immediately evident is the fluctuating trend in the internationalization of research in the food products sector. However, this is due in large part to the problem of small numbers, since the numbers of patents registered by French companies in this industry are very low. Consequently, slight changes are reflected in large percentage increases or decreases. Notwithstanding this qualification, the period since 1983 has witnessed a move towards decentralization of technological activity, to a foreign share closer to that of British food producers (Cantwell and Hodson, 1991). The share of US patents of French firms attributable to overseas invention was 57.8 per cent in the period 1983–86 and 60.3 per cent in the period 1987–90.

The problem of small numbers of patents occurs in most of the industries being considered. This is largely due to the fact that there are fewer French companies represented in the world's largest firms than there are US, Japanese, German or British companies. For example, there are no French firms at

*Table 6.4   The share of US patents of the largest French firms attributable
to research outside France, organized by the industrial group of
parent firms, 1969–90 (%)*

	1969–72	1973–77	1978–82	1983–86	1987–90
Food products	14.29	78.79	14.29	57.78	60.32
Chemicals nes	6.32	6.50	6.45	14.11	14.04
Pharmaceuticals	0.87	3.02	4.91	14.42	3.70
Metals	9.65	8.24	4.73	7.66	9.24
Mechanical engineering	2.94	0.00	0.00	3.45	0.00
Electrical equipment nes	2.31	1.49	1.03	3.23	21.72
Office equipment	18.46	6.40	2.90	0.00	61.80
Motor vehicles	7.24	4.05	3.71	6.07	7.10
Aircraft	10.69	6.32	6.25	4.38	3.46
Other transport equipment	N.A.	N.A.	N.A.	N.A.	N.A.
Textiles	100.00	66.67	69.23	33.33	0.00
Rubber and plastic products	1.00	0.91	0.87	2.70	0.00
Non-metallic mineral products	23.08	29.97	32.75	35.14	38.03
Coal and petroleum products	9.69	8.90	13.60	7.48	5.56
Professional and scientific instruments	N.A.	N.A.	N.A.	N.A.	N.A.
Other manufacturing	N.A.	N.A.	N.A.	N.A.	N.A.
Total	8.19	7.74	7.19	9.20	15.87

Note: N.A. = not applicable.

Source: As for Table 6.1.

all large enough for consideration here in the other transport equipment,
scientific instruments and other manufacturing industries. Altogether, 39 French
firms are included in the study, of which five are in the chemical or pharmaceutical industries, four are in electrical or computer equipment, four are in
motor vehicles, four are in aerospace and two are in non-metallic mineral
products or building materials (see Appendix). By the end of the period, the
problems associated with small numbers of patents were probably avoided
only in the chemical, electrical and office equipment industries. It is only in
these three cases that the number of US patents assigned to large French
firms and attributable to inventions outside France reached about 100 or more
in 1987–90.

The most striking feature of the French corporate case is the marked
increase in the geographical dispersion of technological activity by large
firms in the office equipment and electrical equipment sectors in the late
1980s. Their international shares rose from 18.5 per cent and 2.3 per cent

respectively in the period 1969–72, to 61.8 per cent and 21.7 per cent respectively in 1987–90. It is the firms of these industries that account for the bulk of the increase of the foreign share among the largest French firms as a whole in the late 1980s. These are the fields in which French companies have recently become considerably more international in the spread of technological activity. This has tended to accentuate the variation in the amount of technological activity carried out abroad among different industries. For example, mechanical engineering firms maintain a trend of undertaking most of their research at home; their highest share of US patents attributable to overseas research was 3.45 per cent in 1983–86. In contrast, firms in the non-metallic mineral products sector have long demonstrated a strong tendency towards decentralization starting from a relatively high position of 23 per cent in 1969 and rising to 38 per cent in 1987–90.

The other industry that has significantly contributed to the new internationalization of technological activity in large French firms in the late 1980s is that of chemicals. The share of US patents assigned to the largest French chemical companies that was attributable to technological development outside France increased from 6.3 per cent in 1969–72 to 14.0 per cent in 1987–90. However, for the major French chemical firms the increase in technological activity abroad took place earlier than for their counterparts in the electrical and office equipment sectors. In the French-based chemical industry the share of foreign research had already risen to 14.1 per cent in 1983–86. Despite their somewhat earlier adoption of an international strategy for technological development, the French chemical producers have moved into foreign activity in a less dramatic fashion than have the French electrical and office equipment companies. The share of non-French located technological activity was 14 per cent for the largest French chemical firms in 1987–90, but 22 per cent for electrical equipment firms and as much as 62 per cent for French computer companies in the same period.

With the exception of the food products sector (due to the problem of small numbers just mentioned), the industries with the greatest international dispersion of technological activity at the industrial level are associated with a correspondingly heavy internationalization of the equivalent field of technological activity, as shown in Table 6.5. In these terms French firms carrying out research in non-metallic mineral products, in office equipment, electrical equipment and in certain areas of chemicals have also displayed a strong propensity towards foreign locations. As with Table 6.4, a substantial number of foreign-originating patents is obtained only in the chemical, electrical equipment and office equipment fields. It is again in these areas that around 100 or more patents derived from non-French invention in 1987–90. Sixty-nine such patents were granted to French firms in the field of non-metallic mineral products.

Table 6.5 *The share of US patents of the largest French firms attributable to research outside France, classified by technological activity, 1969–90 (%)*

	1969–72	1973–77	1978–82	1983–86	1987–90
Food products	33.33	42.86	25.00	0.00	33.33
Chemicals nes	6.07	7.86	6.60	10.04	11.52
Inorganic chemicals	4.76	2.73	9.68	0.00	2.20
Organic chemicals	5.29	6.72	3.29	8.43	10.27
Agricultural chemicals	16.67	45.46	58.33	66.67	57.14
Chemical processes	11.18	13.35	9.60	10.17	15.24
Bleaching and dyeing processes	0.00	1.28	12.17	3.13	0.00
Pharmaceuticals	4.55	7.60	11.43	15.81	11.46
Metals	10.40	6.41	8.33	3.86	9.05
Metallurgical processes	4.41	7.45	9.43	1.10	6.93
Other metal products	14.29	5.71	6.98	6.03	10.56
Mechanical engineering	16.15	9.29	9.61	9.21	12.17
Chemical equipment	23.58	13.59	9.27	17.02	20.98
Metal working equipment	8.57	7.14	9.52	6.31	9.30
Assembly equipment	28.89	9.38	22.92	7.14	21.21
Mining equipment	15.00	5.00	21.88	10.00	0.00
Specialized industrial equipment	18.42	12.59	9.18	9.33	14.29
General industrial equipment	8.72	4.91	4.98	6.73	8.84
Electrical equipment nes	1.28	4.91	3.80	4.61	18.62
Telecommunications	2.11	3.23	3.57	3.06	21.77
Image and sound equipment	0.00	4.76	4.00	10.81	30.61
Semiconductors	0.00	0.00	0.00	0.00	6.15
Electrical systems	0.89	2.03	2.58	2.80	19.14
General electrical equipment	8.28	11.37	6.45	8.28	8.82
Office equipment	9.09	2.14	3.14	7.43	55.60
Motor vehicles	8.47	11.65	7.79	12.35	4.08
Aircraft	8.33	0.00	0.00	0.00	2.63
Other transport equipment	0.00	1.47	0.00	9.68	8.82
Textiles	9.09	20.00	25.00	41.67	7.14
Rubber and plastic products	10.77	5.21	5.26	7.41	6.38
Non-metallic mineral products	19.51	20.59	24.32	27.87	35.75
Coal and petroleum products	0.00	8.70	3.39	0.00	1.75
Professional and scientific instruments	5.53	6.47	5.75	14.51	9.04
Photographic equipment	0.00	12.50	23.08	0.00	100.00
Other instruments	5.70	6.30	5.00	14.74	8.31
Other manufacturing	24.32	26.87	12.00	2.04	7.14
Total	8.19	7.74	6.60	9.20	15.87

Source: As for Table 6.1.

In addition, it seems that a clear trend towards an increased internationalization of technological activity has been underway in the electrical equipment, office equipment and organic chemicals sectors. Within the electrical equipment sector, French firms have been especially keen to establish international research in the field of image and sound equipment (radios and TVs), and telecommunications.

The relative internationalization of research by French firms compared with the largest firms of all other nationalities can be seen in Tables 6.6 and 6.7 (which are derived from a comparison of Tables 6.1 and 6.4, and of 6.2 and 6.5 respectively). Table 6.6 shows that by the standards of others, until recently French firms have not been particularly reliant upon research located outside France for any industry in particular. However, this had changed by the late 1980s. The clearest evidence of the relative geographical decentralization of technological activity by French companies can be seen most clearly

Table 6.6   *The share of US patents of the largest French firms attributable to research abroad relative to the equivalent share of the world's largest firms considered together, for each industrial group of parent firms, 1969–90 (%)*

	1969–72	1973–77	1978–82	1983–86	1987–90
Food products	0.85	3.80	0.61	2.34	2.54
Chemicals nes	0.51	0.48	0.48	1.02	0.98
Pharmaceuticals	0.05	0.16	0.29	0.88	0.20
Metals	0.88	0.90	0.43	0.78	0.80
Mechanical engineering	0.28	0.00	0.00	0.24	0.00
Electrical equipment nes	0.23	0.15	0.12	0.33	2.21
Office equipment	3.63	0.75	0.65	0.00	5.50
Motor vehicles	1.48	0.76	2.73	0.85	1.10
Aircraft	5.47	3.11	0.00	1.49	1.39
Other transport equipment	N.A.	N.A.	N.A.	N.A	N.A.
Textiles	15.50	7.85	0.13	7.74	0.00
Rubber and plastic products	0.14	0.12	2.31	0.45	0.00
Non-metallic mineral products	2.00	2.45	1.00	2.73	2.29
Coal and petroleum products	0.59	0.59	0.00	0.49	0.30
Professional and scientific instruments	N.A.	N.A.	N.A.	N.A	N.A.
Other manufacturing	N.A.	N.A.	N.A.	N.A	N.A.
Total	0.79	0.71	0.68	0.83	1.41

Note: N.A. = not applicable.

Source: Tables 6.1 and 6.4.

Table 6.7 *The share of US patents of the largest French firms attributable to research abroad relative to the equivalent share of the world's largest firms considered together, classified by technological activity, 1969–90 (%)*

	1969–72	1973–77	1978–82	1983–86	1987–90
Food products	2.70	2.75	1.68	0.00	2.70
Chemicals nes	0.51	0.64	0.56	0.88	0.85
Inorganic chemicals	0.50	0.29	1.07	0.00	0.20
Organic chemicals	0.41	0.50	0.26	0.73	0.70
Agricultural chemicals	1.45	4.42	5.81	6.43	5.08
Chemical processes	1.05	0.42	0.89	0.92	1.23
Bleaching and dyeing processes	0.00	0.90	0.17	0.21	0.00
Pharmaceuticals	0.28	0.42	0.60	0.78	0.53
Metals	1.15	0.64	0.81	0.33	0.83
Metallurgical processes	0.56	0.90	1.17	0.13	0.86
Other metal products	1.43	0.49	0.57	0.41	0.77
Mechanical engineering	1.44	0.78	0.80	0.70	0.91
Chemical equipment	2.06	1.12	0.87	1.42	1.49
Metal working equipment	0.98	0.74	0.74	0.48	0.74
Assembly equipment	2.48	0.79	1.87	0.66	1.96
Mining equipment	0.92	0.37	2.07	0.73	0.00
Specialized industrial equipment	1.30	0.83	0.57	0.59	0.94
General industrial equipment	1.04	0.49	0.47	0.51	0.69
Electrical equipment nes	0.33	0.54	0.47	0.48	1.97
Telecommunications	0.16	0.28	0.35	0.27	1.98
Image and sound equipment	0.00	0.64	0.52	1.16	3.57
Semiconductors	0.00	0.00	0.00	0.00	0.71
Electrical systems	0.11	0.24	0.35	0.28	1.89
General electrical equipment	1.07	1.45	0.83	1.03	1.13
Office equipment	1.23	0.24	0.41	1.01	7.20
Motor vehicles	1.26	2.33	1.92	1.69	0.71
Aircraft	1.79	0.00	0.00	0.00	1.11
Other transport equipment	0.00	0.19	0.00	0.64	0.88
Textiles	0.82	1.37	1.32	3.81	0.78
Rubber and plastic products	1.13	0.48	0.51	0.67	0.57
Non-metallic mineral products	2.57	2.45	2.61	3.15	3.62
Coal and petroleum products	0.00	0.85	0.45	0.00	0.17
Professional and scientific instruments	0.63	0.70	0.64	1.50	1.06
Photographic equipment	0.00	1.92	5.50	0.00	36.10
Other instruments	0.63	0.64	0.50	1.40	0.86
Other manufacturing	2.57	2.24	1.26	0.14	0.62
Total	0.79	0.71	0.68	0.83	1.41

Source: Tables 6.2 and 6.5.

in the activities of electrical equipment, office equipment and non-metallic mineral products companies. While food products firms can also be included, their relevance tends to be weakened by the small numbers problem discussed earlier.

In the electrical equipment industry, the share of US patents of the largest French electrical equipment firms attributable to research abroad relative to the share of all the world's largest firms had risen to 2.21 by 1987–90 from 0.23 at the beginning of the 1970s, with the greatest increase occurring at the end of the 1980s. The non-French firm international share remained steady in this industry (see Table 6.1), indicating that the change resulted from an increasing tendency towards decentralization by the French firms rather than a change in the behaviour of their non-French counterparts.

In the office equipment sector, by around 1970 French firms were already highly decentralized in their research activity, with over 3.5 times the share of US patents of all other large firms in the study. Following a decline in their relative share during the 1970s and early 1980s, the figure rose to 5.5 by 1987–90. This is clearly far above the French average tendency to decentralize relative to non-French firms, which was 1.4 by 1987–90. Yet the 1987–90 period was the first time in which French-owned firms had an above average degree of internationalization of technological activity (a ratio greater than 1 in Table 6.6). This transformation is essentially due to the new international stance of the leading French electrical and computing companies.

French non-metallic mineral products (building material) firms also increased their relative internationalization of technological activity during this period, despite the increase in the existing levels of overseas technological activity of non-French firms. At the beginning of the 1970s, French firms in this industry were undertaking twice as much of their technological activity abroad compared with non-French firms in the same sector. The figures show that the trend fluctuated in the middle of the period, with evidence of a renewed increase in the relative French decentralization of activity during the 1980s.

Conversely, French textiles and aircraft manufacturers have shown a greater relative tendency towards the geographical centralization of technological activity between 1969 and 1990, despite non-French firms also locating more of their technological activity at home. The data show that French aircraft manufacturers undertook five times as much of their technological activity abroad as did all the world's largest firms during the period 1969–72. This relative share fell steadily throughout the 1970s and 1980s, and by 1987–90 French aircraft companies were exhibiting a below average tendency to decentralize their technological activity relative to all other firms, whose corresponding share of foreign technological activity rose in the middle of the 1980s. Again, however, the data on aircraft manufacturers and their technological activity are subject to the problem of small numbers, mainly because the propensity to patent in the aircraft sector is weak in all countries, and the degree of internationalization itself is everywhere low.

Table 6.7 looks at the same data classified by technological activity. It has already been noted above that French electrical equipment firms have shown a greater tendency to decentralize their technological activity relative to all firms in the industry, and what is evident from Table 6.7 is that research in electrical equipment technologies by French firms has also been subject to a greater relative degree of internationalization than research carried out in this technological area by non-French firms. The main cause of this strong French decentralization in these technological fields is the big increase in the relative proportion of technological activities in telecommunications, image and sound equipment, and electrical systems.

Similarly, while the share of US patents of the largest firms attributable to overseas technological activity in office equipment technologies has remained fairly constant throughout the 1970s and 1980s, the figures for French overseas activity in the same technological field have risen dramatically, especially towards the end of the 1980s. Clearly, French office equipment technology was subject to much greater relative decentralization; by 1987–90, the amount of overseas research in office equipment by French firms was over seven times that for all the world's largest firms considered together.

Following a trend towards the relative internationalization of research activity in textiles technology up to the middle of the 1980s, French firms have started to exhibit a below average tendency to decentralize geographically this type of technology relative to all firms. This relatively low level of activity by French firms in textiles technologies contrasts with the high levels of foreign technological activity by French textiles firms relative to all the world's largest firms in that industry.

An interesting point to note is that while Table 6.6 demonstrated that French non-metallic mineral products companies undertook twice as much overseas technological activity than did all firms in the industry, research by French companies in non-metallic mineral products technologies was over 3.5 times higher than global corporate activity in the same technological field. In aircraft technology, the levels of foreign research activity by both French and non-French firms have fallen substantially between 1969 and 1990, but the trend towards centralization of this type of activity has been most noticeable of all for French firms.

Foreign Firms in France

Turning now to the implications of foreign research by non-French firms for French industry, Table 6.8 presents some evidence on the share of such

Table 6.8 *The share of US patents of the largest non-French firms attributable to research in France, as a proportion of non-French firm patenting due to research in all foreign locations, organized by the industrial group of parent firms, 1969–90 (%)*

	1969–72	1987–90
Food products	1.02	1.73
Chemicals nes	6.36	6.87
Pharmaceuticals	1.96	3.55
Metals	3.18	2.36
Mechanical engineering	2.65	5.91
Electrical equipment nes	10.33	10.07
Office equipment	14.00	8.74
Motor vehicles	9.07	16.68
Aircraft	3.05	3.28
Other transport equipment	30.77	0.00
Textiles	5.13	44.44
Rubber and plastic products	22.00	9.42
Non-metallic mineral products	4.07	2.05
Coal and petroleum products	2.02	3.81
Professional and scientific instruments	12.73	5.56
Other manufacturing	8.99	30.19
Total	6.03	7.66

Source: As for Table 6.1.

research which has been directed to France. Here (and in Table 6.10 below) the activities of large foreign firms in France gave rise to substantial numbers of patents only in the chemicals, electrical equipment, office equipment, motor vehicles and other manufacturing industries. In these five industries the number of US patents assigned to foreign-owned firms but deriving from technological development in France reached about 100 or more in 1987–90.

Table 6.8 shows that the relative attractiveness of France as a location for the technological activity of non-French office equipment firms fell from 14 per cent in the period 1969–72 to 8.7 per cent by the end of the 1980s. Hence the increased international activity of the equivalent French companies was not part of an oligopolistic interaction in which foreign MNCs stepped up their research in France in exchange. However, the share of 8.7 per cent is still above the average for all sectors (7.7 per cent), implying that this is an industry in which foreign research has been relatively attracted to France for some time.

In other words, the greater internationalization of French-owned activity may be viewed as a rather belated response to the long-standing participation of foreign firms in French research. The same is true in the electrical equipment industry; the share of US patents of the largest non-French firms attributable to research in France as a proportion of non-French firm patenting abroad remained relatively high at 10 per cent throughout the period. Non-French firms in the motor vehicle, textile and other manufacturing industries have all increased the amount of technological activity undertaken in France relative to other countries. This trend is most clear for textile firms, in which the figure increased from 5 per cent in 1969–72 to 44 per cent by 1987–90. This rise is interesting given the fact that, as Table 6.1 shows, the world's largest textile firms are exhibiting a growing tendency to centralize their technological activity. Conversely, non-French rubber and plastic products and instruments firms have shown a tendency to move away from France as a location for their technological activity.

Table 6.9 shows that a rise in foreign research in France can also be seen in the equivalent sector of technological activity in textiles but not in motor vehicles. Moreover, the level of non-French corporate research in these technologies undertaken in France as a proportion of the research of non-French firms carried out in all foreign locations is much lower than the figure for all industries in question. This implies that although foreign textile and vehicle companies have recently been more attracted to France as a location for research, their French-based research has not focused on their core technologies, but has been part of a strategy of international technological specialization. Conversely, the French share is much higher for technological activity associated with aircraft than for aircraft manufacturers. In other words, foreign firms outside the aircraft industry have been keen to tap into French strength in technological development in this area.

These pieces of evidence are consistent in that motor vehicle companies (and especially vehicle component manufacturers as opposed to assemblers) often have a substantial interest in aircraft technologies, which are quite closely related to their own basic transport technologies. Thus it is plausible to suppose that some foreign companies in the motor vehicle industry have a strategy of international corporate technological specialization in which they site much of their basic motor vehicle development at home, but they focus on the acquisition of related aircraft technologies in their French-located facilities. This locational strategy would take advantage of France's comparative advantage in technological activity in the aircraft field.

It should be noted, however, that in Table 6.9 (and in Table 6.11 below) large non-French firms are only involved in substantial levels of patenting

Table 6.9 The share of US patents of the largest non-French firms attributable to research in France, as a proportion of non-French firm patenting due to research in all foreign locations, classified by technological activity, 1969–90 (%)

	1969–72	1973–77	1978–82	1983–86	1987–90
Food products	0.00	2.33	7.29	4.12	0.71
Chemicals nes	4.92	4.75	5.30	5.29	4.99
Inorganic chemicals	3.36	2.59	5.06	2.79	0.00
Organic chemicals	4.63	4.98	4.76	5.83	5.31
Agricultural chemicals	13.64	13.63	5.21	2.20	0.91
Chemical processes	5.84	3.98	5.61	4.88	4.59
Bleaching and dyeing process	6.06	3.41	17.00	8.86	17.95
Pharmaceuticals	5.84	9.64	8.84	8.46	6.66
Metals	4.60	5.75	6.76	6.52	7.42
Metallurgical processes	5.60	3.56	7.72	4.48	3.58
Other metal products	3.94	7.18	6.61	7.68	9.59
Mechanical engineering	4.99	6.63	5.73	7.90	8.24
Chemical equipment	4.45	4.73	2.88	5.45	5.44
Metal working equipment	3.94	6.61	5.62	6.04	6.17
Assembly equipment	4.62	3.90	7.42	4.60	2.08
Mining equipment	2.17	2.80	2.76	3.43	11.96
Specialized industrial equipment	5.23	5.26	4.58	7.06	5.46
General industrial equipment	7.16	12.44	9.85	13.27	14.01
Electrical equipment nes	9.01	11.24	11.61	9.45	11.00
Telecommunications	15.70	17.66	19.57	18.24	16.50
Image and sound equipment	5.96	7.27	4.50	4.81	11.46
Semiconductors	7.52	11.81	21.25	11.52	12.13
Electrical systems	7.08	8.83	7.89	6.35	7.72
General electrical equipment	4.75	8.07	8.55	6.35	7.98
Office equipment	12.20	20.95	24.02	13.30	10.32
Motor vehicles	10.53	13.85	14.60	10.89	7.02
Aircraft	11.76	11.11	0.00	30.00	18.18
Other transport equipment	3.16	6.17	1.02	1.69	2.17
Textiles	0.00	1.56	0.00	6.25	6.45
Rubber and plastic products	11.43	8.61	4.48	6.75	2.17
Non-metallic mineral products	4.47	5.17	6.89	5.84	6.57
Coal and petroleum products	2.78	1.77	2.82	3.85	3.14
Professional and scientific instruments	7.75	9.32	7.69	7.33	8.74
Photographic equipment	0.85	2.05	0.95	0.76	4.82
Other instruments	8.69	10.25	8.32	8.03	8.95
Other manufacturing	2.63	5.63	3.65	4.78	8.90
Total	6.03	7.35	7.45	7.44	7.66

Source: As for Table 6.1.

based on their research effort in France in five fields of technological activity. The five fields in question are chemicals, pharmaceuticals, mechanical engineering, electrical equipment, and professional and scientific instruments. It is only in these areas that around 100 or more patents were assigned to foreign firms in 1987–90 based on inventions achieved in France. While in at least some other fields foreign firms may still be engaged in quite extensive technological efforts in France – since, as mentioned earlier, absolute numbers of patents vary between fields with the propensity to patent – low numbers of patents might affect the foreign share ratios constructed in these tables.

Yet high shares of the patenting of large foreign firms attributable to French-located invention are also observed in the electrical equipment technologies, in which there are no difficulties with the absolute number of patents; foreign firms are very keen to use France as a location for their research in telecommunications, semiconductors, and image and sound equipment. This is not fully reflected in the amount of French-based research undertaken by firms in the electrical equipment industry, again pointing towards a strategy of technological specialization across national boundaries. These electrical equipment fields are also areas of French technological strength, such as aircraft development (see Patel and Pavitt (1990), whose discussion is also based on the use of US patent statistics).

The international operations of foreign firms in France are linked to the pattern of their specialization in technological activity. Thus technological specialization has a locational dimension. In this instance it seems that the choice of the fields on which foreign firms concentrate when developing new technology in France is linked to the main sources of local capability in France and in which France can be viewed as a centre of expertise. Foreign firms in France have particularly focused on areas in which public procurement has been important, in telecommunications and aircraft.

In office equipment technologies, non-French firms' share in France as a proportion of their total foreign office equipment technological activity increased throughout the 1970s to 24 per cent and then fell back to 10.3 per cent in 1987–90, less than its original 1969–72 level but still above average and higher than the corresponding figure for office equipment firms.

Table 6.10 looks at the share of research activity undertaken by non-French firms in France relative to all French and non-French large firm activity in France, and shows that the overall proportions remained at similar high levels throughout the 1970s and 1980s. However, there is a marked difference between firms in different industries. The figures are high for office equipment firms throughout the period, rising to 57 per cent by 1987–90 from almost 52 per cent at the beginning of the 1970s. Similarly, non-French motor vehicle firms increased their research in France as a proportion of total

Table 6.10   The share of US patents of the largest non-French firms
              attributable to research in France, as a proportion of the
              number due to research in France by French or non-French
              large firms, organized by the industrial group of parent
              companies, 1969–90 (%)

	1969–72	1987–90
Food products	45.45	28.57
Chemicals nes	33.33	29.20
Pharmaceuticals	18.57	17.98
Metals	6.90	10.22
Mechanical engineering	45.90	42.60
Electrical equipment nes	34.04	33.12
Office equipment	51.81	57.23
Motor vehicles	9.89	36.05
Aircraft	3.31	1.76
Other transport equipment	100.00	0.00
Textiles	100.00	80.00
Rubber and plastic products	25.00	25.00
Non-metallic mineral products	3.23	2.94
Coal and petroleum products	14.43	11.05
Professional and scientific instruments	100.00	100.00
Other manufacturing	100.00	100.00
Total	24.23	27.27

Source: As for Table 6.1.

research in France by all the world's largest firms, from 9.9 per cent in the early 1970s to 36 per cent in 1990. The relative attractiveness of France as a location of technological activity to non-French firms in these industries contrasts with the behaviour of aircraft manufacturers and building materials companies. In these industries, non-French technological activity relative to all firms has remained at very low levels throughout the entire period, implying that foreign firms in these industries are much less inclined to locate their research activity in France than indigenous firms.

Looking at the same data classified by technological activity (Table 6.11), it can be seen that non-French firms have not particularly based their research in France in their core technologies. In the electrical equipment sector, the share of non-French firms' research activity in telecommunications and semiconductors in France relative to that of all the world's largest firms is much

Table 6.11   *The share of US patents of the largest non-French firms*
attributable to research in France, as a proportion of the
number due to research in France by French or non-French
large firms, classified by technological activity, 1969–90 (%)

	1969–72	1973–77	1978–82	1983–86	1987–90
Food products	0.00	60.00	70.00	72.73	9.09
Chemicals nes	21.26	18.50	21.63	21.82	21.30
Inorganic chemicals	5.88	4.46	8.70	6.02	0.00
Organic chemicals	20.16	20.33	22.31	24.64	23.57
Agricultural chemicals	16.67	66.67	50.00	18.18	10.00
Chemical processes	34.78	18.91	22.00	22.91	23.75
Bleaching and dyeing processes	7.41	3.75	27.42	18.42	22.59
Pharmaceuticals	37.31	37.73	40.38	34.89	30.33
Metals	15.76	19.49	22.47	20.72	22.18
Metallurgical processes	17.72	13.00	17.95	12.62	10.48
Other metal products	14.29	23.26	27.27	26.35	29.05
Mechanical engineering	26.50	26.69	23.77	26.99	29.19
Chemical equipment	24.80	20.18	13.84	23.53	27.56
Metal working equipment	14.67	17.61	17.39	17.46	20.41
Assembly equipment	33.33	22.67	38.33	23.53	16.13
Mining equipment	22.73	24.00	13.79	16.28	28.95
Specialized industrial equipment	40.38	30.59	29.37	16.28	25.66
General industrial equipment	23.16	34.26	27.65	29.16	34.53
Electrical equipment nes	29.31	28.07	22.59	25.34	31.90
Telecommunications	43.72	37.69	31.86	37.09	40.85
Image and sound equipment	32.14	16.67	11.11	17.50	39.29
Semiconductors	47.22	52.63	44.16	37.29	40.20
Electrical systems	22.30	24.08	15.88	17.26	22.25
General electrical equipment	14.74	17.98	17.48	19.88	25.30
Office equipment	40.59	43.62	42.96	35.98	45.21
Motor vehicles	12.90	16.51	21.98	31.07	26.56
Aircraft	15.38	3.85	0.00	6.00	5.13
Other transport equipment	5.45	12.99	4.55	9.68	8.82
Textiles	0.00	5.88	0.00	22.22	13.33
Rubber and plastic products	21.62	16.51	9.09	18.03	8.33
Non-metallic mineral products	16.46	19.80	19.42	20.00	20.51
Coal and petroleum products	17.95	7.35	8.06	10.53	9.68
Professional and scientific instruments	28.79	31.58	24.16	26.36	29.77
Photographic equipment	14.29	30.00	9.09	16.67	100.00
Other instruments	29.18	31.62	24.60	26.52	29.19
Other manufacturing	12.50	19.67	10.20	17.24	24.64
Total	24.23	24.73	24.07	25.15	27.27

Source: As for Table 6.1.

higher than is the case for the related figures for electrical equipment firms. Conversely, the figures show that activity in office equipment and motor vehicle technologies by non-French firms in France relative to all firms is lower than the corresponding technological activity by non-French office equipment and motor vehicle companies. The discrepancies between the research activities of firms and their areas of specialization, both in France and around the world, suggest that the world's largest firms are pursuing strategies of international diversification away from their core technology activities into different, but usually related, areas. This will be examined in further detail in the following section.

INTERNATIONAL CORPORATE TECHNOLOGICAL SPECIALIZATION AT THE INDUSTRY LEVEL

Turning now to a consideration of further measures of technological specialization at an industry level, an index of such specialization across different fields of activity, which is often termed an index of revealed technological advantage (RTA), is calculated. The RTA of a firm (or a group of firms) in a particular sector of technological activity is given by its share of US patents in that sector granted to companies in the same industry, relative to the firm's overall share of all US patents assigned to firms in the industry in question. Denoting as P_{ij} the number of US patents granted in the field of activity i to firm (or selected group of firms) j in a particular industry, then the RTA index is defined as follows:

$$RTA_{ij} = (P_{ij} / \Sigma_j P_{ij}) / (\Sigma_i P_{ij} / \Sigma_{ij} P_{ij})$$

The index varies around unity, such that values greater than 1 suggest that a firm (or group of firms) is comparatively specialized in the activity in question relative to the other firms in the same industry. Values less than 1 are indicative of a position of a lack of specialization by the standards of the industry. Just as difficulties can be created when constructing ratios that rely on small numbers of patents, as discussed above, so there are particular problems associated with the use of small numbers when using an RTA index (Cantwell, 1991, 1993b). Due to these problems the analysis is restricted to sectors in which over 1200 US patents were granted to large firms in the industry in question between 1969 and 1990. Sectors that do not meet this criterion are omitted from the RTA values reported in Table 6.12 onwards.

Table 6.12 shows the RTA indices for non-French firms in France as a proportion of all large firms in their particular industry, across each different category of technological activity. For the purposes of Tables 6.12–14 and

Table 6.12 *The revealed technological advantage of non-French firms in France relative to all firms in that industry, across fields of technological activity, 1969–90*

	Chemicals	Electrical	Motor vehicles	Aircraft	Building materials
Food products	0.43				
Chemicals nes	0.70	0.49	0.29	0.50	0.74
Inorganic chemicals	0.15				
Organic chemicals	0.91	0.05	0.00	0.62	
Agricultural chemicals	0.66				
Chemical processes	0.43	0.62		0.53	
Bleaching and dyeing processes	1.71				
Pharmaceuticals	1.89				
Metals	0.76	0.61	2.41	0.92	0.00
Metallurgical processes	0.51	0.71	0.52	0.00	
Other metal products	0.94	0.43	3.45		
Mechanical engineering	2.10	0.50	1.38	1.86	1.60
Chemical equipment	0.47	0.76	1.02		
Metal working equipment		0.36	2.07		
Assembly equipment	0.16	0.55			
Mining equipment					
Specialized industrial equipment	1.40	0.73	1.51		
General industrial equipment	10.99	0.16	1.38	0.63	
Electrical equipment nes	0.47	1.19	0.65	0.83	
Telecommunications		2.44			
Image and sound equipment		0.86			
Semiconductors		1.32	0.00	0.00	
Electrical systems	1.18	0.74	0.68	0.80	
General electrical equipment	0.00	0.69	0.87	2.13	
Office equipment	0.10	1.36	0.24	0.00	
Motor vehicles			0.90		
Aircraft				1.57	
Other transport equipment			0.20		
Textiles					
Rubber and plastic products	0.09				
Non-metallic mineral products	0.17	0.66			1.16
Coal and petroleum products	0.15	0.00	0.00		
Professional and scientific instruments	0.51	0.98	0.58	0.65	
Photographic equipment	0.00	0.19			
Other instruments	0.62	1.11	0.58	0.65	
Other manufacturing	0.79	1.43			

Note: Entries are only provided for the sectors of technological activity in which the world's largest firms in the industry in question were granted 1200 or more patents in the USA between 1969 and 1990.

Source: As for Table 6.1.

6.16–17, the chemical and pharmaceutical companies, and the electrical and office equipment companies are considered together. Also included in this analysis are aircraft firms and motor vehicle and non-metallic mineral products firms. As can be inferred from Table 6.12, sufficient numbers of patents (1200 in the period as a whole) were granted to large firms in 22 fields of technological activity out of 33 in the chemicals and pharmaceuticals industry (not counting aggregate groupings of related fields), in 20 areas in electrical and computer equipment, in 14 sectors in motor vehicles, in 11 fields in aircraft, but in only one separately defined area in building materials.

The technological specialization of non-French chemical and pharmaceutical firms in France relative to that of all chemical and pharmaceutical firms in France is considered. The results show that with respect to their 'core' technologies, non-French firms in these industries are more inclined to base their pharmaceutical research activity in France, but that this is not the case for their chemical activity. France is also relatively attractive as a location for bleaching and dyeing process research and in particular for the development of industrial equipment technology.

For non-French electrical and computing equipment firms in France, most activity is carried out in their 'core' technologies. This might be expected because of the relative strength of French research in a European context in electrical equipment technology which is defence-related or in which state procurement is important, such as in telecommunications (Patel and Pavitt, 1990). The RTA index shows that the specialization of non-French electrical and computing firms in France relative to all firms in this industry is found in telecommunications and semiconductors technologies, and also in other instruments. Overall, France is relatively attractive as a location for all electrical and computing technological activity by these firms, with an RTA of 1.19 for electrical technologies and an RTA of 1.36 for computing technologies.

The data for motor vehicle firms' technological activity suffer from the problem of small numbers, and so, as noted already, the calculations are restricted to just 14 sectors. What can be seen is that non-French motor vehicle firms in France are relatively attracted to France as a base for their research in metal products, general industrial equipment and, to a lesser extent, in motor vehicle technologies.

Unfortunately, the number of foreign patents registered from invention in France by non-French aircraft and non-metallic mineral products firms is very small, and so even when confining the discussion to 11 sectors the results may be misleading. Out of a total of 31 patents registered by non-French aircraft companies, 13 were in mechanical engineering technologies. An RTA of 1.86 implies that France is a relatively attractive location for this type of research by non-French aircraft companies, bearing in mind the low levels of activity recorded. This is also the case for the data available for non-metallic mineral products firms. Of 44 patents registered by these companies, 15 were in the field of general industrial equipment technologies and 11 in the 'core' non-metallic mineral products technology. An RTA of 3.83 for the former and of 1.16 for the latter reflect the relative composition of French-based research in the technological activity of non-French companies.

Table 6.13 looks at the technological specialization of all the activity (at home or abroad) of large French firms in the industries already mentioned. The firms involved are listed in the Appendix. Chemical and pharmaceutical firms in general record the highest absolute level of technological activity in bleaching and dyeing processes, inorganic and organic chemicals and, in broader terms, in the core technologies of chemicals and pharmaceuticals. Of these, French firms in these industries are relatively specialized in inorganic chemical technologies and bleaching and dyeing process technologies. Overall, Table 6.13 reveals that while French chemical and pharmaceutical firms are slightly less inclined to undertake technological activity in chemicals than are other chemical companies, the opposite is true for pharmaceuticals relative to the other largest firms in these industries. French chemical firms are relatively strong in inorganic chemicals, a fact noted by Patel and Pavitt (1990), who also highlight this field as a fast-growing technology. Given that French firms are relatively strong in this sector at home and abroad, this is possibly an area of future growth for these firms. Outside the 'core' chemical areas, French firms show a relative tendency to focus research activity on mechanical fields, and especially in chemical equipment and specialized industrial equipment.

French electrical and computer equipment firms record the greatest absolute level of technological activity in electrical systems, telecommunications and office equipment. Their relative strengths are in the field of telecommunications, with an RTA of 1.58, and electrical systems and devices (1.24). This contrasts with the results for office equipment, in which French firms in these industries display a relative weakness; thus despite the large absolute amount of activity recorded, they are not particularly strong in this area of research.

Hence it is clear that French electrical and office equipment firms are relatively strongest in telecommunications technologies. It has already been noted above that France is considered an attractive location for telecommunications research by non-French firms; Table 6.9 shows that compared with an overall average of 7.6 per cent, the proportion of research by all firms in France undertaken in this field by non-French firms is 16.5 per cent. Furthermore, as seen in Table 6.11, the share of US patents of non-French firms attributable to research in France relative to the total technological activity in France of all the world's largest firms is around 40 per cent, again above the average 25 per cent or so. Thus the specialization of the largest French electrical companies in telecommunications helps to attract non-French

Table 6.13 *The revealed technological advantage of French firms in selected industries, across fields of technological activity, 1969–90*

	Chemicals	Electrical	Motor vehicles	Aircraft	Building materials
Food products	0.61				
Chemicals nes	0.96	0.46	0.40	0.19	1.27
Inorganic chemicals	2.07				
Organic chemicals	0.91	0.18	0.29	0.02	
Agricultural chemicals	0.76				
Chemical processes	0.76	0.55		0.40	
Bleaching and dyeing processes	3.22				
Pharmaceuticals	1.13				
Metals	1.48	0.74	1.46	1.04	0.46
Metallurgical processes	1.09	0.79	0.94	0.76	
Other metal products	1.75	0.66	1.74		
Mechanical engineering	1.42	0.56	1.35	1.45	1.14
Chemical equipment	1.27	0.55	0.88		
Metal working equipment		0.53	1.90		
Assembly equipment	1.18	0.53			
Mining equipment					
Specialized industrial equipment	1.75	0.66	0.69		
General industrial equipment	1.63	0.44	1.46	2.21	
Electrical equipment nes	1.01	1.20	0.72	0.57	
Telecommunications		1.58			
Image and sound equipment		1.12			
Semiconductors		0.69	0.00	0.11	
Electrical systems	0.70	1.24	0.99	0.43	
General electrical equipment	1.44	1.02	0.69	0.61	
Office equipment	0.43	0.94	0.44	0.77	
Motor vehicles			0.73		
Aircraft				2.75	
Other transport equipment			1.26		
Textiles					
Rubber and plastic products	0.66				
Non-metallic mineral products	0.80	0.61			1.12
Coal and petroleum products	0.66	0.68		0.00	
Professional and scientific instruments	0.20	1.12	0.30	1.64	
Photographic equipment	0.05	0.30			
Other instruments	0.80	1.40	0.95	0.93	
Other manufacturing	0.65	0.60			

Note: Entries are only provided for the sectors of technological activity in which the world's largest firms in the industry in question were granted 1200 or more patents in the USA between 1969 and 1990.

Source: As for Table 6.1.

companies in the industry to carry out research into telecommunications technology in France.

French motor vehicle firms are not particularly geared to research in their core technological field. While much of their activity is naturally in this field, the RTA is 0.73, suggestive of a relative weakness compared with their strong technological position in other metal products and general industrial equipment. Some problems with small numbers are encountered again in the data for aircraft and non-metallic mineral products firms. French aircraft companies display a relative strength in the 'core' technology of aircraft, with a high RTA of 2.75. This highlights Patel and Pavitt's point that French relative strength occurs in sectors dominated by state procurement and associated funding of technological activities, such as aircraft. French non-metallic mineral products firms are also relatively strong in their core non-metallic mineral products technology, but their greatest strength lies in chemical equipment and chemical processes.

Table 6.14 looks at the relative technological specialization of French firms outside France. For chemical and pharmaceutical firms, the bulk of their foreign research activity occurs in organic chemicals, pharmaceuticals and other instruments technologies. However, in terms of their relative specialization, the RTAs of organic chemicals and pharmaceutical technologies are low at 0.64 and 0.38, respectively, implying a relative weakness in overseas technological specialization by French chemical and pharmaceutical firms in these fields of activity, despite their comparative specialization in pharmaceuticals at home (Table 6.13). Having seen from Table 6.7 that the degree of internationalization of activity by French firms in these technologies is half the extent of geographical decentralization of non-French firms, these results are not surprising. French firms' technological activities outside France are strongest in other instruments, which has an RTA of 3.09. This is particularly impressive in view of the fact that this is generally an area of technological weakness for French chemical companies (see Table 6.13). Hence they have attempted to compensate for this weakness in their French-based research by developing the instruments technologies they need abroad. This fits with the general tendency for user firms to fulfil their instrument requirements through their international technological activity, as remarked on in connection with Tables 6.1 and 6.2.

In their foreign activity, French electrical and office equipment firms are strongest in office equipment and image and sound equipment, and particularly weak in semiconductors. An RTA of 2.42 in office equipment technologies (Table 6.14) demonstrates that French firms in these industries are much more specialized in this type of technological activity outside France rather than domestically, in which the RTA revealed a relative weakness (Table 6.13). Here again, therefore, French electrical equipment firms use foreign

Table 6.14   The revealed technological advantage of French firms outside France in selected industries, across fields of technological activity, 1969–90

	Chemicals	Electrical	Motor vehicles	Aircraft	Building materials
Food products	1.92				
Chemicals nes	0.77	0.27	0.00	0.00	0.95
Inorganic chemicals	0.34				
Organic chemicals	0.64	0.00	0.00	0.00	
Agricultural chemicals	5.77				
Chemical processes	0.59	0.36		0.00	
Bleaching and dyeing processes	0.19				
Pharmaceuticals	0.38				
Metals	0.25	0.50	1.00	0.23	0.39
Metallurgical processes	0.57	0.26	0.31	0.00	
Other metal products	0.72	0.91	1.37		
Mechanical engineering	0.85	0.75	1.91	1.69	1.13
Chemical equipment	0.63	0.84	1.97		
Metal working equipment		0.59	0.58		
Assembly equipment	2.13	1.23			
Mining equipment					
Specialized industrial equipment	0.88	0.78	0.86		
General industrial equipment	0.98	0.29	2.48	0.48	
Electrical equipment nes	1.24	0.96	0.39	0.71	
Telecommunications		1.33			
Image and sound equipment		2.18			
Semiconductors		0.18	0.00	0.00	
Electrical systems	0.32	0.92	0.44	1.02	
General electrical equipment	1.02	0.42	0.16	0.00	
Office equipment	3.67	2.42	0.00	0.00	
Motor vehicles			0.90		
Aircraft				0.40	
Other transport equipment			0.21		
Textiles					
Rubber and plastic products	0.58				
Non-metallic mineral products	0.42	0.75			1.20
Coal and petroleum products	0.68	0.00		0.00	
Professional and scientifc instruments	2.54	0.75	0.88	0.82	
Photographic equipment	0.00	0.54			
Other instruments	3.09	0.78	0.88	0.83	
Other manufacturing	0.35	0.59			

Note: Entries are only provided for the sectors of technological activity in which the world's largest firms in the industry in question were granted 1200 or more patents in the USA between 1969 and 1990.

Source: As for Table 6.1.

research as part of an internationally specialized network, in which computing technologies are (in relative terms) developed rather more abroad. They are also strong abroad in image and sound equipment, which is not a sector in which they are particularly specialized at home. In general, in their core technologies, these electrical and office equipment firms specialize abroad in office equipment but not especially in electrical equipment, the opposite of the position for French firms' technological activities at home.

The data for both motor vehicle and aircraft companies again suffer from the problem of small numbers, to the extent that the figures for aircraft manufacturers are ignored. The data for the technological activity of French motor vehicle firms outside France point towards a relative strength in general industrial equipment technology, which has an RTA of 2.48 and is also the sector in which most activity is recorded. Once again, this is evidence in favour of a strategy of international corporate specialization, given the lesser degree of focus at home of French motor vehicle companies in general industrial equipment technology compared with their major competitors (an RTA of 1.46 in Table 6.13).

It is possible that strategies of international corporate technological specialization have been reinforced by cross-border inter-company alliances. For one thing, agreements for technological cooperation or exchange between firms are likely to enhance the degree of specialization of each partner, allowing firms to focus more upon their major strengths and to draw upon the experience of collaborators in their respective areas of excellence. Yet it is also feasible that across those fields in which firms continue to maintain a diverse range of activity, this spectrum of areas of technological development comes to be increasingly associated with an equivalent spectrum of international locations, each field being linked to a preferred location. This would occur where the partners in an alliance decide to collaborate in each of the fields they have selected for cooperative effort in the most suitable international location for that branch of activity. However, the contribution to patenting of this type of agreement is still probably quite small relative to the total technological activity of these large firms. In addition, joint work in some alliances is devoted mainly to basic research, which, as suggested earlier, feeds into downstream technological development in each partner company, but which does not itself lead to the immediate creation of technological capability or to patenting.

INTERNATIONAL CORPORATE TECHNOLOGICAL SPECIALIZATION AT THE FIRM LEVEL

Looking at how these changes in the chemical and electrical industries translate to the company level for the three French firms with the largest total numbers of US patents granted (Rhône Poulenc, CGE and Thomson), Table 6.15 shows the share of US patents of each company attributable to research outside France as a proportion of its total research activity. Seven non-French firms in the same industries are included for comparative purposes. The internationalization of Rhône Poulenc's research activity in the mid 1980s reflects a similar story to large firms in the French chemical industry as a whole (see Table 6.4). As will become clear below, this was a time when Rhône Poulenc followed a strategy of the internationalization of production. Its share of research activity undertaken abroad increased dramatically in the period 1983–86, and then decreased slightly at the end of the 1980s. This may be due to the fact that its principal strategy at this time was to increase the number of acquisitions it made, rather than specifically focusing on the internationalization of its activities as such.

Table 6.15 *The share of US patents of the leading French firms attributable to research in foreign research as a proportion of total US patents assigned to the firm in question, 1969–90 (%)*

	1969–72	1973–77	1978–82	1983–86	1987–90
Rhône Poulenc	8.16	6.52	7.27	15.88	14.39
CGE	2.26	2.00	0.91	1.51	34.28
Thomson	2.36	1.14	1.09	3.88	16.40
Bayer	22.95	18.63	16.68	18.75	15.41
Hoechst	16.81	18.17	18.19	24.56	38.16
ICI	18.80	22.63	21.69	26.69	32.63
Ciba-Geigy	38.54	36.49	38.97	40.43	43.92
Siemens	4.07	4.71	7.57	16.58	19.52
GEC	17.25	32.14	27.22	18.18	37.11
Philips	52.30	47.55	46.39	54.03	54.44

Source: As for Table 6.1.

In this respect it can be seen that the data reported in Table 6.15 seem largely to pick up the effect of Rhône Poulenc's international acquisitions in the 1980s (and also those of CGE and Thomson), despite the difficulties that might have been expected owing to the consolidation of corporate groups as of 1984, as described above. The explanation is that most companies central-ize the process of patent applications across many of their affiliates for strategic reasons, such as the avoidance of duplication and the monitoring and exploitation of potential complementarities (Etemad and Séguin Delude, 1985). Thus once an acquisition is made there is often a substantial switch in the assignment of patents away from the acquired affiliate and in favour of the new parent company. This appears to have happened in the case of the companies acquired by these three major French groups in the 1980s. How-ever, to the extent that any of the newly acquired affiliates continued to take responsibility for patent applications, Table 6.15 if anything understates the recent internationalization of these French firms.

As with Rhône Poulenc and the French chemical industry, the substantial increase in international technological activity by large French electrical equipment producers in the late 1980s (Table 6.4) can also be related to the strategies of the major French players, CGE and Thomson, at that time. CGE's strategy of internationalizing production is reflected in the interna-tionalization of its research activities. In the period 1969–72, the share of US patents attributable to research abroad was only 2.26 per cent. This figure declined throughout the 1970s until 1982. Following its successful bid to acquire parts of Thomson and build up its domestic base, and its subsequent strategy of internationalization, the figure increased to 1.51 per cent. How-ever, the most dramatic increase in CGE's internationalization of its techno-logical activity occurred at the end of the 1980s, when its share of foreign research jumped to 34.3 per cent. This clearly reflects a major new departure in strategy of this company, which will be documented further below.

Table 6.15 shows that Thomson's share of US patents attributable to re-search activity outside France also remained at low levels up to 1982. In the mid 1980s, this figure rose slightly but the biggest increase by far occurred at the end of the 1980s. The relative share of Thomson's overseas research activity increased to 16.4 per cent in the period 1987–90, which was also the time when the company bought the consumer electronics arm of GE in the USA, GE/RCA, thereby doubling its size and increasing its international sales, as well as the extent of its technological development located outside France.

Of some of the other leading European companies in the chemical indus-try, Hoechst, ICI and Ciba-Geigy display trends in the internationalization of research that are not too dissimilar to that of Rhône Poulenc, in the sense that their shares of foreign-located research all increased during the 1980s, although beginning from a much higher base. However, the same is not true of Bayer, whose share of activity outside Germany was lower in 1987–90 than it had been in 1969–72. Such conflicting trends help to explain why in the chemical industry in general there was only a rather moderate increase in the degree of internationalization of technological activity in the 1980s (see Table 6.1).

The differences between French and other European firms in the electrical equipment industry are somewhat more marked. While Siemens and GEC certainly saw an increase in the shares of their foreign-located technological development in the 1980s, this occurred rather earlier (in the mid 1980s) for Siemens, and was associated with a much greater volatility in the case of the British GEC. Philips also recorded an increase in the proportion of its research sited abroad in the 1980s, but its degree of internationalization was already at a much higher level than for its major competitors (at around 50 per cent), and the rise of the foreign share in the 1980s did little more than to restore the position that had existed in 1969–72.

Rhône Poulenc

The chemical industry is one in which European performance is strong relative to that of both the USA and Japan. In 1989 the output of the Western European industry was $340 billion in comparison with $275 billion for the USA and $190 billion in Japan. Another important feature of the chemical industry is the extent to which it is already a 'global' industry. Twelve of the 20 largest chemical multinationals, which together account for about a quarter of all world sales, are European. They include some well established firms, such as Bayer and BASF, that have grown historically through internal growth, and others, such as Rhône Poulenc, whose growth has derived from its strategy of acquisitions.

At the beginning of the 1960s, Rhône Poulenc concentrated a large proportion of its production in textiles and pharmaceuticals, with textiles representing more than 50 per cent of sales. Throughout that decade, the company continued with this strategy and also set about acquiring a number of chemical firms because it wanted a presence in as many areas as possible in the new Common Market. This strategy continued until the late 1970s, when a thorough analysis of its corporate strategy revealed that Rhône Poulenc had serious structural problems, stemming partly from the diversification of its activity, which meant that despite a large global size, it was not particularly strong in any one field. Furthermore, given the problems in the textile market in this period, it was decided that textiles accounted for too large a share of global sales, and this was also true for petrochemicals and fertilizers. In addition, Rhône Poulenc was not as internationalized as it wanted, especially in the USA and Japan.

Rhône Poulenc's strategies in the 1980s followed the recommendations of its earlier review. It became more focused in its internationalization, and in particular in its R&D. Furthermore, it was decided that three main areas should form the basis of the company's future growth: pharmaceuticals, agrochemicals and fine chemicals. In order to accelerate this process, numerous acquisitions were made. Between 1980 and 1991, Rhône Poulenc made 68 sales of activities and 91 acquisitions. Furthermore, it sold its basic petrochemicals operation to another French multinational, Elf Acquitaine.

This redefinition of strategy has meant that Rhône Poulenc's position among the world's largest chemical companies has improved from 13th in 1984 to 7th in 1990. Rhône Poulenc has been part of a massive restructuring of the largely state-owned chemical industry. Acquisitions have been central to the spectacular increase in its internationalization. In 1985, 60 per cent of production occurred in France, with the remaining 40 per cent being located overseas. In 1990, 46 per cent of production took place in France, with the majority being undertaken abroad.

This policy of internationalization and acquisitions, according to Cook and Sharp (1991), is explicitly designed to develop Rhône Poulenc to the extent that it can compete in the Single Market. In 1989 Rhône Poulenc was less than half the size of the three German leaders in the industry, and significantly smaller than ICI, Dow or Du Pont. Thus in the years 1986–90, it embarked on a period of acquisitions. These included Union Carbide's agrochemical business, GAF-SSC (an American speciality chemicals business) and, in a deal valued at $3.2 billion, it purchased Rorer, a US pharmaceuticals company. These acquisitions have been accompanied by efforts to integrate all the new activities and sites. This has led to some further restructuring, especially in the USA.

Table 6.16 focuses on the RTA of the company across different technological fields, and shows that relative to other companies in the industry, Rhône Poulenc is specialized in inorganic chemicals, with an RTA of 2.71 and, to a lesser degree, organic chemicals (1.24). This highlights the change in strategy described above, as the company's relative strengths now lie in the fast-growing field of speciality chemicals. An RTA of 0.65 in textiles technologies demonstrates the move away from specialization in this field by Rhône Poulenc.

Rhône Poulenc also seems to have adopted a strategy of international specialization in its technological activity. As shown in Table 6.17, in its foreign research outside France the company is not very active in its two major fields of strength at home, inorganic and organic chemicals. Rhône Poulenc's international research is much more heavily focused on agricultural chemicals, which is also an area of strength at home but to a much lesser extent. Thus Rhône Poulenc has an international network in which foreign affiliates have a well-specified technological role.

Table 6.16 *The revealed technological advantage of Rhône Poulenc, CGE and Thomson, across fields of technological activity, 1969–90*

	Rhône Poulenc	CGE	Thomson
Food products	0.68		
Chemicals nes	1.16	1.23	0.45
Inorganic chemicals	2.71		
Organic chemicals	1.24	0.21	0.19
Agricultural chemicals	1.23		
Chemical processes	0.80	0.64	0.55
Bleaching and dyeing processes	0.47		
Pharmaceuticals	0.82		
Metals	0.35	1.01	0.49
Metallurgical processes	0.29	1.14	0.57
Other metal products	0.39	1.38	0.35
Mechanical engineering	1.19	0.00	0.25
Chemical equipment	1.36	1.32	0.14
Metal working equipment		0.76	0.31
Assembly equipment	1.77	0.68	0.18
Mining equipment			
Specialized industrial equipment	1.16	0.72	0.49
General industrial equipment	0.65	1.13	0.17
Electrical equipment nes	0.70	1.30	1.30
Telecommunications		1.51	1.83
Image and sound equipment		0.39	1.71
Semiconductors		0.25	0.98
Electrical systems	0.58	1.38	1.32
General electrical equipment	1.02	2.00	0.59
Office equipment	0.67	0.26	0.67
Motor vehicles			
Aircraft			
Other transport equipment			
Textiles			
Rubber and plastic products	0.79		
Non-metallic mineral products	1.08	0.83	0.59
Coal and petroleum products	0.55	0.15	1.18
Professional and scientific instruments	0.20	0.91	1.56
Photographic equipment	0.09	1.03	0.39
Other instruments	0.23	1.30	1.74
Other manufacturing	0.41	0.55	1.53

Note: Entries are only provided for the sectors of technological activity in which the world's largest firms in the industry in question were granted 1200 or more patents in the USA between 1969 and 1990.

Source: As for Table 6.1.

Table 6.17   The revealed technological advantage of Rhône Poulenc, CGE and Thomson, from their research facilities outside France, across fields of technological activity, 1969–90

	Rhône Poulenc	CGE	Thomson
Food products	1.59		
Chemicals nes	1.00	0.49	0.22
Inorganic chemicals	0.50		
Organic chemicals	0.83	0.00	0.00
Agricultural chemicals	8.35		
Chemical processes	0.63	0.68	0.31
Bleaching and dyeing processes	0.47		
Pharmaceuticals	1.69		
Metals	0.50	0.56	0.56
Metallurgical processes	0.00	0.58	0.00
Other metal products	0.83	0.51	1.54
Mechanical engineering	0.71	0.95	0.57
Chemical equipment	0.50	1.42	0.27
Metal working equipment		0.66	0.50
Assembly equipment	2.57	0.75	0.57
Mining equipment			
Specialized industrial equipment	0.85	0.58	1.32
General industrial equipment	0.35	0.72	0.18
Electrical equipment nes	0.83	1.17	1.29
Telecommunications		3.06	0.64
Image and sound equipment		0.69	4.88
Semiconductors		0.45	0.11
Electrical systems	0.95	0.88	1.30
General electrical equipment	0.59	0.19	0.85
Office equipment	5.31	0.76	1.55
Motor vehicles			
Aircraft			
Other transport equipment			
Textiles			
Rubber and plastic products	0.84		
Non-metallic mineral products	0.61	1.66	0.63
Coal and petroleum products	0.49	0.00	0.00
Professional and scientifc instruments	0.00	1.22	0.60
Photographic equipment	0.00	0.45	0.69
Other instruments	0.00	1.34	0.59
Other manufacturing	0.00	0.98	0.75

Note: Entries are only provided for the sectors of technological activity in which the world's largest firms in the industry in question were granted 1200 or more patents in the USA between 1969 and 1990.

Source: As for Table 6.1.

CGE

It was in 1974 that a new era in French telecommunications began, to be followed by a period of 'colbertisme high-tech' (Cohen, 1992), in which the French telecommunications network was transformed into one of the most modern and digitalized in the world. The main companies in this field in France at that time were CGE (the holding company of Alcatel) and Thomson. During the 1970s, the aim of CGE was to catch up with its rival, Siemens. It was believed that the way to achieve this goal would be to internationalize in order to stay at the top of an increasingly concentrated market, but Alcatel had to strengthen its domestic base before it could embark upon any kind of international strategy.

The Direction Generale des Telecommunications had attempted to increase the extent of competition in telecommunications between Thomson and CGE, but this proved to be inconsistent with the favoured strategies of both these firms (Sally, 1992). So in 1981, following the nationalization of six leading industrial concerns (including CGE and Thomson) by the new socialist government, CGE made it clear that it wanted to acquire Thomson's telecommunications activities. Following a period of negotiations, it was decided that Alcatel was to buy Thomson's wire, cable and telecommunications operations, while Thomson would get Alcatel's activities in consumer and military electronics. Thus, having achieved its aim of strengthening its domestic operations, Alcatel embarked upon its internationalization strategy.

Its initial ambition was to penetrate the US market and join up with AT&T, but this was to prove unsuccessful. Following this, CGE announced the formation of a new joint venture in 1986, Alcatel NV (registered in Holland), in which it would buy 56 per cent of ITT's world-wide telecommunications operations. This gave CGE an ideal way of gaining access to the new European markets. In the last five years, Alcatel has made further sizeable acquisitions abroad, and has become the second largest telecommunications company in the world, the largest manufacturer in public switching and cables, and the second biggest in transmission equipment. Sales abroad (including exports) represent 71 per cent of its total world sales in 1991, compared with 29 per cent in 1981 and 39 per cent in 1985. Germany is now Alcatel's biggest foreign market with 15.5 per cent of its sales.

Looking at the RTA of CGE across different technological fields, it is clear that its specialization lies in the field of telecommunications, as expected given its position as the second largest company in this field in the world (see Table 6.16). It is also relatively specialized in general electrical equipment and electrical systems. Like Rhône Poulenc, CGE's international research is much more narrowly focused than that at home in France. Abroad the company concentrates on extending its principal technological specialization in telecommunications, as is evident from Table 6.17. In its foreign research it demonstrates little interest so far in following its more general technological concerns in electrical systems and devices, and general electrical equipment.

Thomson

The European electronics industry has experienced far-reaching changes in the last ten years, in terms of the pattern of international trade, the composition of its products and the strategies of its firms. At the beginning of the 1970s, the European consumer electronics industry was characterized by national firms producing and selling in national markets. Partly because of incompatible technical standards in colour television and partly because of differences in national consumer tastes, there was relatively little intra-European trade in consumer electronics products.

This pattern began to change slowly at the end of the 1970s as a consequence of the expanding strength of Japanese industry, which began to erode the market shares of European producers in different electronics sectors. The response of the European firms varied. Some of the smaller ones left the industry, while others (such as Thomson) began a strategy of acquisitions to increase their competitiveness.

Thomson was already a highly diversified electronics group by this stage. In the 1960s and 1970s it had become involved in most major fields of electronics, and by 1981 it operated in about 20 different sectors. This reflected a policy of a spreading of risks. For example, it moved into telecommunications in 1981 when demand in the defence market was expected to fall. However, this presented Thomson with the major problem of higher costs. The cost of R&D was very high because Thomson was required to maintain its position in all its numerous markets. Furthermore, it was faced with the problem of multi-plant coordination and product duplication.

Thus from 1982 to 1992, Thomson, which had been nationalized in 1982 by the French government, managed important changes in its activities. In 1983 it disinvested from civilian telecommunications, which were taken over by CGE as described above. In 1987 Thomson sold its medical systems business to General Electric in the USA, and bought from General Electric its US consumer electronics business, RCA. In this ten year period, the company set about narrowing down its activities so that it could focus on its core business more efficiently. Thus by 1992 Thomson was involved in only three main activities, compared with 22 in 1982.

These three main activities, run by three subsidiaries, were defence electronics (Thomson-CSF), which accounts for 48 per cent of revenue; consumer electronics (Thomson Consumer Electronics; TCE), which accounts for 45 per cent of revenue, with the remaining 7 per cent of revenue coming from home appliances (Thomson Electromenager). More recently still, Thomson has sold Thomson Electromenager, and with it its white goods activities. The focusing of activities reflects a strategic decision to focus on those areas in which the company can be a world leader. Thus TCE is ranked fourth in the world consumer electronics industry, and Thomson-CSF is ranked second in the world defence electronics industry, aided by French government procurement and associated R&D funding in this field (Patel and Pavitt, 1990).

In 1980 Thomson was mainly a French-based group, with international sales representing 45.5 per cent of total sales. Only 13.8 per cent of these sales were products manufactured in foreign subsidiaries. By 1991 Thomson had improved its total internationalization even though its most multinational activity, medical sales, had been sold. International sales represented 70 per cent of total sales in 1991, and over half of these sales were manufactured in foreign subsidiaries. These sales derived mainly from production in Western Europe, but a quarter of sales were in the USA and 10 per cent in the Middle East.

The internationalization of manufacturing obviously affects the internationalization of technological activity. The international organization of R&D was built in the 1980s by the rationalization and coordination of the R&D centres in 17 countries. The main R&D centres of TCE are located in Germany and, to a lesser degree, in France. Outside Europe, R&D centres are located near to the market to deal mainly with adaptation to local conditions. Thus in Asia the R&D centres are specialized in accordance with the specific problems related to local production. Thomson is increasing its location of R&D centres in developing countries. Thus in 1989 a new factory built in Singapore contained an R&D centre.

Table 6.16 shows the RTA for Thomson relative to other firms in the industry. What is most evident is its comparative strength in image and sound equipment, as expected given the growth of TCE. Furthermore, it also reveals Thomson's relative strengths in the field of electrical systems and other instruments. Thomson follows the general pattern of the other leading French companies in establishing an international network which is quite highly specialized in terms of the distribution of research activities. In Thomson's case (see Table 6.17), research outside France is very heavily concentrated in the area of image and sound equipment. This high degree of focus may be attributed to Thomson's relatively recent internationalization, which, as noted above, has been linked to a strategy of emphasizing the consumer electronics segment of the business. Little foreign technological activity is carried out in scientific instruments (in which Thomson is strong at home), and the recent move away from telecommunications is also evident in Thomson's international profile, despite the fact that the firm retains some research expertise in that field in France. However, unlike CGE, Thomson is relatively specialized abroad in research into electrical systems and devices, as well as at home.

CONCLUSIONS

In the 1960s and 1970s, the largest French industrial firms were among the least internationalized in their research, by comparison with their leading European competitors. This has recently been changing quite dramatically. In the mid 1980s the major French chemical companies became more internationalized in their technological activity, and in the late 1980s the main French electrical equipment firms followed suit.

These French companies, and the foreign firms that have located research in France, have constructed international networks of technological activity which are geographically specialized. Foreign research facilities provide a specialized source of support to each MNC's overall technological development. In some cases companies take up technological activities abroad that lie outside their core areas, but which are related to them.

The very strong focus or narrow degree of specialization of the foreign research of the leading French firms may have to do with their comparatively recent internationalization. They have tended to concentrate outside France on selected existing fields of strength, in which their technological competence has already been established. This applies to Rhône Poulenc and its development of agricultural chemicals abroad, CGE in telecommunications and Thomson in image and sound equipment. Other areas of technological emphasis of these companies in France have largely been excluded from their foreign research strategies. Of course, this may well change as these foreign research facilities evolve under French corporate ownership. Over time, the technological profile of French-owned foreign affiliates may become more dispersed, in accordance with local conditions and to take advantage of local sources of expertise and innovation.

This is what we would expect on the basis of the experience of the formation of international networks for technological development in other more mature MNCs, originating from the UK and elsewhere. The broadening out of technological specialization in many of these companies has been linked to international locational specialization, in accordance with the locally specific characteristics of technological development in each site (Cantwell, 1992). The internationalization of technological activity in the French case is also unlikely to be a matter of simply extending the same fields of development abroad, but will increasingly involve international corporate networks aimed at an internationally integrated structure of technology creation.

NOTE

1. The authors wish to thank Frédérique Sachwald for helpful comments on an earlier draft.

BIBLIOGRAPHY

Acs, Z.J. and Audretsch, D.B. (1989), 'Patents as a Measure of Innovative Activity', *Kyklos*, **42**(2), 171–80.

Bartlett, C. and Ghoshal, S. (1989), *Managing Across Borders: The Transnational Solution*, Boston: Harvard Business School Press.

Cantwell, J.A. (1989), *Technological Innovation and Multinational Corporations*, Oxford: Basil Blackwell.

Cantwell, J.A. (1991), 'Historical Trends in International Patterns of Technological Innovation', in J. Foreman-Peck (ed.), *New Perspectives on the Late Victorian Economy: Essays in Quantitative British Economic History, 1860–1914*, Cambridge: Cambridge University Press.

Cantwell, J.A. (1992), 'The Internationalisation of Technological Activity and its Implications for Competitiveness', in O. Granstrand, L. Håkanson and S. Sjölander (eds), *Technology Management and International Business: Internationalization of R&D and Technology*, Chichester: John Wiley.

Cantwell, J.A. (1993a), 'Introduction', in J.A. Cantwell (ed.), *Transnational Corporations and Innovatory Activities*, London: Routledge.

Cantwell, J.A. (1993b), 'Corporate Technological Specialisation in International Industries', in M.C. Casson and J. Creedy (eds), *Economic Inequality and Industrial Concentration*, Aldershot: Edward Elgar.

Cantwell, J.A. (1995), 'The Globalisation of Technology: What Remains of the Product Cycle Model?', *Cambridge Journal of Economics*, **19**(1), February, 155–74.

Cantwell, J.A. and Hodson, C. (1991), 'Global R&D and UK Competitiveness', in M.C. Casson (ed.), *Global Research Strategy and International Competitiveness*, Oxford: Basil Blackwell.

Cantwell, J.A. and Sanna Randaccio, F. (1992), 'Intra-industry Direct Investment in the European Community: Oligopolistic Rivalry and Technological Competition', in J.A. Cantwell (ed.), *'Multinational Investment in Modern Europe: Strategic Interaction in the Integrated Community'*, Aldershot: Edward Elgar.

Cohen, E. (1992), *Le Colbertisme High-Tech: Economie des Telecommunications et du Grand Projet*, Paris: Hachette.

Cook, P.L. and Sharp, M.L. (1991), 'The Chemical Industry', in C.Freeman, M.L. Sharp and W. Walker (eds), *Technology and the Future of Europe: Global Competition and the Environment in the 1990s*, London: Frances Pinter.

Dunning, J.H. (1992), *Multinational Enterprises and the Global Economy*, Wokingham: Addison-Wesley.

Dunning, J.H. and Pearce, R.D. (1985), *The World's Largest Industrial Enterprises, 1962–1983*, Farnborough: Gower.

Etemad, H. and Séguin Delude, L. (1985), 'The Development of Technology in MNEs: A Cross-Country and Industry Study', paper presented at the Round Table on 'International Technical Transfers in Advanced Countries: Multinational Firms and National Policies', University of Paris, Dauphine, September.

Griliches, Z. (1990), 'Patent Statistics as Economic Indicators: A Survey, *Journal of Economic Literature,* **28**(4), December, 1661–707.

Griliches, Z., Pakes, A. and Hall, B.H. (1987), 'The Value of Patents as Indicators of Inventive Activity', in P. Dasgupta and P. Stoneman (eds), *Economic Policy and Technological Performance*, Cambridge: Cambridge University Press.

Hedlund, G. (1986), 'The Hypermodern MNC: A Heterarchy?', *Human Resource Management*, **25**, Spring, 9–25.

Lundvall, B.A. (1988), 'Innovation as an Interactive Process: From User-Producer Interaction to the National System of Innovation', in G. Dosi, C. Freeman, R. Nelson, G. Silverberg and L.L.G. Soete (eds), *Technical Change and Economic Theory,* London: Frances Pinter.

Michalet, C.A. and Delapierre, M. (1975), *The Multinationalisation of French Firms*, Chicago: Academy of International Business Reprint.

Papanastassiou, M. and Pearce, R.D. (1993), 'Les Activités de Recherche des Multinationales Japonaises en Europe', in F. Sachwald (ed.), *Les Entreprises Japonaises en Europe: Motivations et Stratégies*, Paris: IFRI.

Patel, P. and Pavitt, K.L.R. (1989), 'Do Large Firms Control the World's Technology?', University of Sussex Science Policy Research Unit Discussion Paper, January.

Patel, P. and Pavitt, K.L.R. (1990), 'Sources and Directions of Technological Accumulation in France: A Statistical Comparison with FR Germany and the UK', *Technology Analysis and Strategic Management,* **2**(1).

Patel, P. and Pavitt, K.L.R. (1993), 'The Continuing, Widespread (and Neglected) Importance of Improvements in Mechanical Technologies', University of Sussex Science Policy Research Unit STEEP Discussion Papers, No. 2, January.

Pavitt, K.L.R. (1988) 'Uses and Abuses of Patent Statistics', in A. van Raan (ed.), *Handbook of Quantitative Studies of Science Policy*, Amsterdam: North-Holland.

Pavitt, K.L.R., Robson, M. and Townsend, J. (1989), 'Technological Accumulation, Diversification and Organization in UK Companies, 1945–83', *Management Science*, **35**(1), 81–99.

Pearce, R.D. (1989), *The Internationalisation of Research and Development by Multinational Enterprises,* London: Macmillan.

Pearce, R.D. and Singh, S. (1992), *Globalising Research and Development,* London: Macmillan.

Sally, R. (1992), 'Internationalisation and Competitive Challenge: The Case of Thomson Consumer Electronics', paper presented at the EIBA Annual Meeting at the University of Reading, December.

Savary, J. (1984), *French Multinationals*, London: Frances Pinter.

Scherer, F.M. (1983), 'The Propensity to Patent', *International Journal of Industrial Organization*, **1**, 107–28.

Schmookler, J. (1966), *Invention and Economic Growth*, Cambridge, Mass.: Harvard University Press.

Vernon, R. (1979), 'The Product Cycle Hypothesis in the New International Environment', *Oxford Bulletin of Economics and Statistics,* **41**(4), November, 255–67.

APPENDIX: LIST OF FRENCH FIRMS INCLUDED IN THE WORLD'S LARGEST IN SELECTED INDUSTRIES

Chemicals and Pharmaceuticals

Rhône Poulenc
Charbonnages de France
L'Air Liquide
Entreprise Miniere et Chemique
L'Oreal

Electrical and Office Equipment

Generale d'Electricité (CGE)
Thomson
Sagem
CII-Honeywell Bull

Motor Vehicles

Renault
Peugeot
Valeo
Usines Chausson

Aircraft

Aerospatiale
Dassault
Matra
Snecma

Building Materials

Saint Gobain
Lafarge-Coppee

PART III

Innovation and Competitive Advantage

7. Technical change on a global market: competition in solar cell development

Hariolf Grupp

1. GLOBAL TECHNOLOGY APPROPRIATION: MEASUREMENT OPPORTUNITIES AND PROBLEMS

This chapter attempts to contribute to the understanding of the often invisible mechanisms of global creation and appropriation of technological knowledge by innovative firms. It is based on new indicators for technology measurement that reflect also sources of tacit knowledge of innovation on international markets. Although the econometric analyses introduced in this chapter are suitable for the assessment of global effects of technology and competitiveness in general, the empirical analysis is presented in terms of a case study on photovoltaics. After a very brief sketch of modern models of the innovative firm is given, the data samples are discussed. Respective data for three markets and 24 companies are outlined. More than one trajectory of the 'technological paradigm' under consideration is studied in comparison. Technology creation and competitive performance of the firms are put into perspective with the achieved global market penetration of the innovative products. Some general conclusions on science-based firms in rapidly growing worldwide markets are derived.

Photovoltaics is a field of applied engineering; the innovative products constructed from photovoltaic knowledge are commonly called 'solar cells'. In terms of knowledge creation and innovation strategies, photovoltaics is a field of activities with interesting properties as – due to the oil price adjustments of the 1970s – most governments intervened in the respective markets for renewable energy, thus creating coordination problems.

The hypothesis is that the government interactions continue to be particularly strong in photovoltaics and are not overridden by the globalization of modern technology. Thus for firms producing photovoltaic products it is very important to guarantee close interaction with the public research on renewable energy sources and – as photovoltaics is a science-based technology, as will be shown – also with institutions active in basic research. With this background, the quantitative instruments proposed in this chapter are tested in a rather complex case study. On the other hand, when market failure is assumed by governments, as in the photovoltaics case, new analytical instruments are required more than in cases when the price signals from the markets are more reliable.

Traditionally, economics has taken into account only the productivity-raising effect of technological change and technological knowledge. However, innovation has at least the potential to change the variety of business organizations and casual observation suggests that the variety of the economic system has indeed changed quite dramatically (Saviotti, 1994, p. 28) In the case of photovoltaics, these changes since the beginning of the 1970s are beyond doubt. This allows old questions to be answered in a new way and problems not previously on the agenda to be formulated (Nonaka, 1991).

One of these items is the relationship between scientific and techno-economic paradigms. Already in 1962 Machlup had written: 'The production of knowledge is an economic activity, an industry, if you like ... but economists have neglected to analyse the production of knowledge' (Machlup, 1962, p. 9). Freeman *et al.* (1982, p. 47) mention the importance of basic science as a source of radical technological breakthroughs. And – again relevant for the photovoltaics case – Freeman and Perez (1988, pp. 40–66) assume that each techno-economic paradigm is coupled to a specific national innovation system which includes both the scientific infrastructure and national R&D and thus interaction with government.

In the framework of the emerging 'new economics of science' (Dasgupta and David, 1987), codification of knowledge is a step in the process of reducing *complexity* for markets and makes knowledge a non-rival, durable public good. Scientific papers may represent quantified knowledge on science, and patents codified knowledge on technology. For measuring the tacit (Polanyi, 1966), embodied knowledge included in innovative products, measurement of technological characteristics is also required. Here, the newly established technometric concept (Grupp, 1994) may be embarked upon. This requires consultation with technology experts and thus the handling of multi-disciplinarity in industrial economics.

In very general terms, technological innovation is problem-solving. The technological paradigms which relate to products' attributes are progressively developed by socio-economic uses or requirements (for example, for solving the energy crisis in the case of photovoltaics). Companies pursuing innovative activities are strongly selective and cumulative, and direct the appropriation of technical opportunities towards their (future) markets. Because this creates inertia, technological trajectories (Nelson and Winter, 1982; Dosi, 1988) bring about dominant product design configurations (Utterback and Abernathy, 1975).

A dominant design usually takes the form of a new product with given characteristics (in the sense of Lancaster, 1991) that is synthesized from individual technological innovations introduced cumulatively in prior product variants. A dominant design has the effect of enforcing or encouraging standardization so that production economies can be achieved (Utterback and Suárez, 1993). The variety of possible new products is narrowed to few realized products or innovations. Dominant design configurations can be identified in many product lines (for photovoltaic products, see below). These often have the result of drastically reducing the number of performance requirements to be met by a product by making many features implicit in the dominant design and increasing its acceptance by business rivals (*ibid.*).

The technological opportunities may depend on science exogenous to the company, originating from the national R&D infrastructure (R&D institutions other than industrial ones). Networking firms or multinational companies may participate in the knowledge shared by national infrastructures of more than one country. The appropriation of technological knowledge determines the mode of innovative search that each technological paradigm entails (Dosi, 1988, p. 1138). The incentives from the related markets of the relevant sector determine the growth of demand, elasticities of income and changes in relative factor prices.

Differential behaviour of firms within one branch may be influenced by internal learning effects, the innovation strategies decided upon by the corporate executive management, and the industrial structure and size of the firm giving reason for rivalry. Companies differ both in the innovation strategies pursued and in the level of technological performance already mastered. The learning effects include accumulation of knowledge as well as the participation of the firm in the diffusion of knowledge within the national system or internationally. Measuring technological knowledge has to take account of these factors as completely as possible.

At the beginning of the 1980s a series of 'metrics' for evaluating and comparing technological sophistication and quality were proposed. What the author of this chapter coined 'technometrics' in 1985 (Grupp and Hohmeyer, 1986) is a procedure designed along Lancaster's consumer theory (Lancaster, 1991) and is based on the observation that every innovative product or process has a set of key attributes that defines its performance, value or ability to satisfy customer wants. Many of these attributes can be quantified. For instance, in the case of solar cells, such attributes as standard power, voltage, power per unit of area, power per unit of weight and warranty time can all be defined and measured in physical units. Each of these attributes has a different unit of measurement. Problems then arise in aggregating attributes to build a single quality index. Mathematical details of the general procedure are omitted here as they may be found elsewhere (Grupp, 1994). Suffice to say that the technometric indicator surmounts this difficulty by converting each measured attribute into a [0,1] metric, enabling construction of weighted averages, and so on, and permitting comparisons across products, firms, industries and countries. The '0' point of the metric is set as the technologically standard attribute; the '1' point is set as the most technologically sophisticated attribute in existence. Technometric profiles may be used for measuring the firm-specific technological performance level, one of the important determinants for innovation, which includes tacit knowledge. Yet the compilation of technometric data is time-consuming as the specifications are not accessible in data banks. In particular, technometric time-series data are very difficult to obtain and rather costly (*ibid.*). The measure also does not differentiate between the sources of technological know-how. It may be created within the firm by R&D, by learning by doing or learning by using, or by adoption of innovative solutions developed by other industries or firms and embodied in capital equipment and intermediate inputs (Pavitt, 1984).

Besides technometric measurement, therefore, the use of *patent indicators* is suggestive. As patent data represent a widely accepted proxy measure for technology performance (Griliches, 1990) along with technometrics; and as, compared with the latter, they are relatively easy to compile; and further, as they are always assigned to the first innovator but not to the imitator, the adopter or the learning company; it may be assumed that patent data are a good proxy for the explicit and codified firm-specific technology generation process.

In the analysis of global technology appropriation only the part of the inventions for which patent protection has been applied for in several important markets, in particular the triad countries, may serve as a good measure of technology. Thereby, effects originating from the corporate strategy and advantages of companies on domestic markets are taken into consideration. This type of patent search must be based on data from more than one patent office (Schmoch *et al.*, 1988). Together with the more recent patents, the stock of existing intellectual property determines the actual technology levels achieved, as technological knowledge acquisition is a cumulative procedure.

2.   TECHNOLOGY DEVELOPMENT AND STRUCTURES OF THE GLOBAL PHOTOVOLTAIC MARKET

In 1839 the French physicist A.E. Becquerel observed that an electric current in an electrolytic solution increased when the apparatus stood in the sun: the photoelectric effect had been discovered. It took 40 years before this effect was proved to exist also in solids. In 1887 it was explicitly described and named ('codified') by the German physicist, H.R. Hertz. The full theoretical understanding of the phenomenon by Einstein was applied in a 'modern' solar cell at the Bell Laboratories in 1954, when an effectiveness of 6 per cent on silicon substrate was achieved. Photovoltaic engineering became a postwar technology with a market development cycle of about 25 years.

Demand for this new technology came from the extraterrestrial activities of the superpowers. Terrestrial activities benefited from this. Moreover, the technology was able to draw on a great deal of know-how from semiconductor engineering, especially from silicon power electronics. This is why the silicon solar cell still has a considerable development lead over alternative materials. The modern solar cell is a large surface semiconductor element, comprising a charge-isolating structure and electrical contacts for the circuitry. Generally speaking, a cell cannot be routinely used as a source of an electric current: the smallest useful unit is called a module. According to its purpose of application a module has standardized parameters and dimensions and is suitably protected against environmental effects. Photovoltaic systems cover the performance span from microwatt (μW) to megawatt (MW), that is, 12 orders of magnitude.

In terms of dominant design configurations it is customary to distinguish 'thick' cells (for example, those of crystalline silicon) and thin-film cells (for example, those of amorphous silicon). In the manufacture of 'thick' cells there are again two dominant configurations based on either monocrystalline or polycrystalline silicon. Thick cells involve the sawing of rods or blocks of silicon into wafers. Half of the silicon is wasted in this process. Thin-film cells are far less wasteful. Amorphous silicon is now being predominantly used in consumer electronics. The minimodules are supplied directly to the electronic manufacturers and are rarely offered on the seller market (Original Equipment Manufacturers products).

Photovoltaic systems are attractive electricity sources because:

- they contain no moving parts subject to wear and tear;
- they require no fuel;
- they do not pollute the environment in operation;
- they require little maintenance if carefully manufactured and installed;
- they can be produced from silicon, a material available in unlimited quantity;
- they are modular in structure and can serve a broad spectrum of functions.

The eight most important characteristics (with their measuring units) are peak power (W), power variety (ΔW), voltage (standard conditions; V), voltage stability (ΔV), power per unit of module area (W/cm^2), power per unit of module weight (W/kg), lifetime (warranty time; a) and production technology ($/W). This set of technometric specifications was used in 1986 after extensive interviewing of technical experts to compare companies' and countries' performance levels (Grupp *et al.*, 1987). According to this demarcation, market surveys for many brands were published in 1987 and 1992 with data for the above-mentioned specifications of several companies and end-user prices on the German market (Meereis, 1987, revised 1991). The infant photovoltaic industry may be analysed with international data with the help of a branch news service (*PV News*, various issues 1984–93).

The photovoltaic market has expanded over the past 15 years; turnover figures of manufacturing industry show double-figure annual increments. Because of government subsidies and government pilot plants (see below), it is difficult to compare prices on the world photovoltaic markets. It is more common to measure production and module shipments (as a proxy for turnover) in 'megawatts' for the peak electricity to be produced with these modules. Megawatts may be regarded as one of the 'special' statistical units, such as 'number of robots' or 'kilograms of raw materials', used instead of the value of production. Table 7.1 lists the world photovoltaic module production by country of origin. According to Table 7.1 the growth factor of production between 1980 and 1992 is about 18. The growth rates after 1987 are remarkable.

Table 7.1   *World's photovoltaic consumer and commercial module production (MW peak)*

	USA	Europe	Japan	Other than triad	World
1980	2.5	0.3	0.5	–	3.3
1981	3.5	0.8	1.1	–	5.4
1982	5.2	1.4	1.7	0.1	8.4
1983	12.7	3.3	4.3	0.5	20.8
1984	11.5	3.3	6.2	0.6	21.6
1985	7.6	3.7	10.8	1.4	23.5
1986	7.0	4.3	13.4	2.3	27.0
1987	8.7	4.7	12.5	2.8	28.7
1988	11.3	6.9	13.0	4.0	35.2
1989	14.7	7.9	14.2	5.3	42.1
1990	14.8	10.2	16.8	4.7	46.5
1991	17.1	13.4	19.8	5.0	55.3
1992	18.5	16.4	18.8	4.2	57.9

Source: *PV News*, various issues 1984–93.

Most interesting is the breakdown of photovoltaic production by dominant design configurations as introduced below (Table 7.2). The largest segment of photovoltaic production is due to monocrystalline silicon, a niche with strong government procurement, for example, for power supply to satellites. A strong increase is observed for amorphous silicon with wide applications for consumer products. However, there are technical stability problems with degradation in amorphous thin layers and also a certain demand saturation in the consumer market so that, in spite of the tempestuous development of the amorphous material, the future of crystalline silicon should not be prematurely discounted. Polycrystalline silicon modules are cheaper than monocrystalline ones, but their efficiency is lower as well as their lifetime. Still, polycrystalline modules are more durable products than amorphous modules.

Table 7.2   *World's photovoltaic module production by dominant design configuration (%)*

	Monocrystal	Polycrystal	Amorphous	Others
1983	50.2	14.3	14.3	21.2
1988	37.2	22.4	39.5	0.9
1989	42.5	25.5	31.1	0.9
1990	35.3	32.9	31.6	0.2
Breakdown 1990:	100	100	100	100
USA	43.9	35.3	14.3	100
Europe	18.9	38.6	8.2	0
Japan	15.2	22.9	73.5	0
Other than triad	22.0	3.2	4.0	0

Source: As Table 7.1.

Table 7.2 makes one point very clear: the three dominant designs described above cover about 98 per cent of the present markets, with quite stable segments each, so that the general concept of the definition and demarcation of such designs is well justified in the case of photovoltaics. Other designs played a role in the early, exploratory phases of development and may come back in the future.

Price development is difficult to describe. Prices paid per megawatt depend on the power class of the modules. Strong economies of scale are the case. Average final prices per megawatt, which were more than US$ 10 million in around 1980, dropped to about $6 million at the end of the decade. This reduction in prices is certainly less dramatic than the expansion of the related markets.

In terms of market segmentation one can differentiate between three major segments. On the low power side are consumer products for watches, pocket calculators, displays and toys. Capital goods include those for telecommunications (mobile radio, emergency call stations, railway signals, radar, and so on), water handling (pumps, desalination, irrigation, and so on), off-the-grid residential applications (lamplights, air conditioning, heat pumps, water purification, and so on), off-the-grid industrial and commercial applications, and grid-connected and central station applications. The third category is government procurement including orbit, space and defence applications. Table 7.3 indicates the growing importance of consumer products; government procurement is, however, an important market segment for durable products and high prices.

Table 7.3   *World's photovoltaic module production by market niche of application (%)*

	Consumer products	Capital goods	Government procurement
1988	31.5	59.4	9.1
1989	33.0	57.5	9.5
Breakdown 1989:	100	100	100
USA	21.5	46.7	10.0
Europe	10.8	16.5	60.0
Japan	65.5	19.0	12.5
Other than triad	2.2	17.8	17.5

Source: As Table 7.1.

The market segments are not homogeneously distributed in the triad regions. Japan is strongest in consumer products, the United States in capital investment goods, and Europe's strongest customers are governments (by procurement). Why is this so? Following the rapid increase in petroleum prices since 1973, all governments of industrialized nations intended to stimulate renewable energy production. The related so-called 'commercialization programmes' were intended to speed up the process by which renewable energy technologies are developed, tested, demonstrated, produced and disseminated. Obviously, governments made the tacit assumption of market failure. In particular, government R&D managers and administrators pushed the technology prematurely to commercialization status. As a supplement to private efforts rather than a driving force, the government supply-oriented strategies created uncertainty for the companies involved, resulting from the inevitable vagaries of public policy, especially in the United States (Roessner, 1984). Many companies joined government R&D programmes in order to reduce their development costs dramatically.

In later stages of their work, producers of cells and modules were displeased because of an emphasis on R&D from the side of governments which implied that the technology was not commercially ready. Increased R&D efforts also shorten the time before which current technology will become obsolete. Thus some performers believed that fewer public resources should be spent on current technology, in particular in the United States (*ibid.*).

Governments did not only support private R&D but also provided markets and raised public awareness about the technology. Because the United States and European countries were both strong in satellite technology, they concentrated their early photovoltaic R&D on crystalline material; Japan turned instead to amorphous materials which were selected because they lend themselves more easily to mass production (Clark and Juma, 1987, p. 156).

State intervention in all these countries has also been directed at the structure of the photovoltaic industry itself, mainly to consolidate existing financial and market resources so as to strengthen national competitiveness (Krupp, 1992). In France, for example, the state was instrumental in the creation of a single company which is a consolidation of financial and photovoltaic-related capabilities previously held by three different French companies (Clark and Juma, 1987, p. 157). Another public sector application that has not received much attention in the literature is the military application of photovoltaics. There are tactical reasons for using photovoltaics since the recharging of batteries can be done quietly. The United States already sells a large share of its photovoltaic modules to the military under a government procurement programme (*ibid.*, p. 158). This is another area which is insulated from market requirements and which can therefore be used to underwrite the initial high costs of system development.

3. DEVELOPMENT AND STRUCTURE OF GLOBAL PHOTOVOLTAIC KNOWLEDGE

A patent database search to identify the most important producers of company R&D may provide an important piece of intelligence on the distribution of international know-how. As patent applications are legal documents that are valid in only one country, many foreign 'duplications' of domestic priority patent applications are generated. The selection of patent data from only one patent office, therefore, does not always yield an indicator that is representative of the world output of inventions. Duplications of patents can be traced and matched to each other, and so-called 'patent families' may be defined, centring around one invention and bringing together the foreign property rights from all countries of the world.

Table 7.4 gives an overview of the distribution of patents on photovoltaics technology from several countries of origin and on several destination markets. The company level is discussed below. Table 7.4 makes clear that the technology know-how encoded in patents is not the same if the data sources of just one country (patent office) are used. For industrial economics this means that a selection of one national data pool may give misleading results. The countries under investigation pursue quite different globally oriented

Table 7.4   Generation of technology as measured by inventions on designated markets for industrial property, priority years 1970–84

Country of origin	Inventions with domestic applications (1)	Inventions with domestic and foreign applications (2)	All foreign duplications (3)	Outward orientation (2)/(1)	No. of countries protected (average) (3)/(2)
USA	2093	777	4713	37.1%	6.1
Japan	5797	555	1762	9.6%	3.2
EU	1246	718	3830	57.6%	5.3
Germany	570	315	1565	55.3%	5.0
France	365	191	989	52.3%	5.2
UK	193	128	673	66.3%	5.3
Other than triad	339	83	399	24.5%	4.8

Foreign destination markets in per cent of (2)

	USA	Japan	Germany	France	UK
USA	–	68.9	53.6	52.2	49.5
Japan	100.0	–	75.1	58.9	50.1
Germany	64.1	56.5	–	53.0	44.3
France	77.1	58.5	50.1	–	41.5

Source: On-line patent searches; see Schmoch *et al.*, 1988.

innovation strategies. Only parts of their technology know-how will be available on foreign markets.[1]

About two-thirds of the external patent applications of United States companies in photovoltaics are made for the Japanese market. This is the most preferred foreign market for American companies. The major European markets are less completely covered with intellectual property from the United States, with no particular differences between the European countries. Japan directs its foreign patent activities preferably to the United States, the largest OECD market. Fewer intellectual property rights are placed within Europe and here preferably in Germany. In the United Kingdom just half of the Japanese claims than in the United States are upheld. Germany's photovoltaic companies are certainly trying to cover their European neighbour markets with foreign property rights, but Japan seems to be also an interesting market-place for German products. For French companies foreign patent activities are lower, as is technology generation in photovoltaics in general.

This diversified picture of knowledge flows between nations is also found for individual companies. As one has to differentiate between inter-sectoral and intra-sectoral determinants of innovation (Dosi, 1988), a country-wise analysis is not sufficient – the firm level ought to be the primary level of analysis. 'After all, industries do not advance technologies, firms within those industries do' (Chesbrough, 1994, p. 3). However, standard critique is that such analysis on the firm level is biased towards the surviving successful firms, whereas pioneers, merged and acquired units or bankrupts are left out of the sample as there are no data left. As a remedy, it is attempted here to include firms putting out patents on photovoltaics as well, even if they never innovated in the sense that they introduced new products on commercial markets. By this procedure, the list of photovoltaic producers reproduced in Table 7.5 was compiled. The pioneers with patents but no production are mentioned in the column 'knowledge source'. The companies collected in Table 7.5 cover 80 per cent of global solar cell production. The missing firms are mostly located in developing countries such as Brazil or India.

Let us look at the leading American corporation in photovoltaics in terms of patents in 1981–84. RCA is not part of the analysis in subsequent sections, as its amorphous photovoltaic activities have been taken over by Solarex. Energy Conversion Devices (ECD) and Standard Oil jointly founded Sovonics, which is engaged in amorphous technology. The firm has performed contract research for IBM, Atlantic Richfield (ARCO), Sharp and others. Market introduction of own products was announced several times but did not come true. It is likely that ARCO Solar and Sharp (a joint venture with Sharp holding 51 per cent) used ECD as an external knowledge source. The activities of Exxon were marketed by Solar Power until 1983, when Exxon decided

Table 7.5 *List of enterprises in photovoltaics and basic data**

Enterprise	Country	Technology	Production since	German market	Knowledge source
AEG/Telefunken	DEU	m p	1978	yes	own, today Daimler-Benz
ARCO Solar	USA	m p a	1979	yes	own, ECD, today Siemens
BP Solar	ESP/GBR	m p a	(<?) 1983	yes	own, ECD
Canon	JPN	?	1990	no	own, ECD
Chronar	JPN	a	(<?) 1987	yes	own
Fuji Electric	JPN	a	(<?) 1983	no	own, Sharp
Helios	ITA	m	1983	yes	own, Solec
Hoxan	JPN	m	(<?) 1983	yes	own
Kanegafuchi	JPN	a	1984 (?)	OEM (Casio)	own
Kyocera	JPN	p a	1983	yes	own, Mobil Solar, Wacker
Matsushita	JPN	m a	(<?) 1983	no	own, film technology
Mitsubishi	JPN	m a	(<?) 1983	no	own
Mobil Solar	USA	m	1975	yes	own, Tyco
Nukem	DEU	a°	(<?) 1991	yes	own, Univ. of Stuttgart
Photowatt	USA/FRA	m p	1980	yes	own, CGE, Elf, Fuji
Rade Koncar	Ex-YUG	a	(<?) 1992	yes	?
Sanyo	JPN	a	(<?) 1983	no (OEM)	own
Sharp	JPN	m a	(<?) 1983	no (OEM)	own, ECD
Siemens	DEU	m a	1983	yes	own, Interatom, ARCO

Solarex	USA	m p a	1978	yes	own, RCA, Exxon
Solec	USA	m	1977	yes	own, today Pilkington
Sovolco/Boeing	USA	a°	not yet	no	own
Sovonics	JPN	a	(<?) 1987	yes	ECD
Taijo Yuden	JPN	a	(<?) 1983	no (OEM)	own

Notes:

'm' denotes monocrystalline, 'p' polycrystalline and 'a' amorphous silicon technology.

'a°' means amorphous cells based on other materials than silicon.

'<?' indicates that production in the given year is confirmed but probably had already started earlier (lack of information).

The country codes are as follows: DEU = Germany, ESP = Spain, FRA = France, GBR = United Kingdom, ITA = Italy, JPN = Japan, YUG = Yugoslavia.

Sources: *PV News*, various years; Meereis (1987), Grupp *et al.* (1994).

to give up this business. Most of the 'technology inventory' of Solar Power was acquired by Solarex.

Matsushita is a company with a strong patent base but only limited market activities (pilot plants). It is not included in the analysis which follows. Other firms are very specialized (for example, Kanegafuchi on electronic materials). Among the German firms, BASF and Wacker Chemitronic (Hoechst) do not manufacture cells or modules but provide substrate materials. AEG and Telefunken were merged and now belong (together with MBB) to Deutsche Aerospace, a subsidiary of Daimler Benz AG.

Siemens specializes in single crystal solar cells and is the leading German company in this field. It was a late starter in photovoltaics, was not involved in the early satellite activities of other German companies and developed its activities within an affiliated nuclear research establishment. ARCO Solar (an affiliation of the Atlantic Richfield Corporation) established the world's largest production capacity for single crystal modules between 1979 and 1983. As a second major field of activity ARCO also started intensive R&D on amorphous silicon. Hoxan (Hokkusan) expanded its single crystal business around the year 1985 and is one of the few Japanese companies to concentrate on this design, with little activity in the amorphous products field.

The patent data discussed so far indicate R&D activities but are not good proxies for the levels of technological sophistication achieved and thus of tacit knowledge of the respective companies. Technology performance levels may be measured by the technometric approach (see section 1). As an illustration, the technology performance portfolios for the single crystal solar cells of the three leading companies from the United States, Japan and Germany are compared (see Table 7.6). The specifications selected and the data sources (valid for 1987) are given in section 2.

Table 7.6   Technometric performance profiles of single crystal cells by three leading manufacturers (1987)

	Siemens	ARCO	Hoxan
Peak power	1.00	0.63	0.38
Power variety	1.00	0.56	0.05
Voltage	1.00	0.45	0.18
Voltage stability	1.00	0.64	0.87
Area (normalized)	0.86	0.97	1.00
Weight (normalized)	0.87	0.90	0.88
Lifetime	0.44	1.00	1.00
Production technology	1.00	0.97	0.96

The technometric profiles in Table 7.6 look quite different. It is intended to discuss the 1987 data in retrospect in order to make comparisons with subsequent production values possible. Whereas Siemens' products are very strong in the power- and stability-related areas (which are typical requirements for central electricity stations or grid-connected applications), the products are less sophisticated in terms of area- and weight-specific electricity production (this is to say, they are larger and heavier than other products). Obviously the company, starting its photovoltaic activities in a nuclear R&D laboratory, was preoccupied with central electricity production. For mobile power generation, weight and size factors are much more important than for grid-connected installations. Both the ARCO and Hoxan products are strong in these size- and area-specific features but lower in performance specifications concerning power and stability. The products of ARCO, one of the pioneers in this technology, are definitely more sophisticated in power- and stability-related specifications than those of the late starter, Hoxan. The products of both companies seem to be designed for off-the-grid applications which are far more interesting from the market size perspective. Off-the-grid residential, industrial and commercial applications exceeded the central station and grid-connected applications in 1989 by a factor of 12 on the American market (*PV News*, 1990, **9**(2), p. 3). Thus in the three company comparison, Siemens offers high quality products for very small market segments whereas the Japanese and American firms offer medium quality for the larger market segments where some sophisticated specifications are not so important.

This picture for the year 1987 gives a clear indication that the innovation performance of the various companies is quite different. Technology activities and the performance levels achieved differ depending on the market segments aimed at. Nowadays, Hoxan is probably the largest manufacturer of single crystal cells in Japan (whereas most other Japanese companies were innovative in amorphous technology too). The company directed its know-how acquisition into the direction of the most important market segment – other than the market in which Siemens was involved. In 1990 Siemens acquired ARCO Solar from Atlantic Richfield in order to open up a US business (Siemens Solar) but also to complement its own technology, which was streamlined towards markets with little prospects. Reportedly, Siemens has not been successful with its acquisition, as Siemens Solar reduced prices to distributors in 1992 in order to increase sales. The firm went to court against Atlantic Richfield in 1993 claiming that the latter knew about the low commercial revenues of ARCO Solar's products.

Such a 'simple' technology as photovoltaics, with only one principal application, that is, electricity generation, is indeed very complex in terms of technology, is heavily science-based, and is associated with wide-ranging and important spillovers and external effects on other fields of technological knowledge. Country-wise and company-wise, the relevant know-how is codified in various ways (scientific publications, conference proceedings, domestic and foreign patent documents). As for an overview of international activities in photovoltaic technology, one has to be very careful about the preference of innovative firms for certain domestic or foreign markets. This may again be related to the fact that the photovoltaic markets are regulated, that national systems of innovation (and thus corporate access to public research) play a role and that government procurement and subsidies shape the development of this technology. Yet there are effective quantitative tools to throw some light on the situation and to create intelligence on what is going on in this field. Industrial economics can make use of these tools in order to analyse international developments and global innovation.

4.   APPROPRIATION OF GLOBAL TECHNOLOGY BY PHOTOVOLTAIC FIRMS

The technometric indices seem to unfold quite a rich spectrum of diversity within one innovative product group, so that the ranking of priorities and the definition of technology gaps become quite complex. These types of innovation indicator seem to provide important data for industrial economics. How, then, are the technological performance characteristics related to codified technology generation as reflected in patents? In Figure 7.1 those inventions with international significance are compared with the technometric indices for selected photovoltaic companies. All three dominant designs (single crystal, polycrystal and amorphous) are included in the diagram. The selection criterion for patent statistics was that only those inventions for which a foreign duplication at least in the United States, in Japan and in Europe was filed were taken into consideration (see Table 7.4). By this criterion the 'triad' model is applied, requiring protection of intellectual property in each of the triad blocs (Grupp, 1994).

The lessons for clarifying the role global technology knowledge plays for the technology levels to be achieved are two-fold. First of all, in general terms, the more patents with international significance a company takes out, the more sophisticated its product innovations seem to be.[2] On the other hand, some companies, such as Kyocera, Solec, Hoxan and possibly others, offer very sophisticated products on world markets with no comparable patent production.

There are three possible explanations for this observation. First, these companies may have a very good tacit in-house knowledge base in the relevant technology, but rely on secrecy or very short market introduction times and do not care for comprehensive, international protection. Another

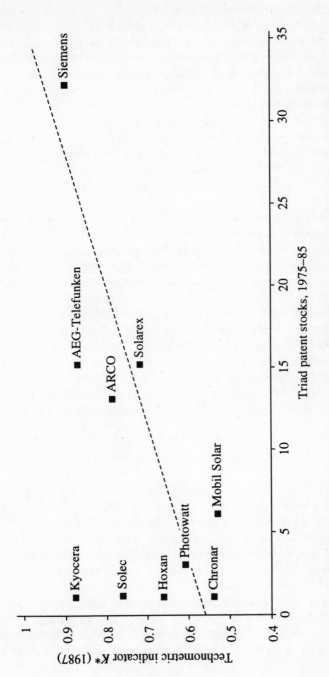

Figure 7.1 Explicit knowledge generation (as measured by triad patents, 1975–85) and technology performance characteristics (1987) of photovoltaic products for ten firms

possibility is that these companies have a strong domestic patent base but do not take out foreign duplications of their inventions, accepting all the associated international market risks. This case can be checked by an analysis of domestic patents and can be ruled out. The third possibility is that the companies produce excellent products from global knowledge external to the company. By acquiring leading-edge companies, licencing, networking and other forms of technology cooperation they may produce innovative products from creative technologies of other firms (including public laboratories).

This is at least partially the case for Kyocera. The firm agreed upon a licencing contract with Wacker in Germany (see Table 7.5) in 1984 and uses technology from Mobil Solar. From Solec it is known that the company belongs to the British Pilkington Group, whereas the global sources of Hoxan could not be clarified. Probably this case is covered by the statistical variance.

From this analysis it is concluded that there are various ways to innovation. Some companies acquire technological knowledge from other, for example global, sources than intramural technology generation and patent protection. But not all companies can do this in photovoltaics, so that for a number of companies a linear relationship between in-house technology generation and technology levels achieved is established. Furthermore, technology generation anticipates technological performance levels for some years. Patent stock data for previous years fit better to the technology levels than the most recent data. This again points to the importance of cumulative and global technology acquisition by firms.

The global 'production function' for technology, as measured by the sophistication levels of innovative products, can be modelled as follows (this is a further development of the basic technometric formulae given in section 7 in Grupp, 1994):

$$K^*(j, k) = \alpha_j E(j, k)^\beta \, T(j, k)^{(1-\beta)} \, \varepsilon_k$$

with k as an index for companies and j as an index for technologies or dominant design configurations. K^* is the notation for the technology performance level (for example, the technometric index), E measures inputs of explicit intramural knowledge (for example, patent stocks, P) and T measures inputs of tacit knowledge including external sources. The elasticity parameter, β, is assumed to be constant, whereas α_j may vary with the technology (for example, patent propensity).

K^* may be measured by technometrics and E by the number of patents (see Grupp, 1994), but there is no way to quantify tacit knowledge T. Also, an appropriate unit of measurement is missing. In the above formula it must be something like 'patent equivalents'. A different procedure is therefore used.

If we assume that both factors – the intramural knowledge base and the technology performance characteristics achieved (which include tacit knowledge from global sources) – are important for innovation and are partly independent of each other, then one should allow for two *independent* variables in explaining innovation statistically. The solution of the measurement difficulties mentioned consists of a replacement of E and T by P and K^*. The latter variables measure different representations of technological knowledge, whereby P excludes tacit knowledge sources and K^* includes tacit as well as explicit knowledge.

Unfortunately, the proxy measures of technological knowledge, K^* and P, are non-pecuniary in nature – they do not represent labour-hours or capital dollars, but rather comparative metrics. This makes conventional production models unusable. A version of linear programming exists, however, that was explicitly built to measure the efficiency of decision-making units (which can be individual firms) and that does allow qualitative inputs. This approach is known as Data Envelopment Analysis (DEA). Essentially, it examines which decision-making units are on the production possibilities frontier (or isoquant) in the knowledge economy and which are not (Charnes *et al.*, 1994).

The result of a DEA model with two inputs (K^* and P) and one output, Y (global production measured as in section 2; the data are from Table 7.1 broken down to the firm level) is included in Figure 7.2. The horizontal axis represents the explicit knowledge dimension generated by intramural R&D. Companies on the left-hand side are efficient insofar as they acquired their knowledge base from outside and converted this efficiently into good production values. The vertical axis represents the technology sophistication level, including tacit and external knowledge. Companies towards the bottom of the diagram achieved sophistication levels which are just right for market demand. The other companies, in the upper part of the diagram, are 'too good' with respect to consumer preferences and market needs. They invested too heavily in their technology, with no pay-off on the markets. The DEA efficiency isoquant thus provides room for two modes of efficient knowledge conversion. There is no reason to establish rank positions for photovoltaics companies (that is, a one-dimensional hierarchy).

Two Japanese companies are at the efficiency frontier because they either licensed relevant technology or their technology strategy strictly aimed at the relevant, growing market segments: these are the two sides of the same coin. The two American pioneering companies, ARCO Solar and Solarex, are also efficient in these terms. Most of the other American and European companies could not achieve similar relations of R&D, know-how, investment and market success, despite the considerable motivation of governments to subsidize renewable energy.

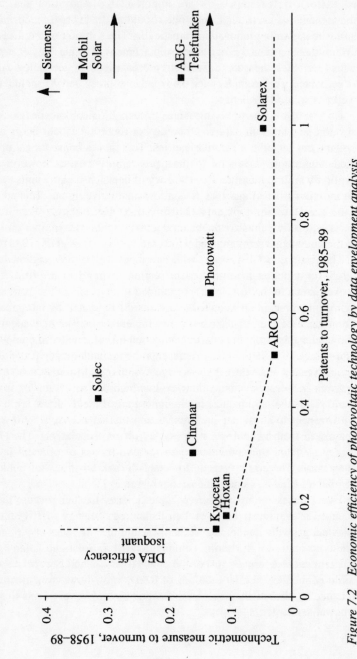

Figure 7.2 Economic efficiency of photovoltaic technology by data envelopment analysis

5. GLOBAL MARKET SHARE GROWTH AND PRODUCT INNOVATION

In a dynamic outlook, it is attempted to explain changes in the (global) market structure by endogenous product progress. It is possible to compare technological product quality increments by looking at the technometric indicators for 1987 in relation to those of 1991 (data sources in section 2). Figure 7.3 presents a comparison of the 1987 and 1991 levels. Overall, the technological levels did not change much in these four years. Along with some improvements, Siemens, Solarex and ARCO reduced some technology performance characteristics considerably by removing very advanced products from the markets (the K^* levels are adjusted to the world standards of 1987 as before (dashed line) even for the products of 1991 in order to achieve comparison). As was argued above, there were hardly any customers for the too far advanced products and the manufacturers reduced product heterogeneity in the course of time. This is an interesting point, as common theoretical models assume technological change always to be progressive and do not take into consideration the opposite case. However, recently Benzoni and Fenoglio (1995, pp. 452ff) published a model that treats such a case. Their model, for the quality dimension on vertically differentiated markets, allows for characteristics of 'overqualification'.

Other companies enhanced the technological quality of their innovation during the time span considered, for example, Hoxan (with monocrystalline cells) and Kyocera. While the reference case for the established products is a steady state in technological performance and withdrawals of companies from advanced market niches are also observed (Mobil Solar), the large number of new entrants to this market is also interesting. The companies with no products in 1987 (for example, Helios, BP Solar, Nukem, Rade Koncar and Sovonics) are not 'learners'; they achieve about the same performance as established producers. Sovonics, a long-established contract research firm for other photovoltaic firms, became an independent manufacturer leading in amorphous technology.

Finally, Figure 7.4 brings into perspective the market dynamics of technological progress (although only for active companies in both periods and without differentiating between the three dominant designs). The new entrants are implicitly included in the econometric analysis, as they diminish the market shares of the traditional manufacturers.

There seems to be a weak correlation, indicating that technologically improved products tend to result in better turnover.[3] Hoxan progressed technologically to a small degree but could not gain a market share increase; Kyocera, in contrast, improved its product quality considerably but expanded its market overproportionally. This is the 'simple' innovation model.

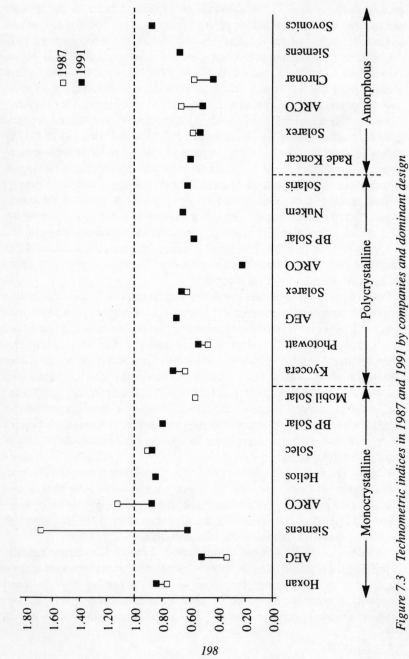

Figure 7.3   Technometric indices in 1987 and 1991 by companies and dominant design

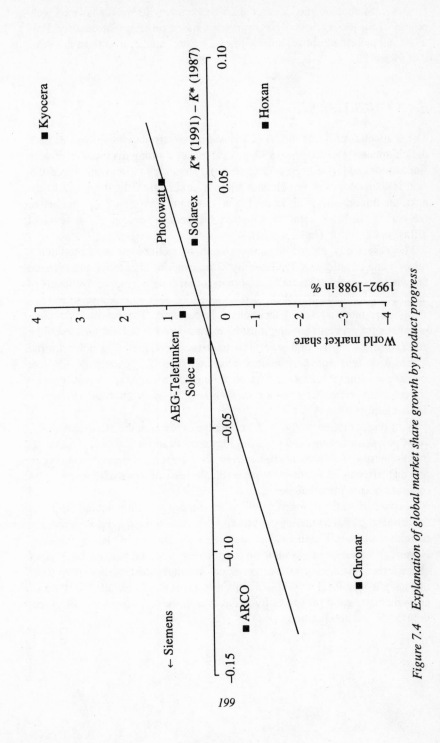

Figure 7.4 Explanation of global market share growth by product progress

However, Siemens gained market share by *removing* its most advanced technology from the markets. The conjectures based on snapshot data for 1987 alone, as presented above, are confirmed by real market events in the years that followed.

6. CONCLUSIONS

The sequential or linear model of innovation which 'undoubtedly goes back to Schumpeter' (Silverberg, 1990, p. 177) makes a strong distinction between 'innovation' and 'diffusion'. As science to technology to innovation to diffusion is understood by the classics to pass unidirectionally from one to the next, the notion is implicit in the linear viewpoint, that 'the faster the better, the earlier the time-point of adoption the better, the higher the level of diffusion the better' (*ibid.*, p. 178).

The case study on global appropriation of technology in photovoltaics raises some questions on the linearity of innovation. Intramural and external knowledge sources are equally important for arriving at competitive levels of technology sophistication. Yet for relevant and growing market segments not always the most advanced technology is required. The innovative search processes for problem-solving must be reconsidered. It did not turn out to be effective to sweep around several distinct market segments which required different designs and performance characteristics. To concentrate too late means spending too much effort on losing knowledge, while too early a convergence may throw away the winning knowledge base (Schmidt-Tiedemann, 1982, p. 19).

With respect to the analysis of knowledge expansion, the statistical analysis of patent documents and of technology specifications offers new measurement opportunities for industrial economics. Science, technology, innovation and diffusion are never entirely separable, at least in cases of science-based innovation as in photovoltaics.

In conclusion, the description of the knowledge economy, including transfer between global technology sources, seems to be quite complex, so that the definition of simple statistical procedures once and for all is not possible. Nevertheless, a network of indicators, which are based on patents, on product characteristics and on turnover figures, can be established, giving an interesting insight into the know-how acquisition process. All in all, this type of analysis bears good prospects for future use in the 'econometrics' of global innovation and competition.

NOTES

1. For the patent search a combination of patent classes and keywords was used; keyword searches in the data pools of the Japanese Patent Office/Tokkyo Cho were not performed but only searches in English, German and the French language. The restricted patent class-based figures for the Japanese domestic applications are therefore not fully comparable with the other data in Table 7.4; however, it is beyond doubt that the outward orientation of Japanese photovoltaic technology is very low.
2. There is an intended lag in the respective data; patent stocks are taken from invention years 1975 to 1985, technometric specification data are for 1987. This is done as patent stock data for previous years fit better to technology levels than the most recent data (see Grupp, 1994).
3. The lognormal relationship tested without Siemens is $\Delta Y_k = h \log K_k^*$ with the variables defined as above and the innovation 'hazard' factor, h. The OLS regression is heteroskedasticity-robust and yields $t = 2.29$ with an error probability of 0.06.

BIBLIOGRAPHY

Benzoni, L. and Fenoglio, Ph. (1995), 'Towards a Concept of Strategy Input: Evaluation and Choice of a Technology in a Vertically Differentiated Market', *International Journal of Technology Management*, **10**(4–6), 441–60.

Charnes, A., Cooper, W.W., Lewin, A.Y. and Seiford, L.M. (1994), *Data Envelopment Analysis: Theory, Methodology, and Application*, Boston: Kluwer Academic Publishers.

Chesbrough, H.W. (1994), 'Firm Level Technology Trajectories: Implications for Industry Innovation', International Joseph A. Schumpeter Society Conference, E1, Muenster, 1994.

Clark, N. and Juma, C. (1987), *Long-Run Economics – An Evolutionary Approach to Economic Change*, London and New York: Pinter Publishers.

Dasgupta, P. and David, P.A. (1987), 'Information Disclosure and the Economics of Science and Technology', in G. Feiwel (ed.), *Arrow and the Ascent of Modern Economic Theory*, New York: New York University Press.

Dosi, G. (1988), 'Sources, Procedures, and Microeconomic Effects of Innovation', *Journal of Economic Literature*, **XXVI**, 1120–71.

Dosi, G., Freeman, C., Nelson, R., Silverberg, G. and Soete, L. (eds) (1988), *Technical Change and Economic Theory*, London and New York: Pinter Publishers.

Einstein, A. (1905), *Theory of Light*.

Freeman, C. and Perez, C. (1988), 'Structural Crises of Adjustment, Business Cycles and Investment Behaviour', in G. Dosi *et al.* (eds), *Technical Change and Economic Theory*, London and New York: Pinter Publishers, pp. 40–66.

Freeman, C. and Soete, L. (eds) (1990), *Explorations in the Economics of Technical Change*, London: Pinter Publishers.

Freeman, C., Clark, J. and Soete, L. (1982), *Unemployment and Technical Innovation: A Study of Long Waves and Economic Development*, London: Pinter Publishers.

Griliches, Z. (1990), 'Patent Statistics as Economic Indicators: A Survey', *Journal of Economic Literature*, **XXVIII**, 1661–707

Grupp, H. (ed.) (1992), *Dynamics of Science Based Innovation*, Berlin, Heidelberg and New York: Springer Publishers.

Grupp, H. (1994), 'The Measurement of Technical Performance of Innovations by Technometrics and its Impact on Established Technology Indicators', *Research Policy*, **23**, pp. 175–93.

Grupp, H. and Hohmeyer, O. (1986), 'A Technometric Model for the Assessment of Technological Standards and Their Application to Selected Technology-Intensive Products', *Technological Forecasting and Social Change*, **30**, 123–37.

Grupp, H., Hohmeyer, O., Kollert, R. and Legler, H. (1987), *Technometrie – Die Bemessung des technisch-wirtschaftlichen Leistungsstandes*, Cologne: TUEV Rheinland.

Krupp, H. (1992), *Energy Politics and Schumpeter Dynamics*, Tokyo, Berlin, Heidelberg and New York: Springer Publishers.

Lancaster, K.J. (1991), *Modern Consumer Theory*, Aldershot: Edward Elgar.

Machlup, F. (1962), *The Production and Distribution of Knowledge in the United States*, Princeton, NJ: Princeton University Press.

Meereis, J. (1987), *Photovoltaik – Marktuebersicht*. Freiburg: Oeko-Institut, Werkstattreihe Nr. 42. Leuchtner, J. and C. Boekstiegel, revised version 1991.

Nelson, R.R. and Winter, S.G. (1982), *An Evolutionary Theory of Economic Change*, Cambridge, MA: The Belknap Press of Harvard University Press.

Nonaka, I. (1991), 'The Knowledge-Creating Company', *Harvard Business Review*, Nov.–Dec., 96–104.

Pavitt, K. (1984), 'Sectoral Patterns of Technical Change: Towards a Taxonomy and a Theory', *Research Policy*, **13**, 343–73.

Polanyi, M. (1966), *The Tacit Dimension*, London: Routledge & Kegan.

PV News, various issues from vol. 3 (1984) to vol. 12 (1993).

Raan van, A. (ed.) (1988), *Handbook of Quantitative Studies of Science and Technology*, Amsterdam: Elsevier.

Roessner, J.D. (1984), 'Commercializing Solar Technology: The Government Role', *Research Policy*, **13**, 235–46.

Saviotti, P.P. (1994), 'Variety, Economic and Technological Development', in: Y. Shionoya and M. Perlman (eds), *Innovation in Technology, Industries and Institutions*, Ann Arbor: The University of Michigan Press.

Schmidt-Tiedemann, K.J. (1982), 'A New Model of the Innovation Process', *Research Management*, March, 18–21.

Schmoch, U., Grupp, H., Mannsbart, W. and Schwitalla, B. (1988), *Technikprognosen mit Patentindikatoren*, Cologne: TUEV Rheinland.

Silverberg, G. (1990), 'Adoption and Diffusion of Technology as a Collective Evolutionary Process', in C. Freeman and L. Soete (eds), *Explorations in the Economics of Technical Change*, London: Pinter Publishers, pp. 177–92.

Utterback, J.M. and Abernathy, W.J. (1975), 'A Dynamic Model of Product and Process Innovation', *Omega*, **3**, 639–56.

Utterback, J.M. and Suárez, F.F. (1993), 'Innovation, Competition and Industry Structure', *Research Policy*, **22**, 1–21.

8. Innovation and competitive advantage

Jonathan Michie and Renée Prendergast

INTRODUCTION

The recent globalization of markets and the accompanying intensification of international competition have been associated with extensive deregulation of economies as well as measures to reduce taxes and government expenditure. This liberalization, taken together with the abandonment of public ownership in both the former socialist and mixed economies, has created a widespread impression that the market system has triumphed and that state intervention in the economy has been shown to be impotent. As Ghai (1994) has pointed out, the structural adjustment programmes embarked upon in virtually all countries in the 1980s were a product of a combination of conjunctural and secular forces. The former had to do with the post-1973 economic crisis; the latter with the continuing world economic integration of the post-Second World War period. The opportunity provided by this combination of crisis and secular trends enabled conservative forces to win acceptance for a political agenda involving the dismantling not only of various controls on the movement of goods and capital, but also of the modern welfare state. However, as Ghai has also pointed out, 'the liberal reforms were not undertaken with the same zeal in all domains' (Ghai, 1994, p. 23). A period which was generally characterized by increasing deregulation also saw intensification of agricultural protection, increasing use of some classes of trade restriction and increasing barriers to the immigration of unskilled persons (*ibid.*). More recently, the intensification of international competition has led to a growing preoccupation with the determinants of competitiveness. Interest is increasingly focused on issues relating to productivity and technical change. While some claim that the same forces make for static and dynamic efficiency so that all that is required is a continuation of the 1980s programme of liberalization and deregulation, others take a contrary view. They argue that the market-oriented reforms of the 1980s have created pressures which lead in various ways to the neglect or undervaluation of assets and structures which are vital for long-term development.

Section 1 of the present chapter examines some of the theoretical arguments made to support the case for deregulation and, perhaps not surprisingly, finds that there is no conclusive case for non-intervention. The possibility of conflict between short-run optimization and long-run development is explored in section 2. It is shown here that, although Schumpeter must be credited with the sharpest and most explicit statement of the possibility of such conflict, it was recognized quite early on in the history of modern economics. Finally, the third section surveys some prominent recent contributions to the literature on competitiveness and technological change, with a view to uncovering some of the mechanisms through which short- and long-run efficiency conflict.

THE CASE FOR DEREGULATION

Neoclassical general equilibrium theory provided the basis for microeconomic policy during the post-war period at least up until the early 1980s. This theory, which emphasized the optimality properties of free market outcomes, also sanctioned a wide range of government interventions designed to deal with market failure. The latter could be due to the absence of a market, the presence of externalities, increasing returns to scale and high transactions or information costs, all of which are ubiquitous features of real economic systems. From the late 1970s onwards, the view that government intervention could provide a means of overcoming market failure was increasingly questioned. For some (such as Hayek, 1944) intervention was to be discouraged because it interfered with individual liberty. For others, what was problematic was the welfare economist's assumption of an autonomous state acting in the public interest. Finally, there was the issue of the state's ability to achieve what it set out to do. Government failure, it was argued, was just as pervasive as market failure and there was no antidote to it (Krueger, 1974; Posner, 1975; Buchanan *et al.*, 1980).

As Chang (1994) has noted, government failure arguments provided a valuable corrective to the naive belief that the benevolent state can solve all market failure problems. However, rather than explore the issue of how state failures can be remedied, many of those contributing to the government failure literature seem to have regarded it primarily as part of a case for non-intervention.

As well as these negative arguments against state intervention, positive arguments were put forward to support the pro-market case. One set of arguments, based on the newly devised theory of contestable markets, seemed to suggest that in sectors where entry was free and exit costless, potential competition could be as effective as actual competition in disciplining market power (Baumol, 1982). All the properties of perfect competition – cost minimization, zero economic profits and price equal to marginal cost – would be reproduced in an industry with two or more firms. Even in natural monopoly, price would equal average costs and there would be cost minimization. This powerful new theory indicated that the scope for effective competition had previously been underestimated and that there were grounds for widespread deregulation in industries such as airlines and freight, where the assumption of complete redeployability or absence of sunk costs (necessary for free entry and exit) was most likely to be met.

The theory of contestable markets suggested that a small number of firms in a market did not necessarily imply a need for government intervention to counteract the effects of market power. It soon became clear, however, that the key requirement of the theory, complete redeployability, was not often met and that in its absence competitive results were unlikely to be achieved (Gilbert, 1989). A rather different case against government intervention and in favour of markets had earlier been put forward by the Austrians. The basis for their rejection of a possible role for state planning was their insistence that the information which is relevant to the making of economic decisions never exists as integrated knowledge but is dispersed in an incomplete and often contradictory form among the individual decision making units of the society. In their view not only is the problem of the central planner made difficult by the dispersed and incomplete nature of knowledge, but planning itself frustrates the operation of those spontaneous market forces which allow agents to become aware of errors in their conjectures. Markets, on the other hand, enable participants to penetrate the deep fog of ignorance that surrounds every economic decision (Kirzner, 1973; Hayek, 1978).

Thus in the Austrian vision, prices emerge as a result of the transactions of the individual participants on the market. These prices convey information about various disequilibria in the market and so also about business opportunities. Alert entrepreneurial types take advantage of these opportunities, and in so doing make money for themselves and improve the degree of coordination in the economy (Kirzner, 1973).

In the hands of Austrians such as Kirzner, the competitive process tends to be depicted as an equilibrating process, although the precise status of the equilibrium is left somewhat unclear. This is problematic given the Austrians' insistence on the superiority of the order achieved by the market process. Questioned about the notion of equilibrium in his system in an interview, Kirzner responded that while he would not claim that there was a built-in tendency for entrepreneurial activity to equilibrate the market under all circumstances, it was a fact of life that economic order was generally achieved (Boehm, 1989). However, as Hurwicz (1984) pointed out in the course of a critique of Kirzner, 'it is difficult to see how, in the absence of stabilizing forces, a *theoretical claim* can at all be made that markets produce efficiency'. Moreover, claims regarding Pareto efficiency of market outcomes and (more damagingly from the Austrian point of view) the use of a 'minimal size message space' applied only in perfectly competitive conditions and were not extendable to other market forms (*ibid.*, p. 85).

Not all Austrian economists accept Kirzner's view of the market process. Some, such as Lachmann, have contrasted market process analysis and equilibrium analysis and have argued that market processes do not converge to an equilibrium (Lachmann, 1976). Lachmann argues that for such convergence to be possible, it would be necessary that the divergence of expectations on which the initial inconsistency of plans rests be gradually turned into convergence. However, this is only possible if expectations are not autonomous and are modified by experience in predictable ways. There is no doubt that unsuccessful plans are revised and that planners learn from experience, but what they learn is not known and different people learn different lessons.

While Lachmann's critique of Kirzner emphasizes diverging expectations, Fehl (1995, pp. 197–205) criticizes Kirzner for overemphasizing arbitrage and failing to take into account two other important driving forces of the market process, namely innovation and production/accumulation. According to Fehl, the market process possesses a spontaneous 'order', but that 'order' is not to be confused with an equilibrium or perfect order. Fehl thinks that a system may be regarded as ordered if it delivers signals to individuals on how to improve their situation or otherwise guides their behaviour. In this view of things, the spontaneous order of the market is constituted by two systems of guidance. The first is the system of legal and moral rules, and the second the system of selection profiles emerging in the market process. The latter includes the various differentiated messages reaching market participants which inform them, for example, whether they should raise or lower prices, increase or reduce production, or enter or leave a market. Thus the selection order is related to the coordination problem, but rather than being concerned with the perfect order of equilibrium economics it is concerned with the process by which order is achieved. This emphasis on selection order makes sense only if the market process takes full account of innovation, because otherwise the market process would eventually come to a standstill and the selection profile of market opportunities would have vanished.

Fehl makes it clear that there is nothing perfect about the spontaneous order in the sense of selection order. As he puts it, the formation, revelation and interpretation of the emerging selection profiles depend on subjective interpretations, expectations and decisions. Consequently they are prone to error and can be characterized by a high level of uncertainty. Market participants may therefore look for new institutions to reduce uncertainty, thereby improving the performance of the market order. Such institutional reform is, of course, often executed by central authority. According to Fehl, this need not represent a departure from spontaneous order. Provided the intention of the state is to improve the existing order (which it may or may not succeed in doing), rather than to create a system as a whole, the emerging order can be characterized as spontaneous as opposed to constructivist (Fehl, 1994).

Far from supporting a non-interventionist programme, Austrian economics thus seems in the end to sanction all kinds of intervention. The only restriction seems to be that the intervention should be piecemeal and that in intention it should be reformist rather than revolutionary. There seems to be no *a priori* way of determining in advance what a good reform would be and only time will tell whether or not a particular reform has achieved its objectives. If a particular reform is unsuccessful, it will not always be clear whether this is because it is a bad reform or whether further reforms are necessary to allow it to achieve success.

The fact that intervention is to be allowed provided it is not constructivist in character, but no other criteria are suggested against which to evaluate any proposed policy, is hardly satisfactory. Should we, it might be asked, allow market participants to reduce uncertainty by placing restrictions on entry? If so, are there circumstances in which we would find this unacceptable?

In evaluating proposed reforms, neoclassical economists use the benchmark of Pareto efficiency. Classical and neo-Schumpeterian economists, on the other hand, use that of economic progress. Assuming winners compensate losers, economic progress will lead to Pareto improvements, though the new position need not be Pareto efficient. Ideally, of course, we would like to exhaust the gains from bargaining and trade as well as maximizing economic progress. But as Schumpeter (1947) and, more recently, Metcalfe (1995) have warned, the two objectives may be fundamentally incompatible in which case it becomes necessary to have a view about which objective is dominant. Over the long run, it is clear that the gains from technical progress dwarf potential efficiency gains. In the short to medium term, the matter may be less clear-cut. If time horizons are short, efficiency gains may dominate the gains from progress. This becomes problematic if the pursuit of short-term efficiency gains reduces the potential of the system for economic progress.

SHORT-RUN OPTIMIZATION AND LONG-RUN DEVELOPMENT

Recognition of the possibility that there might be a conflict between the needs of progress and order has a long history in economics. In order to understand its sources, it is necessary to begin by noting that for the classical economists both economic order and economic development were generated by the general competitive processes in the economy. There was no necessary conflict between the two because of a peculiar circumstance of the times.

This was that the division of labour which gave rise to increased productivity at the same time made labour more mobile between trades, thereby contributing to the perfection of the economic order. All this changed, however, as soon as the use of machinery became the main source of progress. This is reflected in the concern expressed in the writings of Babbage and Senior that the sunk costs associated with the accumulation of physical and human capital would be an obstacle to the mobility of resources which was necessary for the realization of competitive prices (Babbage, 1835; Senior, 1836). Later, attention was focused on economies of scale as the main source of conflict between the needs of order and change. J.S. Mill was troubled by the fact that, owing to technological progress and accompanying increases in efficient firm size, the amounts of capital required to participate in many industries were such as to limit potential competition (Mill, 1848). Like J.S. Mill, Marshall was interested in the implications of technical progress for firm size and hence for competition. The needs of his theoretical framework, however, dictated that the emphasis be on actual as opposed to potential competition. Thus while Marshall recognized that large firms possessed advantages in innovation, both in terms of their greater incentives to innovate and their greater ability to invest in innovative activity, he argued that these advantages would not lead to monopolization because, in most cases, the life cycle of the firm would be adequate to prevent it. In any case, these advantages of large firms applied mainly in the case of 'industries in the early stages of development' where new machinery and new processes were largely devised by manufacturers for their own use. In older, more established, industries, where improvements in machinery were mainly devised by machine manufacturers, small manufacturers might have access to the latest technical developments (Marshall, 1961, I, p. 281). [1]

The incompatibility between progress on the one hand and the perfection of order on the other, which forced itself on the attention of the economists in various guises, was recognized explicitly by a number of social theorists adopting an evolutionary perspective. Herbert Spencer, for example, had asked to what extent the perfecting of arrangements for gaining immediate ends raised impediments to the development of better institutions and to the future gaining of higher ends (Spencer (1889) reproduced in Andreski (1971) pp. 43–6). Clifford (1868) speculated that advantageous permanent changes were always the result of spontaneous actions of the organism. A race at any time, he reasoned, possessed a certain amount of plasticity. Every permanent effect of the environment upon it resulted in the crystallization of some part which was before plastic. As this goes on, the race of animals will bind up in itself more and more of its history and lose the capability of change which it once had. Only the spontaneous activity of the organism by the addition of something which had not been acted on by the environment and which was, therefore, plastic could preserve the capacity for change and, ultimately, survival.

Both Spencer and Clifford were important influences on Marshall's intellectual development. But while Spencer was an advocate of *laissez-faire*, Marshall recognized that the struggle for survival might fail to bring into existence organisms which were highly beneficial. In his opinion, progress could actually be speeded up by judicious intervention which would improve people's character and intellect. These changes might add only a little to the immediate efficiency of production, but they would be worth having if they prepared the way for more effective organization in the future. This was likely to be the case because, given the nature of technological development, demand for complex judgement and intelligence as opposed to purely manual skill, was increasing (Marshall, 1961, I, p. ix).

The Comptian device of separating order and change adopted by Schumpeter in the *Theory of Economic Development* (Schumpeter, 1961) allowed him to sidestep some of the theoretical problems which had created so many difficulties for Marshall and other economists. The circular flow of economic life could be analysed using the Walrasian equilibrium analysis, while Schumpeter's own theory of development, with the entrepreneur at its centre, could be used to explain economic change. But Marshall's theoretical problems reflected the concrete issues discussed by Clifford and Spencer. If these problems seem to disappear in the *Theory of Economic Development* it is only because Schumpeter makes it the task of the entrepreneur to solve them. The entrepreneur, with his superior energy, destroys the existing equilibrium, 'in which every individual is sure of his ground and is supported by the conduct, as adjusted to this circular flow, of all other individuals, who in turn expect the accustomed activity from him' (Schumpeter, 1961, pp. 78–9).

While the focus adopted in the *Theory of Economic Development* tended to conceal the full extent of the conflict between perfect competition on the one hand and the needs of economic development on the other, the same could certainly not be said of *Capitalism, Socialism and Democracy*. Here, Schumpeter accused neoclassical economists of abandoning the classical vision of capitalist society as, 'first and last a process of change' and of concentrating attention on the, 'almost irrelevant question' of whether or not resources were allocated optimally at any given point in time:

> A system ... that at *every* given point of time fully utilizes its possibilities to the best advantage may yet in the long run be inferior to a system that does so at *no* given point of time, because the latter's failure to do so may be a condition for the level or speed of long run performance (Schumpeter, 1947, p. 83).

Basically, Schumpeter's point was that whereas, from a static point of view, restrictive practices may seem to serve only to enrich the sellers at the expense of the buyers, in the context of long-run expansion these same practices may have important stabilizing and incentive functions. This did not mean that all cases of restrictive practice were to be uncritically tolerated on the grounds they were a necessary concomitant of progress. Government regulation remained necessary, but each case had to be evaluated in the context of its contribution to the process of creative destruction (Schumpeter, 1947, pp. 87–110).

The above seems to suggest that insofar as they have considered the problems of both order and development, economists have been troubled by the tensions and contradictions between them. These tensions are, of course, reflections of some very real properties of actual economic systems. As Nelson has remarked, the process of technical change in capitalist societies, at least with the vision of hindsight, appears to be extremely wasteful:

> Looking backward one can see a litter of failed or duplicative endeavours that probably would never have been undertaken had there been effective overall planning and co-ordination. Economies of scale and scope that might have been achieved through R&D co-ordination are missed. Certain kinds of R&D that would have a high social value are not done. Also, because technology is to a considerable extent proprietary, one can see many enterprises operating inefficiently, even failing sometimes at considerable social cost, for want of access to the best technology. (Nelson, 1988, p. 313)

Since innovation processes in capitalist economies are so wasteful, why they have performed so well compared with the socialist economies is something of a puzzle. Nelson takes the view that what makes effective central planning difficult, if not perhaps impossible, is the uncertainty which surrounds the question of where R&D resources should be allocated in a field where technology is fluid. There is always a variety of ways in which existing technologies can be improved and of achieving any particular improvement. Often there will be no agreement, even among experts, about which of these ways is likely to be best. In such circumstances, any attempt to get *ex ante* agreement on the matter may be futile and even counterproductive. It may be best to let the market decide *ex post* which were the good ideas.

The issue of the comparative performance of capitalist and socialist economies in terms of innovation touched on by Nelson is discussed in some detail in Rosenberg (1992). Like Nelson, Rosenberg emphasizes that technological innovation is fraught with uncertainties so that there is no way of knowing *a priori* which alternatives are worth pursuing and which are not. In such a situation experimentation may be valuable, provided means are available for terminating search in directions which have proved unpromising and for limiting the costs of failure. According to Rosenberg, the history of capitalism involved the progressive introduction of institutional devices which facilitated the commitment of resources to innovation by keeping the costs of being wrong within tolerable bounds, while at the same time holding out the prospect of large personal gains if their decisions turned out to be the right ones. These devices included business firms with limited liability for their owners and ownership shares that were easily marketable (Rosenberg, 1992, p. 190). In addition to the incentive structure, Rosenberg pointed to the importance of the freedom to conduct experiments. For such freedom to exist, it was necessary that the economic sphere should attain a degree of autonomy from external forces, especially arbitrary and unpredictable interventions by government (1992, pp. 191–2). Such autonomy is never absolute and other conditions must also be fulfilled if there is to be freedom to conduct experiments. The most important of these, according to Rosenberg, is the existence of a large number of decision-makers, each with insufficient power to influence the outcome of the market evaluation of the new product (*ibid.*).

Arguments in a similar vein to those of Nelson and Rosenberg have been put forward by Pelikan (1988), Eliasson (1991) and Metcalfe (1995), all of whom emphasize that economic self-organization cannot be optimally planned in advance and must involve experimentation through associative trials and errors. In this view of things, picking winners is simply not possible. The job of the policy-maker is to try to create an environment which on the one hand promotes the requisite amount of variety creation but on the other provides appropriate selection mechanisms. This is by no means easy. As Pelikan (1988) notes, a too lax selection will enable errors to survive, whereas a too constrained trial generation will cause absent successes. But while selection processes should not be too lax, they should not be too severe either, or they may prematurely eliminate future successes in temporary difficulties. Consequently there is a role for competent hierarchies which can improve on the short-sighted selection of product markets.

While it is important to emphasize the experimental aspect of economic evolution and technological innovation, some qualifications should also be noted. First, as Dosi (1988, p. 1134) points out, the strongest uncertainty applies to *pre-paradigmatic* phases of technical change. Once a paradigm has been established, the direction of search becomes more focused and uncertainty is somewhat reduced. Secondly, there is evidence that rates of innovation vary substantially between industries (Scherer, 1986). Thirdly, as Rosenberg (1992) recognizes, an environment exhibiting hostility towards experimentation may not be a huge disadvantage if the option of acquiring technology from abroad exists. These qualifications imply that the dangers of activist policy may be less than it would seem at first sight. This is especially the case for developing countries, whose industrialization in the present century has tended to be based on learning or the borrowing of foreign technology (Amsden, 1988, p. 38; Prendergast, 1996, pp. 39–55) but it will also apply to lagging sectors in otherwise industrialized countries.

THE ROLE OF COMPETITION

In considering the relative merits of large and small establishments from an efficiency point of view, J.S. Mill wrote that, in a state of free competition, the matter could be resolved by an unfailing test, namely which size of firm was able to undersell the other (Mill, 1848, p. 134). This view of competition as a selection mechanism is, however, only part of the picture. Adam Smith long ago remarked that increasing competition among producers desiring to undersell one another would cause them to have recourse to, 'new divisions of labour and new improvements of art which might never otherwise have been thought of' (Smith, 1976). Likewise, Schumpeter emphasized that, in capitalist reality as opposed to the textbook picture, the kind of competition that mattered was competition from the new commodity, the new technology, the new source of supply, the new type of organization (Schumpeter, 1947, pp. 84–5). This view of competition as the driving force behind technological and institutional change has been recently reiterated in Michael Porter's influential work *The Competitive Advantage of Nations* (Porter, 1990).

According to Porter, four broad attributes are the main determinants of competitive advantage. These are: factor conditions (skills, infrastructure, and so on); demand conditions; related and supporting industries; and firm strategy, structure and rivalry. These attributes form a mutually reinforcing system in which the effect of one depends on the state of the others. Thus the right factor conditions and the right supporting industries will be necessary if rivalry is to drive the system forward.

Rivalry, particularly domestic rivalry, is an indispensable element in Porter's vision of how competitive advantage is created and retained. Rivalry is important because once advantage is gained, it can only be sustained by a continual search for new things to do and new ways of doing them. According to Porter, powerful forces work against this, particulary in successful firms. Past approaches become institutionalized in procedures, management controls, personnel policy, and so on. Information that would challenge current approaches is screened out or dismissed. It takes powerful pressures to counteract these forces and these rarely come exclusively from within the organization. Companies seldom change spontaneously; the environment jars or *forces* them to change (Porter, 1990, p. 581).

Porter regards domestic rivalry as much more important than foreign rivalry. This is partly because of the direct and personal nature of domestic rivalry. More importantly, domestic rivals face the same basic conditions so that their presence nullifies the advantages of simply being in the nation, and forces firms to seek higher order and perhaps more sustainable competitive advantages. Porter supports his argument on the importance of intense competition from domestic rivals in encouraging the upgrading of a firm's products and processes with a variety of case and country studies. What we also have to consider is the possibility that domestic rivalry will have destructive results. Porter seems to discount this possibility (wrongly in our view) but he does warn of the dangers of identifying competition with perfect resource mobility. Emphasis on resource mobility, he argues, assumes that the productivity of resource utilization in a given industry is given and that consequently it is better for resources to flow to wherever productivity is higher. However, innovation can often boost the productivity of resources employed in a particular trade much more than the gains from reallocating them. It is important to emphasize that the gains from innovation are usually not simply there for the taking and may well require a major investment in restructuring at a time of low current returns and in the face of substantial risk (Porter, 1990, p. 116). 'The alternative, giving up, must be unthinkable if improvement and innovation are to take place' (*ibid.*). This is not to say that commitment is any guarantee of success. Commitment is a necessary condition for innovation, but it is by no means sufficient.

Porter (1992) takes up and develops the theme of commitment in an article on the capital allocation system of the United States. There he shows that, owing to the fragmentation of stakes and short holding periods, shareholders in the USA tend to lack detailed information on companies. Consequently, in making their decisions, they tend to undervalue features of companies which although intangible or difficult to measure are important for long-run success. Fragmentation and short holding periods also limit the ways in which owners and agents can influence management behaviour in the companies whose shares they own. By contrast, Porter claims that German and Japanese shareholders hold their shares permanently. They build up knowledge in the affairs of their companies and encourage continued investment to build up capabilities and increase productivity. While Porter accepts that the Japanese/ German system may lead to overextension of capacity, proliferation of products and a failure to redeploy capital out of weak business, it is much more effective in terms of encouraging the development of firm-specific assets which are vital for long-term success. Overall, Porter claims that the American system for capital allocation is not serving the American economy well and that none of its participants is satisfied. Each group is behaving rationally but all are trapped within a system that serves the interests of no one (Porter, 1992, p. 76). Reform is clearly necessary. Porter takes the view that its main aim should be the creation of a system in which managers will make investments that maximize the long-term value of their companies. But, Porter warns, 'altering the American system will not be easy. There is a natural tendency to limit change to tinkering at the margins, yet systemic change will be necessary to make a real difference' (*ibid.*, p. 82).

The argument that the institutional structure does not provide appropriate incentives for investment in firm-specific assets seems also to apply to the UK system, and may have been exacerbated by the market-oriented reforms introduced since 1979. Discussing the capital markets and corporate control, Franks and Mayer (1991) note that, as in the USA, the UK system is directed towards the promotion of markets and discourages close links between investors and firms. In these circumstances, they argue, correction of managerial failure tends to be associated with changes in ownership and this, in turn, undermines the implementation of informal implicit agreements. In conjunction with the absence of adequate guarantees relating to the rights of employees and managers, this tends to discourage long-term firm-specific investment. Labour market reforms aimed at creating more flexible labour may also have acted to discourage investment in firm-specific skills, although this tendency should be partly offset by some improvement in the returns to human capital investment which has accompanied these reforms (Beatson, 1995).

The issue of whether the competitive environment promotes innovation or cut-throat price-cutting has been discussed independently by Lazonick (1991). Lazonick argues that the key determinant of whether or not the firm's decision-makers choose an innovative strategy is the extent to which, 'they control an organisational structure that they believe provides them with the capability of developing productive resources that can overcome the constraints they face' (Lazonick, 1991, p. 328). Such structures include not only the internal organization of firms themselves and their relationships with the public authorities, but also networks of relationships between firms in a particular industry or cluster of industries.

Lazonick's emphasis on the need for control over the requisite organizational structure derives at least in part from his own work as an economic historian, particularly his work relating to the failure of the British cotton industry to innovate in the late 19th and the 20th centuries. Referring to a period of stagnation following the end of the post-Second World War boom, Lazonick characterizes the situation in the following terms: 'The fundamental problem was an industry mired in its own highly competitive and vertically specialised structure, lacking any internal forces to set organisational transformation in motion' (Lazonick, 1986, p. 35). The vast majority of businesspeople in the cotton industry had neither the incentive to participate nor the ability to lead in the internal restructuring of their industry (*ibid.*, p. 45). Given this absence of leadership from within private industry, what was required was the visible hand of coordinated control not the invisible hand of the self-regulating market (Elbaum and Lazonick, 1986, pp. 10–11).

The parallels between Lazonick's discussion of the British cotton industry and Porter's discussion of the system of capital allocation in the United States at the present time will be obvious. In both cases, sets of institutions which evolved over considerable time periods locked participants into behaviour which was irrational and unprogressive from the point of view of technological progress. Both situations require systematic rather than piecemeal institutional reforms.

Rather than dwell on the issue of systematic as opposed to piecemeal reforms, we would like at this point to ask to what extent is it possible for firms, and indeed industries, to avoid being locked into a particular set of structures or technologies? To a substantial extent the answer to this question depends on the sources of lock-in. In some cases, where a superior technology is available and the source of lock-in is network externalities, the problem is primarily one of coordination (Arthur, 1988). In other cases, matters are more complex, involving capability failures in addition to coordination failures. This leads to the question: are there ways in which firms can develop the capability to enable them to innovate, or at least adapt for their own purposes innovations made elsewhere? According to Carlsson and Jacobsson (1994) the creation of the necessary competence requires a great deal of investment in the firm's own absorptive capacity as well as in its links to other actors in the technological system of which it is a part. These investments, they argue, should not be restricted to those technologies which constitute the technology base for the firm's existing products, but should go beyond them in order to increase awareness and reduce the risks of a locking-in effect. Unfortunately, however, it is clear that, at the present time, there is widespread neglect of competence-creating investments. Firms in the USA and UK have become adept at downsizing and restructuring and managing their bottom line, to the neglect of the creation of new products and markets (Hamel and Prahaled, 1994; Applebaum and Berg, 1996). This may be a product of the general competitive environment and the capital allocation processes in the countries concerned, but it has also been argued that this sort of behaviour is simply a matter of firms failing to exercise their 'corporate free will' in responsible ways (Stopford and Baden-Fuller, 1992). While there may be some truth in the view that the failure to invest in long-run development can be attributed to a lack of managerial competence and vision, this is hardly the whole truth and it may be necessary to examine ways in which investments in firm competence and flexibility can be encouraged and preserved. In Korea, this has been done by allowing, and even encouraging, collusive behaviour in industries that need to increase R&D or improve product quality (Chang, 1994, p. 112). Clearly, other instruments, including subsidies for R&D, might also be used.

The issue of the relationship between industry structure and the capacity for innovation is a complex one. On the one hand, there is evidence that forms of long-term relationship between independent firms may be superior to vertical integration as a means of coordinating the activities required for innovation, especially where these activities involve a high degree of techno-logical 'strangeness' (Gomes-Casseres, 1994, p. 63). These new forms of alliance are prevalent in high technology industries, and there are indications that they contribute most to innovative performance when they involve a dense network of interpersonal relationships and internal infrastructures that enhance learning, unblock information flows and facilitate coordination by creating trust and by mitigating perceived differences of interest (Porter, 1990, pp. 152–3; Moss Kanter, 1994, p. 97). It is widely recognized that Asian companies have been particularly adept at developing and using inter-firm relationships and that failure to do so is a particular weakness of North American firms. Thus Moss Kanter (1994, p. 97) refers to American firms as taking a narrow, opportunistic view of relationships. Similarly, Porter (1991, p. 527) refers to relationships between US firms as being opportunistic and notes that skill transfers and the sharing of market insights takes place only sporadically.

But while there is evidence that networks and groups of firms can increase the scope for innovation, it is clear from our earlier discussion that they do not always do so. As noted already, the problem may be due to coordination failure and/or capability failure. A good example of the latter comes from the highly successful Taiwanese electronics industry. In the main, the industry is made up of small and medium-sized enterprises which concentrate almost exclusively on the manufacturing function to the neglect of areas such as marketing and R&D which are necessary for the upgrading of their techno-logical level (Gee, 1993; Chou, 1995). As a result, the role of the state has been extremely important in building competence in advanced electronics, with leadership of the industry vested in public research organizations and public enterprise (Wade, 1990).

By contrast, in the Japanese case, intervention is mainly aimed at facilitat-ing the creation of convergent technological expectations, thereby reducing risk but also leaving a good deal of space for competition among technologi-cally leading firms (Wade, 1990; Porter, 1991).

While industry structure and, related to that, firm-level competence are important for innovative performance, it is necessary to note that, in general, firms' ability to change strategic orientation is constrained by the nature of their existing capabilities. Thus Oscarsson (1993), in a study of 57 large OECD firms, found that while most diversified their technological base, only about 20 per cent of these expanded into new product areas. This tendency towards lock-in even in large firms with strong R&D bases suggests that there is considerable scope for intervention to promote technological and product diversification. An important task here is the early identification of technological opportunities and the creation of a framework in which these opportunities can be tested in practice. This may involve improving the incentives for firm diversification through advanced procurement policies (Carlsson and Jacobsson, 1994). It may also involve such things as investments to create appropriate skill and research bases in advance of industry need. Creation and facilitation of networks of firms and networks involving both firms and other institutions may also be important. As Carlsson and Jacobsson (1994) note, technological policy in a new but relatively promising field may have to be comprehensive and concern itself with the functioning and strengthening of the system as a whole.[2]

CONCLUSION

In the post-Second World War period, the world economy has become increasingly globalized. In the 1950s and 1960s, the driving force behind this was the rapid growth of international trade facilitated by arrangements agreed at Bretton Woods. With the partial breakdown in the latter in the 1970s, the leading role was taken by flows of capital financed by the commercial banks. Following the onset of the debt crisis, the latter declined in importance and the leading role in economic integration passed to the transnational enterprises. These enterprises not only dominate world trade but, by the 1990s, the sales of their foreign affiliates were almost double world exports (Ghai, 1994). This globalization of economic activity necessitated a carving out by capital of a greater sphere of freedom for itself, with a dismantling of the obstacles to its movement and development. In turn, this freedom of movement led to constraints on the ability of states to manage their economies, to impose taxes, to vary interest rates and so on, with the result that globalization has come to be associated with the dominance of market forces and the free play of competition.[3]

What we have tried to show in this chapter is that there has always been a tension between the role of competition in promoting economic order and its role in stimulating economic development. In general, it is important not to overestimate the capacity of central authorities to intervene in the innovation process given the high levels of uncertainty surrounding the development of new products and processes. But the crux of the matter is the difficulty of achieving efficiency in production while at the same time preserving space for the exploration of new possibilities or relatedly preserving the flexibility to respond when new possibilities are created elsewhere. Without competition, there is no reason to change but, paradoxically, an excessive emphasis on market-type flexibility can lock firms and industries into existing products and routines of production. Once lock-in occurs, very substantial reforms may be necessary before development once again becomes possible.

NOTES

1. Russo's (1985) research on the Italian ceramic tile industry lends support to Marshall's views on this point.
2. These policy issues are discussed in detail in Archibugi *et al.* (1995).
3. For an analysis of these developments in the global economy and what they imply for economic policy, see Michie and Grieve Smith (1995).

REFERENCES

Amsden, A.H. (1988), 'Private Enterprise – The Issue of Business–Government Control', *Colombia Journal of World Business*, **23**, Spring, 37–42.

Amsden, A. (1989), *Asia's Next Giant*, Oxford and New York: Oxford University Press.

Andreski, S. (ed.) (1971), *Herbert Spencer: Structure, Function and Evolution*, London: Michael Joseph.

Applebaum, E. and Berg, P. (1996), 'Financial Market Constraints and Business Strategy in the USA', in J. Michie and J. Grieve Smith (eds), *Creating Industrial Capacity: Towards Full Employment*, Oxford: Oxford University Press.

Archibugi, D., Carlsson, B., Jacobsson, S., Metcalfe, S. and Michie, J. (1995), *The Internationalization of the Innovation Process and National Innovation Policies: A Survey of the Literature*, Cambridge: ESRC Centre for Business Research.

Arthur, W.B. (1988), 'Competing Technologies: An Overview' in G. Dosi *et al.* (eds), *Technical Change and Economic Theory*, London and New York: Pinter Publishers, pp. 590–606.

Babbage, C. (1835), *On the Economy of Machinery and Manufactures*, reprinted 1963, New York: Augustus M. Kelly.

Baumol, W.J. (1982), 'Contestable Markets: An Uprising in the Theory of Economic Structure', *American Economic Review*, **72**, 1–15.

Beatson, M. (1995), *Labour Market Flexibility*, Sheffield: Employment Department, Research Series No. 48.

Boehm, S. (1989), 'Interview with Israel Kirzner', *Review of Political Economy*, **1**.

Buchanan, J., Tollison, R. and Tullock, G. (eds) (1980), *Towards a Theory of the Rent Seeking Society*, College Station: Texas A&M University Press.

Cantillon, R. (1931), *Essai sur la Nature du Commerce en General* (ed. H. Higgs), London: Macmillan.

Carlsson, B. and Jacobsson, S. (1994), 'Technological Systems and Industrial Dynamics – Implications for Firms and Governments', paper presented at the international J.A. Schumpeter Conference, Munster, Germany, 17–20 August.

Casson, M. (ed.) (1990), *Entrepreneurship*, Aldershot: Edward Elgar.

Chang, H.-J. (1994), *The Political Economy of Industrial Policy*, Basingstoke: Macmillan.

Chou, T.-C. (1995), *Industrial Organisation in a Dichotomous Economy*, Aldershot: Avebury.

Clifford, W. J. (1868), 'On Some of the Conditions of Mental Development', discourse delivered at the Royal Institution, March 6; published in K. Pearson (ed.), *The Common Sense of the Exact Sciences by William Clifford Kingdom*, newly edited (1947) by J.R. Newman, London: Sigma Books Ltd.

Dahmen, E. (1970), *Entrepreneurial Activity and the Development of Swedish Industry 1919–1939*, translated by A. Leijonhufvud, Homewood: Richard D. Irwin, Inc. for the American Economic Association.

Dosi, G. (1988), 'Sources, Procedures and Microeconomic Effects of Innovation', *Journal of Economic Literature*, 26, 1120–71.

Dosi, G., Freeman, C., Nelson, R., Silverberg, G. and Soete, L. (eds) (1988), *Technical Change and Economic Theory*, London and New York: Pinter Publishers.

Elbaum, B. and Lazonick, W. (1986), *The Decline of the British Economy*, Oxford: Clarendon Press.

Eliasson, G. (1991), 'Modelling the Experimentally Organised Economy', *Journal of Economic Behaviour and Organisation*, 16, 153–82.

Fehl, U. (1994), 'Spontaneous Order', in P.J. Boettke (ed.), *The Elgar Companion to Austrian Economics*, Aldershot: Edward Elgar.

Franks, J. and Mayer, C. (1991), 'Capital Markets and Corporate Control: A Study of France, Germany and the UK', *Economic Policy*, 20, 191–235.

Gee, S. (1993), 'Global Restructuring and Economic Development Strategies in Taiwan and South Korea', in C. Brundenius and B. Goransson (eds), *New Technologies and Global Restructuring*, London: Taylor Graham.

Ghai, D. (1994), 'Structural Adjustment, Global Integration and Social Democracy', in R. Prendergast and F. Stewart (eds), *Market Forces and World Development*, Basingstoke: Macmillan.

Gilbert, R.J. (1989), 'The Role of Potential Competition in Industrial Organisation', *Journal of Economic Perspectives*, 3, 107–27.

Gomes-Casseres, B. (1994), 'Group Versus Group: How Alliance Networks Compete', *Harvard Business Review*, July–August, 62–74.

Hamel, G. and Prahalad, C.K. (1994), *Competing for the Future*, New York: McGraw Hill.

Hayek, F.A. von (1937), 'Economics and Knowledge', *Economica*, new series, 4, 33–54.

Hayek, F.A. von (1944), *The Road to Serfdom*, London: George Routledge & Sons Ltd.

Hayek, F.A. von (ed.) (1978), 'Competition as a Discovery Procedure', *New Studies*, London: Routledge and Kegan Paul.

Hurwicz, L. (1984), 'Economic Planning and the Knowledge Problem: A Comment', in J. Cunningham Wood (ed.), *Fredrick A. Hayek: Critical Assessments*, London: Routledge.

Hurwicz, L. (1989), 'Mechanisms and Institutions', in T. Shiraishi and S. Tsuru (eds), *Economic Institutions in a Dynamic Society: Search for a New Frontier*, Basingstoke: Macmillan for the IEA, Chapter 4, pp. 87–104.

Kirzner, I. (1973), *Competition and Entrepreneurship*, Chicago: University of Chicago Press.

Kreuger, A. (1974), 'The Political Economy of the Rent-Seeking Society', *American Economic Review*, 64, 291–303

Lachmann, L. (1976), 'On the Central Concept of Austrian Economics: Market

Process', in E.G. Dolan (ed.), *The Foundations of Modern Austrian Economics*, Kansas: Sheed & Ward, Inc.

Lazonick, W. (1986), 'The Cotton Industry', in B. Elbaum and W. Lazonick (eds), *The Decline of the British Economy*, Oxford: Clarendon Press.

Lazonick, W. (1991), *Business Organisation and the Myth of the Market Economy*, Cambridge: Cambridge University Press.

Lazonick, W. (1993), 'Industry Clusters versus Global Webs: Organisational Capabilities in the American Economy', *Industrial and Corporate Change*, **2**.

Marshall, A. (1961), *Principles of Economics*, ed. C.W. Guillebaud, 2 vols, London: Macmillan.

Marshall, A. and Paley Marshall, M. (1979), *The Economics of Industry*, London: Macmillan.

Metcalfe, J.S. (1995), 'Technology Systems and Technology Policy in an Evolutionary Framework', *Cambridge Journal of Economics*, **19**, 25–46.

Michie, J. and Grieve Smith, J. (eds) (1995), *Managing the Global Economy*, Oxford: Oxford University Press.

Mill, J.S. (1848), *Principles of Political Economy*, edited 1909 with an Introduction by W. Ashley, London: Longmans, Green and Co.

Moss Kanter, R. (1994), 'Collaborative Advantage: The Art of Alliances', *Harvard Business Review*, July–August, 96–108.

Nelson, R. (1988),'Institutions Supporting Political Change in the United States', in G. Dosi *et al.* (eds), *Technical Change and Economic Theory*, London and New York: Pinter Publishers, pp. 312–29.

Oscarsson, C. (1993), 'Technology Diversification – the Phenomenon, Its Causes and Effects', Doctoral dissertation, Department of Industrial Management and Economics, Chalmers University of Technology, Goteborg, Sweden. Cited in Carlsson and Jacobsson, *op cit.*

Pelikan, P. (1988), 'Can the Innovation System of Capitalism be Outperformed?', in G. Dosi *et al.* (eds), *Technical Change and Economic Theory*, London and New York: Pinter Publishers, pp. 370–98.

Porter, M.E. (1990), *The Competitive Advantage of Nations*, London and Basingstoke: Macmillan.

Porter, M.E. (1992), 'Capital Disadvantage: America's Failing Capital Investment System', *Harvard Business Review*, Sept.–Oct., 65–82.

Posner, R. (1975), 'The Social Costs of Monopoly and Regulation', *Journal of Political Economy*, **83**, 807–27.

Prendergast, R. (1996), 'The Environment for Entrepreneurship', in R. Auty and J. Toye (eds), *Challenging the Orthodoxies*, Basingstoke: Macmillan, pp. 39–54.

Rosenberg, N. (1992), 'Economic Experiments', *Industrial and Corporate Change*, **1**, 181–203.

Rothwell, R. and Zegveld, W. (1982), 'New Ventures and Large Firms; the Search for Internal Entrepreneurship', Chapter 6 of *Innovation and the Small and Medium Sized Firm: Their Role in Employment and in Economic Change*, London: F. Pinter, reprinted as reading no. 20 in M. Casson (ed.) (1990).

Russo, M. (1985), 'Technical Change and the Industrial District: The Role of Interfirm Relations in the Growth and Transformation of Ceramic Tile Production in Italy', *Research Policy*, **14**, 329–43.

Scherer, F.M. (1986), *Innovation and Growth. Schumpeterian Perspectives*, Cambridge: MIT Press.

Schumpeter, J.A. (1947), *Capitalism, Socialism and Democracy*, second edition, London: George Allen and Unwin Ltd.

Schumpeter, J.A. (1961), *The Theory of Economic Development*, translated by R. Opie, Oxford: Oxford University Press.

Senior, N.W. (1936), *An Outline of the Science of Political Economy*, reprinted 1951, London: George Allen and Unwin Ltd.

Shiraishi, T. and Tsuru, S. (1989), *Economic Institutions in a Dynamic Society: Search for a New Frontier*, Basingstoke: Macmillan for the IEA.

Smith, A. (1976), *An Inquiry into the Nature and Causes of the Wealth of Nations*, Vol. 1, 1976 edition edited by R.H. Campbell, A.S. Skinner and W.B. Todd, Oxford: Clarendon Press.

Stopford, J. and Baden-Fuller, C. (1992), *Rejuvenating the Mature Business*, Harvard: Harvard Business School Press.

Teece, D. (1988), 'Technological Change and the Nature of the Firm', in G. Dosi *et al.* (eds), *Technical Change and Economic Theory*, London and New York: Pinter Publishers, pp. 256–81.

Wade, R. (1990), *Governing the Market*, Princeton: Princeton University Press.

9. Technological competitiveness in an international arena

Jeremy Howells and Jonathan Michie

INTRODUCTION

There is no single, consensus view of the globalization of technology, any more than there is a single agreed perspective on globalization more generally (see Chapter 1 refs, Dicken, 1992, p. 101). The emergence of a single conceptual core to explain such a process may be particularly unlikely due to the nature of globalization itself; rather than developing as a single phenomenon, the globalization of technology displays different (and perhaps even divergent) paths between sectors, functions, technologies, nations, firms and patterns of trade and investment. Firms are also reacting differently to these different sets of circumstances, and are choosing to deploy their technological resources differently from each other. These corporate decisions are in turn influenced by the perceived scope for shaping technological developments. Much of the focus of academic research has naturally been on large firms and the ways they have advanced and reconfigured their structures; this is not surprising given that they are seen as the major 'movers' and 'shakers' on the global technological landscape.

For smaller firms, freedom of action may be more restricted (although not necessarily; see Dicken, 1994, p. 111). Their ability to globalize their technology, or even to deal with the globalization of technology, may be much more limited, especially if they have no overseas subsidiaries. Joint ventures and licencing are likely to be the main tools of their globalization route, either in the domestic market to defend their existing market structures, or overseas to extend the reach of their products and services. Laggard firms risk seeing rivals entering their existing markets with newer, more innovative products, capturing their market share. The 'winds of creative destruction' may be increasingly 'foreign'. Former domestic patterns of technology generation, transfer and utilization may be breaking down, leading to more open technological regimes.

UNEVEN FORM: GLOBAL–LOCAL 'DEEPENING' AND 'HOLLOWING' IN TECHNOLOGY

Although globalization may be leading to more open technological systems, there is still a significant local dimension in the globalization process where 'local' characteristics remain important and where indeed there may be a deepening of relationships between firms and their technical 'task' environments. Institutional systems and settings – whether they be national or regional in orientation – remain key, representing a 'bonding' element to companies. Indeed, foreign firms often (although not always) slowly assimilate and integrate with the local innovation system (see, for example, Young *et al.*, 1994). They start contributing to the indigenous innovation system and hence further enhance its overall shape and profile. However, how far do inward investors reinforce existing patterns where domestic innovation systems are already strong and competitive? Or do they rather enter and establish themselves in fields where the innovation system is weak? There has been much debate about which sectors are most likely to look to invest in overseas markets, and about the impact this will have on the existing local/ national technical capacities.

Thus Siemens made a major investment in 1997 in the North East of England in a new semiconductor plant, an industrial and technology field where Britain is weak technologically.[1] However, at the same time, Pharmacia (Sweden) and Upjohn (USA) have, after their merger in 1995, located their new headquarters, and other higher technical and strategic functions, in Britain, further strengthening the role of pharmaceuticals in the UK innovation system. The latter certainly appears to continue a long-term positive or 'virtuous' cycle of technological accumulation (Dunning, 1988, p. 139). However, both have obviously strengthened the UK's technological position, although from very different sectoral standpoints in terms of indigenous technological capability and competitiveness.

The pharmaceutical industry in Britain is an instance of a virtuous cycle, but equally there are examples of 'vicious' cycles in terms of the impact of overseas investment on a nation's technological capability. This would be where the technological capacity of a host country is weak in the sector concerned and where new inward investment by foreign companies may drive out local competition and actually reduce local technological capability still further (Dunning and Cantwell, 1985). Trying to deduce, still less forecast, the impact of these investments on the indigenous technological capability of a nation or region is extremely difficult. However, this is only one aspect of the long-term trajectories of innovation within countries and localities. Most of the discussion of virtuous and vicious cycles of technological investment in host countries has concentrated on new, 'greenfield' investments. The impact of 'brownfield' investments, where foreign companies acquire indigenous firms and their technical expertise, and the actual closure of facilities by overseas companies of their foreign facilities, are also aspects of this process which have been largely neglected by researchers. In terms of brownfield investments, the UK is again a case where the potential problems of overseas technological acquisition have been highlighted (Howells and Charles, 1989). More recently, deregulation has continued to create problems for indigenous UK industry, with the telecommunications manufacturing industry being a particular case in point. However, one area where such deregulation did stimulate innovative solutions to many of the technical problems thrown up by having so many new local and long-distance telecommunications service providers, which frequently had to use each others networks, was in ISDN switching technologies which allowed different operators to link between each. A series of new, small UK-owned firms was set up which developed these technologies and soon gained a world lead in this field. Since 1995, however, seven of these leading companies specializing in ISDN technology have been acquired by foreign, mainly US, companies. How far this lead established by the UK in ISDN technology will continue is now in doubt.

Another neglected aspect in the influence of foreign investment on indigenous technological development is that of facility closure. Well-established foreign companies with good indigenous technical links and strong technological records may decide to close down research and technical facilities in a country and effectively 'exit' from that country's national system of innovation. This may occur not only in weak technological sectors. This again can be seen with reference to Britain, where the UK has sectors (such as consumer electronics) where innovative capability is weak and sectors which have strong innovative records (such as chemicals and pharmaceuticals) an example of the former case (of exit from weak innovative sectors) would be the 1995 closure of Texas Instruments's key manufacturing and technical centre in Bedford, while examples of exit from strong innovative sectors would include the closure of G.D. Searle's research and manufacturing operations in High Wycombe in the mid 1980s and the closure by other foreign drug companies of their UK R&D and production activities. Reasons for such closures are often highly specific, in many cases being associated with periods of restructuring within the firm or sector concerned. Nevertheless, these 'exiting' patterns can be as important to the technological capability of countries and regions as the more widely publicized 'entry' patterns of foreign investors.

Again there may be no single prescriptive path for a country for identifying or forecasting such changes in indigenous technological capability and the role of foreign investors in that change. Indeed different patterns may emerge and run together simultaneously. Each country's firms tend to embark on a changing pattern (both strengthening and weakening) of technological accumulation which will have certain unique characteristics (Patel and Pavitt, 1994, p. 767), and this influences not only their home country but overseas countries as well. Thus although there are distinctive sectoral variations in the degree of overseas research and technical capacity, firms themselves also display significant variations in the way they manage and configure their overseas technical capabilities. Some multinationals allow a high degree of research and technical autonomy, to the extent that these overseas units have global research and production mandates for their company in certain businesses and technologies. Others follow much more constrained and limited international technological structures. However, regardless of their different strategies and structures towards overseas technology, all are still strongly influenced by their historical path dependencies and their indigenous technological and cultural environments (Chapter 3, this volume). As Dicken (1994, p. 117) has noted in a more general context: 'TNCs are not placeless, all have an identifiable home base, a base that ensures that every TNC is essentially embedded within its domestic environment'. This is echoed by Kozul-Wright (1995, pp. 160–63), who reaffirms that geography still matters and that geographical place will continue to remain important in the emerging system of international production. In this sense, therefore, the global underlines the local and makes the analysis of local variations in technological capacity all the more important if the process of the globalization of technology is to be understood.

KEY THEMES IN THE GLOBALIZATION OF TECHNOLOGY

It could be argued that the paradox of the globalization of technology is that it emphasizes the particular, the special and the local rather than the general, the commonplace and the international. There are three central interlinking themes which recur in debates over the nature and extent of the globalization of technology and on which (arguably) the concept of such technological globalization rests. The three themes centre on:

1. The issue of the *mobility and immobility* of assets and, related to this, the issue of 'embeddedness'.
2. Associated with the above, the issue of the *reproducibility and transferability* of knowledge, information and know-how, in turn linked with tacitness and 'stickiness' (see Chapter 1, this volume).
3. The issue of *homogenization and specialization* in technological capability.

A key element in determining the nature and extent of the globalization of technology is how far technological assets are mobile or immobile. In a sense all assets are 'mobile' in that new investments, techniques or research teams can be relocated, or newly established, overseas (Krumme, 1969). The focus on asset mobility within the context of technological innovation has tradition- ally centred on the 'harder', embodied and more quantifiable technological assets, especially research and manufacturing establishments, and more par- ticularly, on the components that make them up (that is, the plant and equip- ment and the new products that are generated or manufactured by them). Barriers to such movement have often been viewed in terms of traditional diffusion processes, focusing on when and where overseas expansion would take place. An assessment of the feasibility and motives of such moves and the barriers to them is undoubtedly important, and data availability on these moves remains poor; however, this is by no means the only element of asset mobility and performance, nor the most significant issue.

Thus more recently, attention has moved on to not so much the feasibility of, or barriers to, such movement, but whether the shift of technological assets overseas might actually jeopardize the successful generation of new technologies. This in turn introduces the issue of transferability and repro- ducibility. Often, embodied technical assets have been moved or set up as new in overseas sites but then shown to be less effective. Thus although the components (the plant and machinery and the products being manufactured) themselves were outwardly the same – with companies having world-wide standards on equipment and suppliers – it was found that their performance in terms of output and costs could still vary substantially and their quality was poorer. Equally, R&D units were found to be less successful even though they had similar resources devoted to them. Such companies found it difficult to transfer and reproduce these research and manufacturing abilities even though the specific assets were similar. The focus, therefore, shifted towards non-tangible and tacit assets involved in technological innovation and its reproduction in terms of manufacturing. It also shifted to the *ensemble* of technical assets (and how firms managed and integrated them together) rather than the individual components themselves. It has been increasingly sus- pected, although difficult to quantify, that it was the tacit, disembodied ele- ments and the 'integrative know-how' of firms managing the ensemble of technical assets that were less mobile and harder to transfer and reproduce elsewhere rather than the embodied, codified and formal technical compo- nents (see Chapter 1, this volume).

If these important intangible assets are difficult to transfer and reproduce, technological specialization is likely to remain, and indeed grow, with glo- balization. These assets may become more interlinked and be owned and controlled by foreign firms, but their place-based nature remains. The flows of technology, whether traded or non-traded, within or between firms, will grow, and increased specialization, rather than homogenization, will occur. However, although this scenario provides some support for Michael Porter's (1990) argument (see Chapter 1, this volume), it does not necessarily reject that of Robert Reich's (1991) view either. The use of 'global webs', and more particularly information and communication technologies, by multinationals is likely to be the best way to exploit the immobility of such key technical assets globally. The main difference is that Porter views his global vision largely on an inter-firm basis, with firms exploiting the specialist technical know-how advantage of localities or nations on an inter-firm, network basis. By contrast Reich's vision is of the giant multinational corporation and how it employs its internal assets to exploit best these localized centres of knowledge. Here exploitation of such immobile assets is based on intra-firm locational specialization in terms of technologies, sectors and functions of the firm (R&D, sales, marketing and production), and their configuration and coordination.

The key point is that the competitive advantage of firms and of the economies from which they operate is something which is built up by conscious policy action by firms, governments and others. It is not determined by some sort of natural, resource endowment-determined comparative advantage. And as the economy becomes more globalized, any competitive advantage gained (or lost) will have that much greater effect on market shares, output, and employment levels and living standards. Thus far from being swept aside by the forces of technological globalization, economic and industrial policy is becoming more, not less, important. And central to this need for active government – nationally, locally and globally – lies technology and innovation policy.

NOTE

1. The following discussion uses recent UK examples, but we would argue that there are equally valid examples in other developed economies around the world.

REFERENCES

Cantwell, J. (1989), *Technological Innovation and Multinational Corporations*, Oxford: Basil Blackwell.
Dicken, P. (1994), 'Global–Local Tensions: Firms and States in the Global Space-Economy', *Economic Geography*, **70**, 101–28.
Dunning, J.H. (1988), *Multinationals, Technology and Competitiveness*, London: Unwin Hyman.

Dunning, J.H. and Cantwell, J. (1985), 'The Changing Role of Multinational Enterprises in the International Creation, Transfer and Diffusion of Technology', paper presented to the Conference on Innovation Diffusion, Ca' Dolfin, Dorsoduro 3825/E, Venice.

Howells, J. and Charles, D. (1989), 'Research and Technological Development and Regional Policy: A European Perspective', in D.C. Gibbs (ed.), *Government Policy and Industrial Change*, London: Routledge, pp. 23–54.

Kozul-Wright, R. (1995), 'Transnational Corporations and the Nation State', in J. Michie and J. Grieve Smith (eds), *Managing the Global Economy*, Oxford: Oxford University Press, pp. 135–71.

Krumme, G. (1969), 'Notes on Locational Adjustment Patterns in Industrial Geography', *Geografiska Annaler*, **51B**, 15–19.

Narula, R. (1993), 'Technology, International Business and Porter's "Diamond": Synthesizing a Dynamic Competitive Development Model', *Management International Review*, **33**, 85–107.

Patel, P. and Pavitt, K. (1994), 'Uneven (and Divergent) Technological Accumulation among Advanced Countries: Evidence and Framework of Explanation', *Industrial and Corporate Change*, **3**, 759–87.

Porter, M.E. (1990), *The Competitive Advantage of Nations*, New York: Free Press.

Reich, R.B. (1991), *The Work of Nations: Preparing Ourselves for 21st-Century Capitalism*, New York: Knopf.

Young, S., Hood, N. and Peters, E. (1994), 'Multinational Enterprises and Regional Economic Development', *Regional Studies*, **28**, 657–77.

Index